BATTLE FLAGS
of the WARS *for*
NORTH AMERICA, 1754–1783

Foreign Armies and Regiments

STEVEN W. HILL

STACKPOLE
BOOKS

Essex, Connecticut
Blue Ridge Summit, Pennsylvania

STACKPOLE BOOKS

An imprint of The Globe Pequot Publishing Group, Inc.
64 South Main Street
Essex, CT 06426
www.globepequot.com

Distributed by NATIONAL BOOK NETWORK

British Library Cataloguing in Publication Information available

Library of Congress Cataloging-in-Publication Data

Names: Hill, Steven W., author.
Title: Battle flags of the wars for North America, 1754–1783 : foreign armies
    and regiments / Steven W. Hill.
Description: Essex, Connecticut : Stackpole Books, [2025] | Includes bibliographical
    references.
Identifiers: LCCN 2024014771 (print) | LCCN 2024014772 (ebook) |
    ISBN 9780811776738 (cloth) | ISBN 9780811776745 (ebook)
Subjects: LCSH: United States—History—Revolution, 1775–1783—Flags. |
    United States—History—French and Indian War, 1754–1763—Flags. |
    Standards, Military—France. | Standards, Military—Great Britain. |
    Standards, Military—Germany. | Standards, Military—Spain. | Flags—
    United States—History.
Classification: LCC E289 .H66 2025 (print) | LCC E289 (ebook) | DDC 355.1/5—
    dc23/eng/20240404
LC record available at https://lccn.loc.gov/2024014771
LC ebook record available at https://lccn.loc.gov/2024014772

Printed in India

For my wife, Reva,
my powerful partner for over 50 years,
whose unwavering love and support have made this book possible.

NESCIT PERICULA

G.D.1908.

Table of Contents

Previously unpublished watercolor of unidentified Hessian Fahne, by Gherardi Davis, 1906. Gherardi Davis papers, Manuscripts and Archives Division, The New York Public Library.

Acknowledgments

The present work is the product of nearly fifty years of research. As I neared retirement in 2020 and began to seriously collect and collate my sources (photographs, etc.), to at long last write the book I had so long been planning, I was surprised to find among the files, not only partial outlines and some tentative introductory materials, but letters to prospective publishers as far back as the 1980s! So I can only assume that many people whom I have worked with and corresponded with and received help and information from over that long span will be inadvertently left out of these acknowledgments. Nevertheless, there are certainly many individuals and organizations to whom and to which I am grateful for their part in making this book possible.

Colonel J. Craig Nannos, of the Pennsylvania National Guard, member of the Company of Military Collectors and Historians, and curator of the First Troop Philadelphia City Cavalry Armory, has been a valuable source of information and running interference with museums and collections in Philadelphia, Pennsylvania in general, and the US Army and Army National Guard, for too many years for either of us to want to count.

Josh Bucchioni, formerly of Colonial Williamsburg, has sent much useful and interesting information, has read some of my drafts, and been generally helpful and supportive of my efforts to get this book done. Don Troiani, historical painter, has been a friend for many, many years, and has always been very generous with information from his research and collections.

Meredith Mann, of the New York Public Library, Special Collections, was extremely helpful in retrieving and going through the collected papers of Gherardi Davis, whose *Regimental Colors in the War of the Revolution,* has stood as the primary source on the topic since its publication in 1907, with supplemental additions in 1910. Looking through Davis's original correspondence with German archivists was incredibly helpful for the sections on Hessian and Braunschweig flags.

Among British sources, I would especially like to thank Dr. Julie Holder and Dr. Calum Robertson of the National Museums Scotland, for information and wonderful photos of several regimental colours and especially for closeups of the remnants of the Seventy-First Fraser's Highlanders, which I believe have never before been looked at by flag researchers specifically to create an accurate reconstruction. Retired Captain Mick Holtby, curator at The Royal Lancers & Nottinghamshire Yeomanry Museum, sent much useful information and answered several questions on the uniforms and guidons of the Seventeenth Light Dragoons and British guidons of the period in general. Jennifer Marshall, archivist at the Black Watch Museum in Perth, sent me photos I had not previously seen, and which were invaluable in sorting out colours of the Forty-Second Regiment, Royal Highlanders. Many thanks to Scott Flaving, regimental archivist, Duke of Wellington's Regiment Museum, and Eli Dawson, curator, Calderdale Museums, both of Bankfield Museum in Halifax, United Kingdom, for photographs and helpful information on the colours of the Thirty-Third Regiment. Also special thanks to Kate Thaxton, Curator, Royal Norfolk Regimental Museum, who answered questions and sent info that helps correct many inaccurate assumptions and reconstructions of British colours. The staff of the Shropshire Museum in Shrewsbury—several curators ago—was very forthcoming in both photos and information. Special thanks also to Alex Welirang, Military Historian and Photographer, as well as Colonel (retd) Michael Dudding, Chairman of the Royal Fusiliers

Memorial Chapel Committee, and Major (retd) Mick McCarthy MBE, Regimental Area Secretary, RHQ Fusiliers, for information, photographs, and measurements of colours of the Seventh Regiment, Royal Fusiliers on display at the Church of the Holy Sepulchre, London.

Alejandro M. de Quesada Jr. of Tampa, Florida, and Josh Phillips of Heritage Conservation LLC were both very helpful in the reconstruction of the King's Colour of the Fourth American Regiment.

Ruby Fougere and Daniel Pitcher of Parks Canada, Fortress of Louisbourg National Historic Site, Louisbourg, NS, answered questions on the manuscript drawings of French drapeaux in their collections and forwarded useful information on the disposition of the French drapeaux captured at Louisbourg in 1758.

On Hessian colors, many thanks to Frédéric Aubert, France, assisted by Michael Zahn in Germany, who offered a trans-Atlantic friendship and much insight on some of the more obscure sources, and made a compelling and convincing argument that all Hessian regiments had white Leibfahnen. As covered in the section on Hessian Fahnen, that was decidedly *not* the opinion of earlier researchers, including Hessian and other German authors. Thanks also to Marcus Jae, Germany, for onsite research in Hessian Archives, and unselfish sharing of it, almost twenty years ago—but still invaluable to the present book.

The section on Spanish banderas simply would not, or could not, have been written without the incredible assistance of Luis Sorando Muzás, the resident expert on Spanish military flags at the Museo del Ejército in Toledo, Spain. Luis saw a post on Facebook of one of my reproductions and my plans to catalog and publish a book on colors of foreign regiments in the American War of Independence, and without knowing me at all, kindly offered to assist in any way he could on the Spanish banderas. And he certainly followed through.

And finally, I very sincerely thank my wife, Reva Karen Strudeman Hill, without whose support and indulgence the present work would never have been completed. Thank you, my dear, for putting up with late nights in the sewing room or at the computer, research trips too numerous to list, visits to museums and historic sites you could have done without, and your unwavering good cheer and positive support for such an arcane and/or esoteric undertaking.

Introduction

Regimental Flags of Foreign Armies in North America, 1754–1783

Thou art beautiful, O my love, as Tirzah,
comely as Jerusalem, terrible as an army with banners.
—SONG OF SOLOMON 6:4

This study covers regimental flags—colours, drapeaux, Fahnen, or banderas, in the languages of the troops which carried them—of foreign regiments in the battles and campaigns fought in North America during the period of the wars of empire, 1754 through the end of the American War of Independence in 1783. Its purpose is to give an accurate picture of how these colors actually looked at the time of their use, rather than as worn and dilapidated mementos of battles fought two centuries ago. It attempts to correct mistakes and misunderstandings that have crept into the literature on the topic from the very earliest sources, including some of the standard reference works. As William H. Prescott, America's first great historian, explained his purpose in 1847, "I have attempted to seize the characteristic expression of a distant age, and exhibit it in the freshness of life."[1]

The colors of a regiment were almost sacred to the soldiers to which they belonged and deserve to be properly recorded. Each was carried by a junior officer or officer-cadet, and their loss was considered a great calamity and lasting shame. During the period under study, there are many examples of colors being burned or spirited away rather than surrendered, even after a battle nobly fought and fairly lost. Those colors taken in battle were usually sent to the home country to be displayed as marks of honor to the troops that had captured them.

During the French and Indian War, 1754–1763 (known as the Seven Years' War in Europe) and the American War of Independence 1775–1783, no fewer than nine European kingdoms and principalities had regular troops engaged in conventional warfare in North America: Britain, France, Spain, and the German states of Ansbach-Bayreuth, Anhalt-Zerbst, Braunschweig (Brunswick), Hesse-Hanau, Hesse-Cassel, and Waldeck. There were many militia and irregular units active in North America during this period as well, but these generally did not carry colors, or if they did, nothing is known of them. The flags and colors of American units, except those raised in America as part of the British Army during the French and Indian War, and five Loyalist regiments raised during the War of Independence and officially placed on the American Establishment of the British Army, are outside the scope of this work.

Throughout this work, I have attempted to portray the flags as they would have looked in life. To do this, I have worked as often as possible from extant originals, artistically undoing years of neglect or questionable conservation and reconstruction or correcting, where necessary, earlier artistic license or conventions that have accrued over the years and given many original flags a historic portrait very different from their actual appearance. Where the originals no longer exist, I have used contemporary descriptions, comparisons to other originals of the same general style or period, and details from contemporary styles of decorative painting or embroidery. Artistic tastes change dramatically over long stretches of time, and the ways flags are made and embellished change as well, generally mirroring the tastes and conventions of the times. To take one example: the fleur-de-lis prominent in many French flags of the eighteenth century have a very large, pronounced, and bulbous central leaf compared to what is now considered a properly dimensioned and attractive design. Researchers in the nineteenth century thought of the fleur-de-lis as being tall, slender, and elegant, and that is how it was drawn. In the twentieth century the fleur-de-lis have become more compact and symmetric. But in each case, the later drawings have tended to reflect the tastes of the time the drawings were made rather than the original flags they were meant to portray. I have tried to capture the original appearance of such details—regardless of how awkward they may appear to modern eyes—rather than re-drawing them to what I think is more attractive and appealing now.

In many cases, of course, we cannot know the exact appearance of a flag, having only a record of its use, a description in words, or an obviously flawed contemporary or later drawing. This is where reconstruction must be a reasonable interpretation based on other flags from the same period, likely area of manufacture, period styles of painting or embroidery. It must be understood that in many cases, there is not one absolutely correct answer. In many cases, we not only lack the original flag, but we have conflicting authorities describing one flag differently—sometimes even based on contemporary eyewitnesses. Here we must take several things into account: How credible is the eyewitness? How unbiased is the historian? Is the discrepancy something as simple as describing a gold detail as "embroidered" when we know from extant examples that such flags were actually painted? Are two accounts actually describing two different flags? Flags were issued, lost, repaired, re-issued, and replaced on an entirely random basis, and a new flag given to an old unit might look quite different from the one it was replacing. A French flag with fleur-de-lis *semé* (uniformly sprinkled) on its central cross may have had sixty or more during one period and only forty-eight when a new flag was presented. A British colour with a small and compact Union wreath at its center in 1775 may have had a replacement colour in 1780 that had a Union wreath twice the size and partially spilling over the edges of the red cross onto the white. In some cases, all we can do is make a best guess, and give the reasons why. In every such case, I have tried to make my reasoning clear. To again quote Prescott: "I have suffered the scaffolding to remain after the building has been completed. . . . I have shown to the reader the steps of the process by which I have come to my conclusions. Instead of requiring him to take my version of the story on trust, I have endeavored to give him a reason for my faith." [2]

The most obvious difference between this work and most earlier works on the topic is that I have chosen to *not* use line drawings, except where they are used to define patterns or general characteristics of whole classes of flags. There are very few photographs of originals of the period, and those that do exist show very old, damaged, and sometimes reconstructed flags. Therefore, I have used photographs of modern reproductions, computer-assisted reconstructions, or, in a very few cases, paintings of the colors in question. While line drawings can give a very accurate plan or model of a particular flag, they do not give an accurate impression of the flag's actual appearance. Flags in life do not have black lines separating the different colors or different elements of their design (except for Spanish flags of the period, which had black cable stitched along many of the seams to delineate and highlight their designs). In fact, the opposite is often closer to the truth—flags in life can have large sections of a single color pieced together, and while these seams are generally not shown in line drawings, they are often very obvious on the real item. The large single-color field of British regimentals may be made of three or four panels seamed together. The red cross so prominent in the center of British Union colours, or the white cross of the French drapeaux, are not seamless pieces of cloth cut into the shape of a cross; they are pieced together, and in real life, the double or quadruple layers of cloth in the seams and the stitching holding them together are often very apparent. Obviously, I have not made some three hundred individual flags for this book, but with the production of a model of at least one of each major type, additional flags required only the substitution of one color for another, or one slightly different wreath, or a regimental numeral. In the cases where a different central design or other motif was superimposed on a photograph of an actual flag already photographed, the added elements were painted at full size and then downsized on the computer to fit. For those interested, I have made a note in the picture captions of any that were completed as full-sized flags, then used additionally as a basis for others of the same pattern.

GENERAL NOTES ON THE CONSTRUCTION OF MILITARY COLORS

Most flags used by troops in the field throughout the period this book covers were made of very tightly woven silk. There were different names used at different times and places, but generally, all silks used for flags would now be considered different grades of taffeta, though some cavalry flags were made of damask or other figured silks. The silks used for these flags varied greatly in quality and weight; there are examples of complaints of flags falling to pieces in the field, the embroidery falling out, or the paint causing the silk to crack. At the same time however, colors were expected to last within a regiment for many years, or generations, and often did. Silk at the time was quite standardized at a width of approximately twenty-eight English inches, seventy to seventy-one centimeters in modern measurement, although some British and most German flags were made using eighteen to nineteen-inch widths. These two widths, twenty-eight modern inches and eighteen to nineteen modern inches, seem to have been quite constant throughout the period, even if the units used to measure them differed. There was no standardization of measurements used in different parts of Europe, so the same nominal width might be listed differently in different places. A French inch was a bit bigger than an English inch, for example: silks manufactured in France were regulated at twenty-seven French inches (*ponces*) but would still be seventy to seventy-one centimeters in modern measurement. And of course, then as now, the standards were not always met, and variations of an inch or more, either wider or narrower, would be commonplace. It must also be remembered that all sewing and embroidery during the period was done by hand. Embroidery, by modern standards, often used excessively large stitches and sometimes cut the silk so completely that the embroidered sections broke away. The relatively strong selvage of the silk, as it came from the loom, was often used for the top and bottom edges of a flag so that it would not have to be hemmed. While most flags had their sizes prescribed by tradition or regulation, in life they often varied by several inches larger or smaller, depending on the widths of silk available and how many pieces had to be seamed together, with each seam taking up a little bit of the nominal width.

NOTES ON TERMINOLOGY

While I have used the generic term "flags" when discussing common characteristics of flags of the period, or of my treatment of them within this book, the more specific terms in the language of origin are used in the different sections on each country—hence "colours" for the British, "drapeaux" for the French, "Fahnen" for the German, and "banderas" for the Spanish. In American English, all of these flags would be considered "colors" as they are the unique and distinctive flags carried by individual regimental units rather than generic flags that represent a nation, an army, or an ideal.

English is also used for all military terminology except in the case of the nomenclature of the flags themselves; for example, each company (an English word) in a Hessian regiment would carry a "Leibfahne" or a "Kompaniefahne," but not a "Body Fahne" or a "Company Fahne." In addition, in the case of some of the German states in the period we are addressing, Frenchified terms such as "Compagnie" were used instead of their common German equivalents. I have chosen to ignore these as simply complicating things even more.

GENERAL OBSERVATIONS ON COLORS, THEIR DEFINITION, AND USES

"Colors," as distinct from "flags," are individual and unique to a body of soldiers, generally a regiment, or, in some cases, a battalion, the permanent organizations on which all armies of the period were based. Colors are so closely associated with regiments and battalions that such organizations are often termed "color-carrying units." Smaller units, such as companies in the infantry, companies or troops in the cavalry, and companies or batteries in the artillery, might carry guidons or markers of various types, but these are not considered colors. While not common until later periods, designating flags for brigades, divisions, or corps would also not be considered colors.

The term "colors" derives from the traditions of heraldry, where a knight in full armor, or members of his retinue, could be identified literally by the colors on their shields, their tunics, their horse dressings, and the like. When regiments and then entire national armies began to be uniformed in distinctive clothing of various colors, individual regiments came to be identified by the colors of the flags flying above them. In various internal wars in Britain in the seventeenth century, whole sections of an army were defined by the colors of their flags and sometimes their sashes and other individual accoutrements. On the continent, regiments raised by nobles or corporate entities such as cities or cantons began to use flags based on the colors of the nobles or corporations who paid for them. With the rise of national armies, regimental colors became much more regulated and generally settled on traditional colors or symbols of the nations to which they belonged. By the time of the period of this study, virtually all regimental colors had strong national designs and motifs that readily identified their unit's national origins, if not the monarch or armies they were currently serving.

And yet, colors were unique in that each was a specific physical flag, not an idea or pattern or design, like a uniform, that could be reproduced in a number of sizes or shapes. A British Union flag can be made in many different sizes and many different fabrics, it can have a pole sleeve, or grommets to attach to a halyard, the central red cross may be broad or skinny, the white cross may run accurately from corner to corner or be haphazardly placed almost parallel to the top and bottom of the flag, but it will be readily identifiable as a British flag. It may even have a wreath and the name of a regiment at its middle, but that will not make that flag a color. Even the most perfect reproduction of a flag carried by the Ninth Regiment of Foot in 1776, for example, will not be the colors of that regiment. It will only be a representation, more or less authentic or accurate. Only the flags that the regiment actually carried in service can be said to be that regiment's colors.

"Colors" in English can be either singular or plural. A single regimental flag could be called colors simply because it generally did indeed comprise more than one literal color. In American, British, French, and Spanish regiments or battalions during the period we are exploring, the unit generally carried a pair of flags. This pair is also referred to as the regimental colors, giving rise to the confusion. It is equally correct to say for example that "Ensign X carried the King's Colour at the Battle of Y," as to record that "Ensign X carried the King's Colours (plural) at the battle of Y." In either case, it is clear that Ensign X was carrying only one flag. When an account tells us that "the colours were in danger of being captured," we can only surmise from the context whether we are talking about one flag or two. French, German, and Spanish do not have this problem—the terms for colors in these languages follow the normal singular/plural rules of the tongue: "drapeau/drapeaux" in French, "Fahne/Fahnen" in German, and "bandera/banderas" in Spanish. (While I have avoided the use of the term throughout this book, "stand of colors" is and was also used interchangeably to mean either a single flag with its staff and tassels, or in its plural sense to denote the *pair* of flags with their staffs, generally carried by a regiment.)

The basic unit of organization for all armies of the period under consideration was the regiment. A regiment was considered a permanent organization. Even though, in practice, they were created and disbanded routinely, regiments were permanent in the sense that they had an individual identity and remained intact even as the higher and lower organization of an army might shift and change depending on its mission or needs. A regiment had a name, sometimes from its original commander, sometimes from its current commander, sometimes from the locale in which it was raised, or a number based on its seniority, or both.

Technically, the regiment was an administrative unit, and the battalion was the tactical, or combat, unit. Most regiments of the period had a single battalion, so in practice and in many documents, the terms regiment and battalion were used interchangeably. Some regiments had two or more battalions, which were almost never fielded together in a single army. During the French and Indian War of 1754–1763, the French Army in North America was composed entirely of second battalions; the first battalion of each of the named regiments fighting in America remained in its home department in France. During the American War of Independence, however, the French and Spanish regiments were the exception; each was composed of two permanent battalions fielded together as a single tactical unit. The size of a regiment or battalion varied by nation and will be addressed in the section on that nation's colors.

British Regimental Colours in North America

INTRODUCTION: BRITISH REGIMENTAL COLOURS, 1743–1800

Prior to 1743, British regiments were generally known by the names of their colonels, and each regiment's colours, procured by each individual colonel, were embellished with designs entirely at his whim, often with elements of his personal or family coat of arms. In 1743, the first of a series of royal warrants and regulations standardized British colours in several important ways that still obtained at the time of the wars in North America: (1) the first colour of each battalion was to be the Great Union, (2) no color would display any designs except those approved, and specifically *not* any part of the arms of their colonels, (3) the second colour was to be the color of the regimental facing and display a small union in the upper canton next to the staff, (4) except those regiments specifically authorized Royal devices or "ancient" badges, colours would display in their centers the rank of the regiment painted in gold, in a Union wreath of roses and thistles on one stalk. Regiments with their uniform facings in red or white were to have a regimental colour with white field overlaid by the red cross of St. George. Colours with an all-red field were reserved for the Guards regiments. Descriptions were given for regiments with special devices and ancient badges: the approved Royal device replaced the Union wreath in the center on both colours, the rank of the regiment was to be in Roman numerals in the upper corner near the staff, and the ancient badges were to be displayed in the other three corners of the regimental colour only. The cord and tassels of all colours were to be crimson and gold.

Warrants and drawings prepared in 1747, 1749, and 1751 reiterated the points made in 1743, authorized for the first time the devices to be "painted or embroidered," and included watercolor paintings for those regiments allowed ancient badges. These dates are often cited individually, but in fact, they refer to a single set of rules prepared by Colonel Robert Napier, Adjutant General (AG) of the British Army, in 1747, delivered to the Clothing Board in 1749, and published in 1751. Each painting included a label or scroll on the colour for regimental motto, although not all regiments had a motto at the time. It is unreasonable to suppose, however, that flags were made, presented, and carried with blank scrolls, and no original colour so made has yet come to light.

The AG's watercolors were not exact in their proportions, but Napier also included a carefully drafted scale drawing that showed the exact sizes of the component parts of the King's Colour, including the Union wreath sized to fit entirely within the thirteen-inch wide cross of St. George (see illustration). The standard drawing did not include a motto scroll. It is often mistakenly claimed that before the Warrant of 1768 the size of the colours was not officially stated; the scale drawing accompanying the 1751 regulation clearly indicated both length and width. It also gave precise dimensions for the pike, spear-head, and the cord and tassels.

Detail, *The Redoubt, Battle of Bunker Hill, June 17, 1775,* **by Don Troiani, 2009, oil on canvas.**
Photo courtesy of the artist.

Fig. 16.—Diagram of a King's Colour, 1747.

A B. Six feet six inches.   B C. Six feet two inches.   D E. One foot one inch.   E F. Five inches.   G H. Nine inches.

Length of the pike (spear and ferrule included), nine feet ten inches.   Thickness of the pike at top, five-eighths, and at bottom seven-eighths of an inch.

Length of the cords and tassels, three feet, each tassel four inches.   Length of the spear, four inches.

Colonel Napier's scale drawing of 1751, reprinted in Milne, *Standards and Colours of the Army*.

Another document generally overlooked was published in 1758. In that year fifteen new regiments were created from the second battalions of those regiments which had them, and a circular letter was published to fix the facing colors and lace of the uniforms and the colours to be carried. This was the first description of colours for regiments faced in black—there had been none in 1751. Colours for these regiments were to be a black field overlaid with the red cross of St. George. This document also specified that the rank (designating number) of the regiment would be "on crimson" in the center of the colours. Prior to this all colours had their rank painted or embroidered directly on the silk field regardless of its color. The well-known Warrant of 1768 basically restated the provisions from the earlier documents and added two regiments to those allowed ancient badges and special devices. It also reduced the size of the colours by two inches on the pike, so that properly made colours would thereafter be six feet six inches flying, and six feet deep on the pike.

Extant colours from the period tend to be fairly close to the regulation size, though King's Colours with their many separate pieces of silk sewn together are often a bit smaller. Due to how silk was manufactured, regimentals had to be built up of panels of a single color. Four panels of eighteen-and-a-half-inch wide silk as used in German flags would come out at almost exactly seventy-two inches. The small Union canton of approximately twenty to twenty-two inches square would have to be mitered into the second panel from the top. An alternative was to use standard twenty-eight-inch widths of silk cut down to three equal panels of approximately twenty-four inches to achieve the regulation size of seventy-two inches. This was easier for the flag-maker because the Union canton could be just a little bigger and simply rest on the seam between the first and second panels rather than having to be sewn around an inset corner. Some of the rococo pattern described below were made of two pieces of approximately twenty-seven inches—within the standard variation for cloth nominally made to be twenty-eight inches—and a top panel of about nineteen to twenty inches, with the Union canton made correspondingly smaller, again so as to obviate the problem of mitering in the corner. It might be pointed out that at this period the Royal Navy did not even bother to describe the sizes of flags for the different sizes of ships in feet and inches, simply saying how many widths of bunting were to be used, since bunting was always of a standard size: twenty-two inches wide up to about 1800, eighteen inches thereafter. (The actual term used was "breadth." A breadth was equal to one-half a standard width of bunting, eleven inches up to about 1800, nine inches after.)

The colours for infantry were of a heavy silk taffeta of a fairly plain weave—in some cases a slight ribbing effect can be seen as there were fewer warp threads per inch than weft. Colours throughout this period did not have fringe. After about 1760, designs were generally embroidered, though painting was still authorized. In either case the reverse of the flag would have appeared as a mirror image of the obverse—the embroidery thread or paint went straight through the fabric. On flags before 1758 the regimental number also would have appeared backward on the reverse of the colours. The addition of the red cartouche in 1758 allowed the regimental title to be painted correctly on both sides of a solid painted red panel or embroidered correctly on two separate pieces of red silk appliquéd on opposite sides of the flag. There remained a problem on colours for regiments that had an ancient badge or device at center and the regimental number in the upper canton near the staff. Whether painted or embroidered, these would continue to read correctly only on one side and backward on the other. Some regiments got around this problem by having the regimental rank embroidered in a small silk cartouche appliquéd to both sides.

All British colours were made with a separate pole sleeve. This was almost always red on the King's Colour; of surviving regimental colours, they are about evenly split between those with a red sleeve and those with a sleeve matching the color of the field. Although the pole was tapered, the pole sleeve was not. On some colours there was a small eyelet whip-stitched into the sleeve near the top. The cord of the cord and tassels could be passed through this eyelet, run round the staff, and passed through its own loop, thus both tightening the pole sleeve around the pole and keeping the cord and tassels from slipping down the staff. The pole, called a pike for infantry, was nine feet ten inches from the bottom of the brass butt ferrule

Example of union mitered into field made of four eighteen- to nineteen-inch panels. Lower edge of union extends about two inches into second panel. On flag made of three panels, the seam connecting top two panels simply runs along bottom edge of union. (Author's photo).

to the top of the spearpoint. The spear was to be four inches high. Based on surviving examples, this was generally interpreted as the blade itself—most spears on British colours are about seven to eight inches tall counting the ferrule that the spear blade screws into. Most of the spears of the period of this study were teardrop shaped with four sections cut out to leave a cross with a rounded cross-piece inside. A second less common style had a different arrangement of cutouts such that what was left was more of a rounded "X" than a cross. The ferrules were also of two general types—either fairly slender with two rings and a flared top somewhat like a cannon barrel, or somewhat stouter with a heavy ridge or ring near the bottom, a slight taper, and a flared cap at the top, much like modern military-style finials. Either type of spear might be screwed into either type of ferrule. There does not seem to be any system as to which regiments got which spear type. The spears were rather plump and round-bottomed through the end of the eighteenth century, those of the early nineteenth century tended to be narrower and more straight-sided. British spears are generally drawn far too large and narrow in secondary illustrations. All colours included cord and tassels, nominally six feet from end to end, usually red with metallic gold netting over the wooden tassel core and a bushy brush-cut silk fringe of red with gold highlights. Most tassels were straight-sided, sometimes with a very slight taper, and a separate bead on top, rather than bottle-shaped, as became popular in the next century. The cords suspending the tassels were very thin and might be either woven cord or braided ropes of red and gold. There was a slide to keep the cords from flying about in separate directions, though it appears that in some cases, the cords were simply knotted together.

Reproduction British spear and tassels circa 1750–1800. (Author's photo).

Mounted troops carried standards or guidons, much smaller than colours, so as to be manageable on horseback. Standards were almost square, guidons longer and swallow-tailed, but the terms were often used interchangeably. While both British cavalry regiments in the American War of Independence were light dragoons and carried guidons, inspectors in 1769 and 1771 listed them as standards in the reports.

Each mounted regiment had a King's Standard or guidon, and two or more squadron standards or guidons. The King's were the same for all regiments; only the regimental rank and color of the fringe varied. The Warrants of 1751 and 1768 were identical in their descriptions of both King's and second standard or guidons; the Warrant of 1768 added specific details for regiments that had not yet existed at the earlier date. For the King's or first standard or guidon: "Crimson, with the Rose and Thistle conjoined, and Crown over them in the Centre. His Majesty's Motto, *DIEU ET MON DROIT*, underneath. The White Horse, in a Compartment, in the First and Fourth Corner; and the Rank of the Regiment, in Gold or Silver Characters, on a Ground of the same Colour as the Facing of the Regiment, in a Compartment, in the Second and Third Corners." The "compartment" was an oval or rounded rectangle cartouche with gold frame. Some King's guidons had the regimental rank in a small wreath of roses and thistles rather than the prescribed compartment.

Like the regimental colours of infantry, the second and third standards or guidons were the same color as the facings of the regimental uniforms. The color or colors of the fringe were specifically listed for each regiment. Both mounted regiments that served in North America had a "particular badge" and a motto, in addition to its numerical rank. The wording of the warrant was ambiguous: "the Badge of the Regiment in the Center, or the Rank of the Regiment, in Gold or Silver Roman Characters, on a Crimson Ground, within a Wreath of Roses and Thistles on the same stalk. The Motto of the Regiment underneath." The serial clauses separated by commas allow for several interpretations. Judging by the few existing guidons that survive the period roughly from 1760 to 1816, those with numerals or lettering of a regimental name usually have the figures in accordance with the warrant on a red ground within a wreath of roses and thistles. Those with a regimental badge are about equally split between those having no wreath and those with a wreath, which is generally not a complete circle and varies considerably in design and execution from one flag to the next. But in all cases, the badge is directly on the ground color of the guidon; none has the badge on a red ground within a wreath.

The warrant goes on: "The White Horse, on a Red Ground, to be in the First and Fourth Compartment, [same as the King's Standard or guidon] and the Rose and Thistle conjoined upon a Red Ground, in the Second and Third Compartments. Those Corps that have a particular badge, are to carry it in the Centre of their Second and Third Standard or Guidon, [nothing about a red ground, or a wreath] with the Rank of the Regiment on a Red Ground, within a small Wreath of Roses and Thistles, in the Second and Third Corners." When there is a wreath incorporated around the central badge, the compartments for the regimental number are made like those with the white horse rather than the regulation small wreaths. The third squadron of the regiment was designated by a numeral 3 on a small red medallion below the motto.

Not counting the fringe or the pole sleeve, standards were twenty-seven by twenty-nine inches, guidons twenty-seven by forty-one inches to the extreme outer ends. The guidons of light dragoons were "to be of a smaller size," but appear to have been generally of the same size as all other mounted troops, perhaps a bit shorter to the ends of the swallowtail. The lance was nine feet including the spear and butt ferrule, the spears of various patterns, but mostly like those on the infantry colours. Lances for the "smaller" guidons of the light dragoons were presumably shorter, but no specified size is given. Both standards and guidons generally had cord and tassels, sometimes with elaborate knots in the cord to take up the extra length.

Standards were made of figured silk damask, surrounded by heavy fringe, double sided, being two layers of silk back-to-back, even though the designs were the same on both sides. Guidons were of plain silk and were a single layer. Throughout the period under study, guidons had a very rounded fly end, with a narrow cut about nine to ten inches deep at the midpoint. For some unknown reason, most guidons were made of two pieces of standard twenty-seven to twenty-eight-inch wide silk sewn together vertically, top to bottom, selvage to selvage, and the top and bottom edge of the flag rolled and hemmed. To produce a guidon nominally twenty-seven inches on the staff, why not just use the usual twenty-seven to twenty-eight-inch width of silk as manufactured, and cut it as long or short as required? Instead, guidons were made like square standards with additional silk added for the swallowtail. In addition, the designs painted or embroidered on them were generally centered not at the optical center of the entire flag, but at the center of the squarish portion of the flag to the left of the cut of the swallowtail. Pole sleeves were generally of the same color as the field, usually added as a separate piece, though sometimes the leading edge of the field was simply rolled over and sewn down. Most had a small whip-stitched eyelet near the top for the cord of the cord and tassels to pass through. The designs were usually very heavy embroidery, although the guidons of both mounted regiments that served in North America during this period were painted.

While most drawings, paintings, or reproductions of British standards or guidons of the period 1751–1815 are reasonably accurate, with only details to quibble over, British infantry colours are routinely misrepresented in secondary works in three ways that lead to a very inaccurate idea of what they looked like in life:

1. The central designs are drawn far too large in proportion to the whole flag.
2. The colours are drawn, particularly the King's Colours, with the white fimbriation—the white strips that separate the red cross of St. George from the blue field of the flag—far too narrow, and often as not, the white corner-to-corner cross of St. Andrew far too wide. These mistakes are often compounded by the fact that most colours during the period of the American War of Independence were made with just the opposite attributes: their white fimbriations were *wider*, and the St. Andrew's cross *narrower*, than per regulation.
3. The central designs are drawn so freely as to give the impression that there was little regularity among the regiments. In fact, there were standardized designs, each theoretically approved by the King, almost certainly associated with individual makers, which account for by far the largest number of colours that survive from the period, suggesting that those colours which have not survived, would nevertheless have been very much like those that have.

Unfortunately, the standard references used for most secondary works are unintentionally misleading. Samuel Milne Milne's *Standards and Colours of the Army* has been the standard reference on British colours since its publication in 1893. Milne's desire to adequately portray the salient points of art and design in British colours, however, led him to draw the designs on the flags much larger than they would appear in life. While Milne clearly stated his purpose in the introduction to his book, apparently very few have bothered to read it. British colours have been drawn ever since with their central motifs far too large in relation to other parts of the overall design. In book after book, the central Union wreath is shown spilling far out over the white fimbriation of the central cross on the King's Colour or filling virtually the entire field of regimentals. Milne's drawings might also be faulted for ignoring accurate proportions between the crosses and the white fimbriation on the colors, another mistake common to most later depictions.

Apart from the oversized central design, most reconstructions of period British colours undersize the width of the white fimbriations and oversize the width of the St. Andrew's cross. According to Napier's standard drawing, the fimbriations—the white strips that separate the red cross of St. George from the blue field of the flag—were to be five inches wide. The white corner-to-corner St. Andrew's cross was to be nine inches wide. If all these pieces are made exactly to the standard, then the cross and its white fimbriations would be twenty-three inches, or very close to one-third the entire width of a seventy-two-inch wide flag.

Original King's Colour, 1761. The Colonial Williamsburg Foundation. Museum Purchase.

King's Colour, 1751, with Milne-style exaggerations. From regimental history published in 1930.

Regimental colour, 1780. From Milne's *Standards and Colors*, showing drastically oversized central device. This particular flag was originally dark blue, which Milne points out. But as with oversized details, later authors have looked at the pictures and not read the words—this flag has sometimes been redrawn with the field all white.

With the nine-inch wide cross of St. Andrew also taking up considerable space in the overall field of the flag, the triangles of blue are actually relatively small. During most of the period 1760–1786, most King's Colours were made with the fimbriation wider than called for, and the St. Andrew's cross much narrower, all being close to six inches wide. This was probably due to some supposed economy in using the standard widths of silk, but this is merely speculation. Around 1790, the St. Andrew's cross again began to be made as per Napier's warrant, only to be superseded in 1801 by the need to include the red cross of St. Patrick counter-charged with it. The white fimbriation on either side of the St. George's cross on the King's Colours continued to be made about six inches wide well into nineteenth century, though there are examples of colours with the regulation five inches. The Union cantons of the regimental colours were simply small editions of the King's Colour with all parts roughly in the same proportions.

An oddity of British colour design is that the central devices are always considered as a single unit and centered from top to bottom of the colour. Where a wreath or shield or some other insignia is surmounted by a crown, for example, the main insignia will be placed lower than center on the flag so that the single unit of device *and* crown will appear centered. See Eighty-Fourth Royal Highland Emigrants or Seventh Fusiliers in the American War of Independence as examples. Drawings in secondary sources tend to place the main device dead center and the crown above. It is also found that some colours were made back-to-front, with the pole on the right-hand edge of the flag. In general, this would not even be noticed, except on those colours with special devices at their centers and the regimental number painted or embroidered in the upper canton next to the staff, where the numerals would run from left to right *toward* the staff. The Seventh Royal Fusiliers is an example. The Sixtieth Royal Americans was also made this way, as was a colour for a second battalion of the Forty-Second Regiment raised in 1780. On all three of these colours, the Royal garter at center was made correctly on the reverse of the colour; when viewed from the front with the pole to the left, the buckle on the garter is on the right, opposite of what it should be. All the lettering reads correctly on both sides, however, because it is done on double layers of silk and appliquéd to both sides of the colour.

From fairly early on, most British colours seem to have been made by a relatively small number of firms in England and Ireland. Patterns of design and workmanship are clearly evident—in fact the quality control among colors made to the same pattern is quite remarkable. And while Colonel Napier's drawings would seem to impose a specific interpretation of the Union wreath, it appears that different firms may have vied for dramatic effect while staying within the letter, if not the spirit, of the law. The earliest authenticated colours comport reasonably well to Napier's drawings, but by about 1761, the central wreaths had expanded in richness, complexity, and overall size.

Though few original colours survive from the period of the French and Indian War, it appears that early on at least, the Union wreath was still generally small and close to Napier's model. The regimental number was placed directly on the silk field. What is claimed to be the oldest surviving colour in the British Army belongs to the Ninth Foot. The flag itself was presented to the regiment in 1772, but the embroidered central wreath was taken from an earlier colour presented in 1757 or 1759. The wreath is almost circular and measures only eleven inches across at the widest point, even smaller than the pattern wreath shown on Napier's original scale drawing. The new directive of 1758—coming after many regiments were already

Center of regimental colour, Ninth Regiment, circa 1757 (Milne).

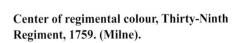

Center of regimental colour, Thirty-Ninth Regiment, 1759. (Milne).

Center of regimental colour, One-Hundred-Third Regiment, 1760. (Milne).

deployed in North America—necessitated a new design to incorporate a crimson cartouche or shield of some type within the Union wreath. This also gave makers the opportunity to update their designs to better suit the changing tastes of military style and the society at large.

Embroidered designs, first authorized in the Warrant of 1751, began to appear around mid-decade. Colours prepared for the second battalion of the Fourth King's Own regiment in 1756 were embroidered, as was the small central wreath of the Ninth regiment generally dated about 1757.

The new embroidered designs were also the first to incorporate natural or realistic garden-style roses in place of the heraldic roses shown in Napier's standard drawing. The Thirty-Ninth Regiment was presented with embroidered colours in 1759 which included both natural and heraldic roses. The regimental number was embroidered directly on the green silk, suggesting that this pattern predated the letter of 1758 specifying the rank of the regiment to be "on crimson." The number within a florid rococo-style cartouche frame, however, is very similar in design to those in the more common patterns described below. The lettering included "REGT," now placed above rather than below the Roman numerals of the regimental rank. While no other flags of this pattern have survived, this nevertheless strongly suggests a standard pattern in which only the numerals need be changed to make a new colour for a new regiment. Colours using the same wreath but made after 1758 probably incorporated a red silk panel into the frame at center. Another in the evolution of embroidered designs was made for the 103rd Regiment raised in 1760 and disbanded at the end of the Seven Years' War. This colour featured a smallish wreath, but a crimson shield bordered in yellow, and roses and thistles, all virtually identical in size and shape to those of the rococo pattern described next. This particular example was reconstructed from the embroidery only, the original silk having rotted away, so the exact layout is somewhat suspect.

The most common of the new standardized patterns has been called the "rococo" pattern for its asymmetric, rambling, natural appearance. The roses are realistic or natural in execution rather than stylized heraldic roses. There are at least eleven extant or otherwise authenticated colours of this pattern, reliably dated between 1761 and 1786. The earliest known flags with this pattern were presented to the Thirty-Third Regiment in 1761 and to the Ninety-Sixth Regiment raised for service in India in the same year, and the latest to the Seventy-Third Foot (formerly 2/42) in India in 1786. The rococo is the most common pattern found on British colours during the American War for Independence.

With only one known exception, all of the rococo colours were embroidered. Although there are small discrepancies in detail, the wreaths are perfectly regular, and must have been laid out with a stencil or tracing. In a few cases the pattern is reversed, or mirror image from the standard. The wreaths are carefully designed to stay within the red cross of St. George on the King's Colour and are of identical size and shape on the regimentals. Wreaths on the regimentals are routinely drawn oversized and completely out of proportion in secondary works.

The central cartouche of the rococo pattern seems to occur in three sub-styles. In about 1770, elements of the embroidered frame began to be made to include two trailing tendrils that come down and twine around the stems of the wreath. A few of this type also had only three rather than four roses on one side of the cartouche, the missing rose replaced by additional leaves, and the little buds terminating each half of the wreath crossing over one another at the top. These variations are probably due to different manufacturers following a standard pattern for the wreath and putting in their own aesthetic touches. Since the central cartouche is of red silk appliquéd on both sides of the flag, the regimental designation always reads correctly on both sides.

The single known exception to the above is a painted regimental colour belonging to the Fiftieth Regiment, dating from 1763. Although the designs of both wreath and cartouche on this flag are similar

Center of original King's Colour, Ninety-Sixth Regiment of Foot, 1761.
Embroidery in colored silk and metallic threads. The Colonial Williamsburg
Foundation. Museum purchase.

Rococo-style wreath with tendrils, 1772. Note that there are only three roses to the left of the cartouche. This is actually the reverse of this colour; in most cases, the branch with five roses is on the left, or the pole side of the flag. (Milne)

to and about the same size as the embroidered rococo pattern, they differ in detail—neither seems to have been an exact model for the other. Unlike most other painted colours, the designs on this flag are painted on a solid red cloud background within the red cross of St. George and are in gold rather than natural colors.

The second common standardized type, presumably from a single source in England, or possibly Ireland (there are references to colours being made in Dublin), was presented to the Eighty-Second, Ninety-Third, and Ninety-Fifth Regiments in 1778 and 1781. The Seventy-Sixth Regiment also had colours of this pattern, as shown in James Peales's painting, *Washington at Yorktown*. Other regiments raised around the same time and place would likely have had similar colours. Another colour of the same pattern, but with two roses obscured or replaced by a motto scroll, was presented to the Seventy-First Regiment when it was re-ranked from Seventy-Third in 1786. The Seventy-Sixth and Eighty-Second have their regimental numbers in Arabic numerals, the other known examples use the traditional Roman numerals.

Colours of this pattern belonging to the Ninety-Fifth were carried against the French invasion of Jersey in 1781 and are the major focus in John Singleton Copley's monumental *The Death of Major Peirson*,

Illustration from photograph of originals, showing new symmetrical pattern wreath introduced circa 1778. The use of Arabic rather than Roman numerals is very unusual in British colours, but not related to pattern of the wreath. (Ross)

COLOURS OF THE
OLD 82D, OR DUKE OF HAMILTON'S REGIMENT
ONE OF SEVEN REGIMENTS RAISED IN SCOTLAND
IN 1778, AND DISBANDED IN 1783-84.
THE 82D WAS CHIEFLY RAISED IN LANARKSHIRE

The new pattern circa 1778–1786, the same as shown in Ross print of Eighty-Second, Duke of Hamilton's Regiment. (Milne)

painted in 1783. Copley was known for his meticulous attention to detail in uniform and equipment and may well have had the original colours to work from.

The wreath on this pattern is neat and symmetric, with the left and right sections virtually identical, as well as much larger than the rococo type. The cartouche is virtually identical to the pattern of the 103rd Regiment of 1760 described above. The wreath is almost circular, and no attempt is made to fit it into the center of the St. George's cross—this is the earliest pattern in which the wreath spills out onto the white fimbriation on the King's color. Nevertheless, none of the foliage or flowers reaches anywhere near the diagonal St. Andrew's cross nor the blue field. The same wreath on the regimental colour is identical in size and at its highest point is still below the level of the small union.

As mentioned above, the rococo pattern survived until the mid-1780s. It was completely replaced about 1790 by a much simpler wreath and heater-shaped shield. The new design was about the same in overall size as the style described above—the roughly circular wreath lapped over onto the white fimbriation, but still no part extended onto the St. Andrew's cross or the blue field. This design, with only minor variations, and of course updated in 1801 to include the red cross of St. Patrick and shamrocks for Ireland in the wreath, remained in use until after the Napoleonic period. The design was often painted; though painting had been authorized from the earliest warrants, its use had been fairly rare after about late-1750s. Two extant flags of this pattern, preserved in Canada, have been mistakenly, or hopefully, identified with at least one famous regiment of the American War of Independence, which is why it is mentioned here.

A Note on Colors Used in British Colours

The colors of silk used in British regimental colours followed the colors of the regimental facings—the collars, cuffs, lapels, and sometimes turnbacks of the uniform coats. In general, these were clear primary colors, white, buff, red, yellow, green, blue, and black. Those regiments with more specific shades, such as "gosling green" for the Fifth Regiment of Foot, "bright yellow" (Tenth), or "pale yellow" (Twentieth and Twenty-Sixth) were so noted in the various warrants issued during the period. One regiment (Thirty-Fifth) was faced orange, and one (Fifty-Ninth) technically among the red-faced regiments, was described in different lists as "pompadour" and "purple."

Buff at the time was more yellowish than now, and relatively light. Buff colours, as they aged, might be misidentified as either white or yellow by impartial contemporary observers. White would never have been snow-white or typing-paper-white, as silk can only be bleached so much before losing all strength but would certainly appear very white when sewn into a flag with reds and blues, or as the main color of a flag with a large red cross superimposed. Royal blue, used for the colours of Royal regiments, was also generally not so dark as we might now think of it; it was a deep blue, but not navy, and often not even especially dark. King's Colours, and the small Union cantons of regimentals, generally used blues not so dark even as royal blue, though the main blue dyes of the time—indigo and Prussian blue—were not perfectly colorfast and faded with time. This fading seems to have reached a natural maximum fairly soon, however, and would then remain the same virtually forever. There were, of course, a few exceptions in which the blues were very dark indeed, but unless the originals are still extant, all reconstructions in this book assume the standard colors available. Though the terms "crimson" and "red" were used more or less interchangeably in the various warrants and regulations pertaining to colours, the red silks used were generally more crimson than scarlet, more toward the blue end of the range, and certainly darker and more intense than the scarlet coats of the soldiers.

A Note on British Regimental Titles

Great Britain was among the first nations to identify its regiments by numbers corresponding to their seniority, or earliest date of establishment. Before the Warrant of 1743, regiments had been officially known by the names of their current colonels, though a few regiments even then had informal traditional titles associated with them, such as the "Buffs" for their (at the time) distinctive uniform facings, or the "Inniskillings," based on the regiment's origin and the area where the bulk of its recruits were enrolled. While day-to-day orders and other military records continued to address regiments by the names of their colonels well into the period of the French and Indian War, the regiments' official titles were effectively fixed as numbers in 1743. Regiments up to number Forty-One were relatively secure by this point, but in 1748–1749 two events occurred: the Forty-Second Regiment was disestablished, allowing the Highland Regiment, then numbered the Forty-Third, to become the Forty-Second, and ten regiments of Marines were deleted from the official seniority list for infantry; thus a number of regiments were suddenly moved up eleven spaces from where they had ranked in 1743. As new regiments were formed, they took the next number in sequence, and if these were later disbanded, as happened to the provincial regiments numbered Fifty and Fifty-One early in the French and Indian War, the regiments numbered above would be re-designated so that there was always an unbroken chain of rank and seniority.

More leeway was given to the titles of new regiments raised for specific emergencies. While these were officially numbered in sequence above whatever was the highest number in service at the time they were raised, they often adopted colorful titles which were then sometimes reflected on their colours. Secondary or territorial titles were authorized for most regiments after 1782, but these did not come into widespread use or appear on colours until after the Napoleonic period. Nevertheless, many histories will anachronistically use popular titles that were not necessarily associated with the regiments in question until much later—calling the Forty-Second Highland Regiment the Black Watch, for example, or placing the Worcestershire Regiment at the Boston Massacre in 1770.

A Note on Sources

Official records regulating British colours include the Warrant of 1743, the Warrant of 1751, including Napier's pattern book for the regiments allowed special badges (sometimes referred to as the Windsor book because of where it is preserved), the circular letter of 1758, the Warrant of 1768, and documents requiring the updating or replacing of all regimental colours to reflect the new Union in 1801. As mentioned above, the Warrant of 1751 included an accurate drawing of a model King's Colour. Napier's drawings for individual regiments, however, do not show correct proportions or details, but only give a general idea of what was allowed, not exactly as it ought to look, let alone how it really looked when made and carried. However, a fairly large number of original flags of the period still exist, and many pertinent generalizations can be gleaned from these. Where artistic renditions or interpretations of particular unit colours are found, whether in Napier's drawings, in archives, or in old book plates for example, they can be compared to and understood in relation to known originals.

Unlike the numerous conflicting documents and drawings of French and German flags of the period under study, no comprehensive contemporary collections purporting to represent the colours of every individual British regiment exists. Since only certain listed regiments were to have special devices, and all other colours were to be the same except for the color of the regimental flag and the rank painted or embroidered at the center, this should not be surprising. Luckily, there are numerous mentions of colours in regimental inspection reports made over many years, and these will often give the year that colours were issued. By warrant, British colours were to show only officially sanctioned designs, and this seems to have been reasonably well enforced. Approved designs arose and remained in vogue for several years, then were gradually replaced by newer patterns, which would stay in use for another long period. By comparing the dates given for new colours for such-and-such regiment with the prevailing pattern in use at the time, a fairly accurate picture can be drawn of that regiment's colours during a particular period.

Two works from the end of the nineteenth century are very useful in that they have numerous photographs of originals or drawings made from originals. Andrew Ross's *Old Scottish Regimental Colours* was published in 1885. The plates are uniformly excellent and appear to have been made from photographs. It includes a few colours that were carried in North America and examples of many more from the same period, giving a good overall idea of the general characteristics and appearances of the colours of the time. Samuel Milne's *Standards and Colours of the Army* has been the standard reference on British colours since its publication in 1893. It has much useful information and many good photographs, but as mentioned above, Milne chose to draw the central designs of the colours much larger than they ought to be, and this has led to much confusion and misrepresentation ever since.

Regimental Colors in the War of the Revolution, published in 1907 by American historian Gherardi Davis, who had corresponded with Milne, gives information on British colours, and includes photographs and drawings of three that were actually carried in America. Unfortunately, Davis does not go into much detail, claiming that a description of the specifics of pattern or design among the British colours would be "probably . . . impossible, and in any event not especially interesting." Davis also left several fine watercolors that have been widely published in *The American Heritage* histories of the Revolution. Overall, Davis shows too few British colours to draw generalizations, and perhaps following Milne, some of his drawings show the component parts of the colours out of proportion. Other original or documented contemporary sources on individual colours are noted under the entry for that unit.

Cecil C. P. Lawson's three volume *History of the Uniforms of the British Army*, published in 1940 and 1941 (Vols. I and II) and 1961 (Vol. III), includes much useful information on the colours, including visual descriptions of some manuscript sources, tabular formats of the Warrants of 1751 and 1768, and descriptions and drawings of some extant colours not found in other sources.

BRITISH COLOURS IN THE FRENCH AND INDIAN WAR, 1754–1763

Only a few British colours exist from the period 1754–1763, which spans both the French and Indian War in America and the Seven Years' War in Europe. Not a single colour has survived from the regiments that served in North America during that time. Therefore, all the colours described below are reconstructions, based on contemporary warrants and other documents describing what *should have* existed, and existing examples of contemporary British colours produced and used during the same period in Europe, the British home isles, or imperial campaigns in fields around the world. The reconstructions are guided by the principles set out in the introduction, namely that those few examples, when taken together, clearly suggest that there were standard models used far more often than one-off or unique flags made for individual regiments. Apart from the First (Royal) Regiment, and the Twenty-Seventh Inniskillings, no other regiments serving in North America during this period had Royal devices or ancient badges assigned by warrant, although both the Forty-Second Highland Regiment and the Sixtieth Royal Americans adopted badges which were only later officially described and authorized. The colours shown for most units, therefore, are based on the color of the uniform facings, the dates the regiments arrived or were absent in America, and standard patterns that can be reliably associated with specific dates. If a regiment was already in America in 1755, for example, I have not suggested their colours were of a pattern that has been authenticated no earlier than 1759 for a regiment that remained in Britain.

First (Royal) Regiment

The second battalion of the First (Royal) Regiment served in North America from May 1757 to April 1761. The First Battalion remained in Britain and participated in the Seven Years' War.

The First was one of the regiments allowed Royal devices and ancient badges after the standardization of colours in 1743. From the Warrant of 1751: "The First Regiment, or the Royal Regiment. In the centre of their colours, the King's cypher, within the circle of St. Andrew, and crown over it; in the three corners of the second colour the Thistle and Crown. The distinction of the colours of the second battalion is a flaming ray of gold descending from the upper corner of each colour toward the center." While not specified in the written description, the King's cypher was on a blue background on both colours. The thistles and the circle of St. Andrew with the motto of the Scottish kings, *NEMO ME IMPUNE LACESSIT* (No One Harms Me With Impunity) were ancient devices based on the regiment's origins in Scotland.

According to regimental records, a new set of colours was prepared for the regiment sometime between the first publication of the new rules in 1747 and the official publication of the Warrant in 1751. The new colours were probably painted, embroidery not coming into fashion until some years later. The King's cypher at this period was quite plain, the foliated script of later colours also not yet being in vogue. As the regulations did not specify, the thistle and crown in the earliest colours were placed in the corners of the second colours with their tops pointing toward the center. (This was changed in 1801, apparently much to the annoyance of the officers and soldiers of the regiment.) A regimental colour dated 1756–1758 belonging to the second battalion of the Fourth, or King's Own Regiment, displays the flaming ray of gold as actually starting from the upper corner of the flag, cutting completely across the small Union canton. This seems to be the only example of such a colour, however, and in most cases the golden ray on any second battalion's regimental colour was indicated merely by a little tail of it showing at the lower corner of the union.

King's Colour, Second Battalion, First (Royal) Regiment. Flag reproduction by author.

Regimental Colour, Second Battalion, First (Royal) Regiment.

King's Colour, Second Battalion, First (Royal) Regiment. Illustration from Milne, *Standards and Colours*, showing the oversized depiction of central design common to all Milne's drawings.

Regimental Colour, First Battalion, First (Royal) Regiment. Illustration from Milne, *Standards and Colours*, showing the oversized depiction of central design common to all Milne's drawings. Because this drawing represents the First Battalion, it does not have the flaming ray of gold.

Fifteenth Regiment of Foot

The Fifteenth Regiment of Foot arrived in North America in 1758. Its uniform facings were listed as yellow. The regiment had been long in service and presumably had colours based on the new regulations introduced 1747–1751. These would likely have been painted, closely following Napier's model, with the regimental numerals directly on the silk, rather than on a red panel or cartouche. This regiment also served in the American War of Independence.

King's Colour, Fifteenth Regiment of Foot.

Regimental Colour, Fifteenth Regiment of Foot.

Seventeenth Regiment of Foot

The Seventeenth Regiment of Foot arrived in North America in 1757. The uniform facings as noted in the Warrant of 1751, in the column "Distinction in the same colour" were grayish white. Per the warrant, the regimental colour was white with the red cross of St. George. There is no suggestion at any time throughout the regiment's long history, that the white silks of the regimental colours were grayish white. The regimental historian P. D. S. Palmer wrote in 1930, in *The Colours of the Seventeenth, or the Leicestershire Regiment of Foot*, "It is presumed that, as a result of these alterations (the directives and Warrants of 1747–1751), the Colonel of the Regiment, John Wynard, ordered new Colours to be made, which were taken into use in 1751 in Ireland." These remained with the regiment until 1766. The central device of both colours would have been fairly plain, probably painted, and closely following Napier's model. This regiment also served in the American War of Independence.

King's Colour, Seventeenth Regiment of Foot.

Regimental Colour, Seventeenth Regiment of Foot.

The Twenty-Second Regiment of Foot

The Twenty-Second Regiment arrived in North America in 1756. Its regimental facings were pale buff, probably much like the French color "isabelle." The regimental colours, following the Warrant of 1751, would have been close to Napier's model, painted, and with the regimental number directly on the silk rather than in a red cartouche. This regiment also served in the American War of Independence.

King's Colour, Twenty-Second Regiment of Foot.

Regimental Colour, Twenty-Second Regiment of Foot.

Twenty-Seventh Inniskilling Regiment of Foot

The Inniskilling Regiment of Foot was originally raised in Enniskillen (the name is variously spelled throughout the documents of the period). County Fermanagh, Northern Ireland, and maintained its strength primarily with new recruits from the same area. Its uniform facings were buff. In the Warrant of 1743, by which most other regiments were effectively renamed as numbers based on their rank or seniority, the Twenty-Seventh was one of the few singled out as "distinguished by particular devices, and therefore not subject to the preceding articles for colours." This was clarified by the Warrant of 1751: "Twenty-seventh, or the Inniskilling regiment. Allowed to wear in the center of their colours a castle with three turrets, St. George's colours in a blue field, and the name 'Inniskilling' over it." The actual Enniskillin Castle had only two prominent turrets, which were high on the walls—colours made for the regiment in 1807 had a more accurate rendering of it—but AG Napier apparently used a standardized heraldic castle rather than trying to portray the real one. Unlike other regiments with an associated Royal or ancient badge, the regimental colour of the Inniskillings did not have corner devices. Napier's watercolor of the authorized pattern included the regimental number in Roman numerals in the upper corner near the pike on both colours. It also included a blank motto scroll, but as mentioned in the introduction, there is no good reason to believe that regiments that did not have a motto at the time carried flags with a blank scroll. Milne's drawing in 1893 does not include a scroll.

According to inspection returns, the regiment received new colours in 1754. These were probably painted, embroidery not becoming general for colours until later in the decade. The Inniskillings were sent to North America in 1756. This regiment also served in the American War of Independence.

King's Colour, Twenty-Seventh Inniskilling Regiment.

Regimental Colour, Twenty-Seventh Inniskilling Regiment.

Twenty-Eighth Regiment of Foot

The Twenty-Eighth Regiment of Foot arrived in North America in 1758. Its uniform facings were bright yellow. Without further evidence, it can be assumed that the regiment carried colours as authorized by the Warrant of 1751. The colours likely were painted, their basic pattern fairly close to what Napier published as the model in 1751. This regiment also served in the American War of Independence.

King's Colour, Twenty-Eighth Regiment of Foot.

Regimental Colour, Twenty-Eighth
Regiment of Foot.

Thirty-Fifth Regiment of Foot

The Thirty-Fifth Regiment of Foot was the only regiment in the British Army with orange as the color of its regimental facings. Originally raised in Belfast, and maintained and recruited entirely in Ireland, the regiment was strongly Protestant, at least in its early years, and had been rewarded by King William III, a champion of the Protestant cause, with special permission to adopt orange for its uniform facings and regimental colour. As shown in contemporary illustrations, the regimental facings at the time of the French and Indian War were a fairly deep burnt orange; the regimental colour would have been made in the same hue. There are no records of presentation of colours at any specific dates prior to the nineteenth century. When the regiment departed for North America in April 1756, it probably carried colours with the central designs painted, close to the standardized pattern published in the Warrant of 1751. This regiment also served in the American War of Independence.

King's Colour, Thirty-Fifth Regiment of Foot. Flag reproduction by author, used in the movie *The Last of the Mohicans*, 1992.

Regimental Colour, Thirty-Fifth Regiment of Foot. Due to requirements of film company, this orange colour was not used in *The Last of the Mohicans*. A regimental colour for the Thirty-Fifth does appear on screen, but it was made royal blue rather than the correct deep orange.

Fortieth Regiment of Foot

The Fortieth Regiment of Foot had been created in Nova Scotia in 1717 and was maintained entirely in Canada and other parts of North America until the last years of the French and Indian War. Its regimental facings were buff. There is no evidence to suggest if or when its colours were replaced to be in compliance with new warrants or other directives. Nevertheless, it is unlikely that colours would have been procured locally, so it seems reasonable to suppose the regiment was sent new colours sometime after the Warrant of 1751 fixed a new standard pattern. This regiment also served in the American War of Independence.

King's Colour, Fortieth Regiment of Foot.

Regimental Colour, Fortieth Regiment of Foot.

Forty-Second Regiment of Foot, The Royal Highland Regiment

The Forty-Second Regiment of Foot, the Royal Highland Regiment, was created in 1739 by amalgamation of several independent companies of Highland militia and was originally numbered the Forty-Third Regiment of Foot. Its designation became Forty-Second Regiment in 1749 on the disestablishment of the first regiment to hold that number. This was the same time that new regulations were being promulgated on regimental colours, and there is no reason to doubt that colours of the newly described pattern were presented to the Forty-Second soon after its renumbering. The regimental facings at this time were buff—the regiment was not designated Royal until 1758—and while the regiment was uniformed in the Highland style, there was nothing in the Warrant of 1751 to allow for special distinctions on Highland regimental colours.

The Forty-Second arrived in North America in June of 1756, with relatively new colours, the regimental colour being buff. In 1758 a second battalion of the Forty-Second was raised in Scotland, and concurrently King George II conferred the title of Royal Highland Regiment. The uniform facings of both battalions were from then forward to be blue. New colours were made for the new battalion, presumably as later detailed in the Warrant of 1768, which probably authorized in writing what was already in use: "The 42nd, or Royal Highlanders. In the centre of their colours the King's cipher within the garter, and crown over it; under it, St. Andrew, with the motto, *NEMO ME IMPUNE LACESSIT*, in the three corners of the second colour [blue] the King's cypher and crown." By this date, the cypher would have assumed its flowing brush-script or foliated style, very different from the block-like lettering on the First Royal Regiment's colours, but was probably not doubled and reversed as on later colours.

It is unknown whether there was one set of colours made, or two, with one set for each battalion. Perhaps it was supposed even at the time, that one set of colours would soon enough be used by a re-combined regiment to replace the out-of-date colours then on campaign with the First Battalion in America. It is also not known whether the second battalion had the "flaming ray of gold descending from the upper corner of each colour," as authorized for other regiments with a second battalion. Based on later colours of the regiment, it also seems likely that cypher, garter, and crown were surrounded by the Union wreath of roses and thistles on the new colours of the Forty-Second. A regimental historian writing in 1936, in an extended article on "The Colours of the Black Watch," in the magazine *The Red Hackle*, commented on the Warrants of 1751 and 1768: "In the case, however, of a Royal Regiment, which the 42d became in 1758, the centre badge of both colours consisted of the Royal cypher G. R. (or later V. R.) within the garter, surmounted by the crown and surrounded by the Union wreath." This is not what either warrant actually states, but from time to time they were interpreted this way—surviving colours prepared for the second battalion of the Fourth King's Own Regiment in 1756 are examples. In addition, all other colours of the Forty-Second known to the historian at the time did indeed have the Royal devices surrounded by a wreath.

After serving in the West Indies, the Second Battalion was reunited with the original regiment in North America in 1759, and as both battalions had suffered great loss in their separate campaigns, they were united as a one-battalion regiment. Possibly the colours carried by the Second Battalion were at this point simply passed on to and carried by the regiment as a whole. The Second Battalion was formally disestablished in 1763. None of these colours has survived. According to *The Red Hackle*, they were stored in the Grand Store House of the Tower of London and were destroyed in a fire in 1841. This regiment also served in the American War of Independence.

King's Colour, Forty-Second Regiment of Foot, circa 1756. Flag reproduction by author, used in movie *The Last of the Mohicans*, 1992.

Regimental Colour, Forty-Second Regiment of Foot, circa 1751. Flag reproduction by author, used in movie *The Last of the Mohicans*, 1992.

King's Colour, Forty-Second Royal Highland Regiment, circa 1758.

Regimental Colour, Forty-Second Royal Highland Regiment, circa 1758. (Flag reproduction by author)

Forty-Third Regiment of Foot

The Forty-Third Regiment of Foot arrived in North America in 1757. Its uniform facings were white; per the Warrants of 1743 and 1751 its regimental colour was white with the red cross of St. George throughout. The regiment had originally been numbered the Fifty-Fourth, however, and renumbered only in 1749 on the disbandment of eleven regiments from the Army's seniority list. Thus, new colours were undoubtedly procured right at the time the new regulations and Warrants of 1747–1751 were being promulgated to fix proper designs. This regiment also served in the American War of Independence.

King's Colour, Forty-Third Regiment of Foot.

Regimental Colour, Forty-Third Regiment of Foot.

Forty-Fourth Regiment of Foot

The Forty-Fourth Regiment of Foot embarked from Ireland for North America in January 1755. The regimental facings and regimental colour were yellow. The Forty-Fourth had been renumbered from Fifty-Fifth in 1749, when the original Forty-Second Regiment was disestablished and ten regiments of Marines were removed from the Army seniority rolls, so it is likely the regiment had relatively new colours in North America, probably painted, and very close to Napier's standard drawing from the Warrants of 1747–1751.

The Forty-Fourth was one of the two British regular units (the other was the Forty-Eighth) badly mauled at the Battle of the Monongahela, better known to Americans as Braddock's Defeat, on July 5, 1755.

Braddock's Army had been separated into a "flying" column, which included most of the companies of both Forty-Fourth and Forty-Eighth regiments, to march ahead, and a main body with the camp followers, heavy baggage, and some of the heaviest guns, to follow. Presumably to allow both forces to have colours on the march, the flying column was accompanied by the King's Colour of the Forty-Fourth Regiment, and the buff regimental colour of the Forty-Eighth. David L. Preston records in *Braddock's Defeat*, published in 2015, that these colours were uncased and displayed as rallying points during the confused combat of the battle, in which the British flying column was ambushed and virtually annihilated by a combined force of French troops and American Indian warriors. It is hard to credit, that in the well-documented chaos of the British defeat, when all order and unit cohesion was lost, with huge numbers of dead and wounded and catalogues of lost cannon, muskets, uniforms, even General Braddock's secret papers, that the two British colours were somehow saved. Nevertheless, they are nowhere specifically mentioned as lost, and various comprehensive lists of British colours lost from the 1690s to the present day never mention the Forty-Fourth or Forty-Eighth regiments in America. It is possible that one or both colours were lost during the battle itself but recovered and returned to regimental survivors with the main army. Preston mentions that five days after the disaster a soldier of the New York Independent Company "found" a pair of colours, which he turned in to a sergeant of his unit. No further information on these colours was noted. If they were regimental colours, it was not noted to which unit they belonged, but it is unlikely that any of the small American units had carried colors into the

King's Colour, Forty-Fourth Regiment of Foot.

Regimental Colour, Forty-Fourth Regiment of Foot.

fight. In any event, no report of the battle specifically listed colours lost, nor lost and subsequently returned to the regiment to which they belonged. In 1758, "English Colours, taken from Gen'l Braddock," were reportedly seen by a Virginia officer in a Potawatomi Indian town, but there is no way to know whether these colours were British infantry colours either. Preston suggests in a footnote that they may have been simply one of the British friendship flags carried in Braddock's wagons with other gifts to present to Indian chiefs.[1] This regiment also served in the American War of Independence.

Forty-Fifth Regiment of Foot

The Forty-Fifth Regiment of Foot was another of the very early regiments to be sent to North America, arriving in Nova Scotia in 1747. The regimental uniform facings and the regimental colour were deep green. The regiment had originally been ranked as Fifty-Sixth in seniority but was renumbered Forty-Fifth in 1749, when the original Forty-Second Regiment was disestablished and ten regiments of Marines were removed from the Army seniority rolls. This, of course, necessitated new colours, which were just then being carefully defined by the Warrants of 1747–1751. The new colours were probably painted and would have been fairly accurate representations of Adjutant General Napier's models from the new warrant. This regiment also served in the American War of Independence.

King's Colour, Forty-Fifth Regiment of Foot.

Regimental Colour, Forty-Fifth Regiment of Foot.

Forty-Sixth Regiment of Foot

The Forty-Sixth Regiment of Foot arrived in North America in the summer of 1757. Its uniform facings were yellow. The regiment had originally been numbered the Fifty-Seventh, but was moved up in rank in 1749, when the original Forty-Second Regiment was disestablished and ten regiments of Marines were removed from the Army seniority rolls. Colours reflecting the regiment's new rank, and of the patterns just then being laid down by the Adjutant General, would have been issued shortly thereafter. As a newly re-designated regiment, the Forty-Sixth most likely carried its original colours in America. This regiment also served in the American War of Independence.

King's Colour, Forty-Sixth Regiment of Foot.

Regimental Colour, Forty-Sixth Regiment of Foot.

Forty-Seventh Regiment of Foot

The Forty-Seventh Regiment of Foot arrived in North America in 1750, exactly at the time colours were being addressed by Adjutant General Napier in 1747–1751. The regiment's facings were white, the regimental colour white with the red cross of St. George. The regiment had originally been numbered Fifty-Eighth, and been renumbered in 1749, when the original Forty-Second Regiment was disestablished and ten regiments of Marines were removed from the Army seniority rolls. With the conjunction of having to change the regimental name on the colours, as well as organizing to be deployed overseas, it seems likely that new colours were issued to the regiment shortly before its departure. This regiment also served in the American War of Independence.

King's Colour, Forty-Seventh Regiment of Foot.

Regimental Colour, Forty-Seventh Regiment of Foot.

Forty-Eighth Regiment of Foot

The Forty-Eighth Regiment of Foot embarked from Ireland for North America in January 1755. The regimental facings and regimental colour were buff. The Forty-Eighth had been renumbered from Fifty-Ninth in 1748–1749, when the original Forty-Second Regiment was disestablished and ten regiments of Marines were removed from the Army seniority rolls, so it is likely the regiment had relatively new colours in North America, probably painted, and very close to Napier's standard drawing from the Warrants of 1747–1751. The Forty-Eighth was one of the two British regular units (the other was the Forty-Fourth) badly mauled at the Battle of the Monongahela, better known to Americans as Braddock's Defeat, on July 5, 1755.

Braddock's Army had been separated into a "flying" column, which included most of the companies of both Forty-Fourth and Forty-Eighth regiments, to march ahead, and a main body with the camp followers, heavy baggage, and some of the heaviest guns, to follow. Presumably to allow both forces to have colours on the march, the flying column was accompanied by the King's Colour of the Forty-Fourth Regiment, and the buff regimental colour of the Forty-Eighth. David L. Preston records in *Braddock's Defeat*, published in 2015, that these colours were uncased and displayed as rallying points during the confused combat of the battle, in which the British flying column was ambushed and virtually annihilated by a combined force of French troops and American Indian warriors. It is hard to credit, that in the well-documented chaos of the British defeat, when all order and unit cohesion was lost, with huge numbers of dead and wounded and catalogues of lost cannon, muskets, uniforms, even General Braddock's secret papers, that the two British colours were somehow saved. Nevertheless, they are nowhere specifically mentioned as lost, and various comprehensive lists of British colours lost from the 1690s to the present day, never mention the Forty-Fourth or Forty-Eighth regiments in America. It is possible that one or both colours were lost during the battle itself but recovered and returned to regimental survivors with the main army. Preston mentions that five days after the disaster a soldier of the New York Independent Company "found" a pair of Colours, which he turned in to a sergeant of his unit. No further information on these colours was noted. If they were regimental colours, it was not noted to which unit they belonged, but it is unlikely that any of the small American units had carried colors into the fight. In any event, no report of the battle specifically listed colours lost, nor lost and subsequently returned to the regiment to which they belonged. In 1758, "English Colours, taken from Gen'l Braddock," were reportedly seen by a Virginia officer in a Potawatomi Indian town, but there is no way to know whether these colours were British infantry colours either. Preston suggests in a footnote that they may have been simply one of the British friendship flags carried in Braddock's wagons with other gifts to present to Indian chiefs.[2]

King's Colour, Forty-Eighth Regiment of Foot.

Regimental Colour, Forty-Eighth Regiment of Foot.

Fiftieth Regiment of Foot

The Fiftieth Regiment of Foot was a provincial regiment, raised in December 1754 in the New England colonies and commanded by William Shirley, governor of Massachusetts. Despite being raised entirely in America, the Fiftieth was ranked on the British Army establishment. The uniform facings were red, and thus the second colour was white with the red cross of St. George superimposed. The Fiftieth (Shirley's) and the other new provincial regiment, the Fifty-First (Pepperrell's) were both surrendered in their entirety at Oswego in 1756, their colours and men being made prisoners of war in Montreal. Rather than attempt to reconstitute the two provincial units, they were disestablished and dropped from the Army rolls, allowing several other newly raised regiments to move up two spaces in seniority. The colours lost at Oswego were reportedly recovered at the capture of Montreal in 1760 and sent back to England. What became of them thereafter is unknown.

King's Colour, Fiftieth Regiment of Foot (Shirley's).

Regimental Colour, Fiftieth Regiment of Foot (Shirley's).

Fifty-First Regiment of Foot

The Fifty-First Regiment of Foot, known also as Pepperrell's Regiment and sometimes as the Cape Breton Regiment, was raised in the New England colonies in December 1754 under William Pepperrell, who had led the provincial troops that took the Louisbourg fortress in 1745. Although raised entirely in America, the regiment was ranked on the British Army establishment. The regiment had red uniform facings, and thus its second colour was white with the red cross of St. George superimposed. The Fifty-First (Pepperrell's) and the other new provincial regiment, the Fiftieth (Shirley's), were both surrendered in their entirety at Oswego in 1756, their colours and men being made prisoners of war in Montreal. Rather than attempt to reconstitute the two provincial units, they were disestablished and dropped from the Army rolls, allowing several other newly raised regiments to move up two spaces in seniority. The colours lost at Oswego were reportedly recovered at the capture of Montreal in 1760 and sent back to England. What became of them thereafter is unknown.

King's Colour, Fifty-First Regiment of Foot (Pepperrell's).

Regimental Colour, Fifty-First Regiment of Foot (Pepperrell's).

Fifty-Fifth Regiment of Foot

The Fifty-Fifth Regiment of Foot was raised in 1755 and posted to North America in 1757, arriving in early July. Its uniform facings were green. The regiment had originally been numbered Fifty-Seventh but was renumbered Fifty-Fifth in 1756–1757 on the disestablishment in December 1756 of the Fiftieth and Fifty-First Regiments, which had been captured at Oswego in August of that year. The Fifty-Fifth's colours were probably altered or new colours issued shortly after the change in rank and prior to departure for America. This regiment also served in the American War of Independence.

King's Colour, Fifty-Fifth Regiment of Foot.

Regimental Colour, Fifty-Fifth Regiment of Foot.

Fifty-Eighth Regiment of Foot

The Fifty-Eighth Regiment arrived in North America in spring of 1758. It had been raised as the Sixtieth Regiment of Foot in 1755 but was renumbered the following year after the capture of the Fiftieth and Fifty-First Regiments at Oswego and their subsequent disestablishment. The uniform facings of the Sixtieth, now Fifty-Eighth, were black. There had been no regiments faced with black when the Warrant of 1751 was published, and some sources suggest that the two new black-faced regiments (the Fifty-Second, which became the Fiftieth, was the other) created in the interim between the Warrant of 1751 and the Warrant of 1768, which clearly describes colours for regiments faced in black, would have been white with a red cross, like those of regiments faced in white or red. This seems to overlook the circular letter of 1758, however, which described for the newly created Sixty-Fourth Regiment, also faced in black, "Second Colour black, St. George's Cross throughout, union in the upper canton." It seems unlikely that two regiments newly raised and given black facings, would have been given colours of white and red, completely at odds with the Army-wide practice of colours matching the uniform facings, and then been commanded, retroactively as it were, to change to black by an order only two years later describing even newer regiments. It seems more plausible that the 1758 description simply specified for the Sixty-Fourth what was already in use by the Fiftieth and Fifty-Eighth. In any event, the newly designated Fifty-Eighth Regiment would have received new (or altered) colours on its redesignation in mid or late 1756, prior to its embarkation for America.

King's Colour, Fifty-Eighth Regiment of Foot.   **Regimental Colour, Fifty-Eighth Regiment of Foot.**

Sixtieth Regiment of Foot, the Royal American Regiment

The Sixtieth, or Royal American Regiment, was created by special act of Parliament in early 1756 for the rapidly escalating war in North America. Originally ranked Sixty-Second, the regiment was renumbered in February 1757 after the Fiftieth (Shirley's) and Fifty-First (Pepperrell's) regiments were disestablished following their capture at Fort Oswego. Although its name suggests being raised primarily in America, its officers were recruited from Britain and throughout Protestant Europe (held to be sufficiently antagonistic to Catholic France) and many of its private soldiers from Europe or among recent European immigrants to British North America. The regiment originally comprised four battalions. The first and second battalions were complete by September 1756. All four battalions were organized and trained entirely in America. It is unknown exactly when colours arrived for them from Britain.

As a Royal regiment, the facing color of the uniforms was blue, and the second colour of each battalion was blue. As late as 1940, two original colours of the Fourth Battalion of the regiment were on display in the Museum of the Royal United Services Institution in Whitehall, where they were described and sketched by Cecil C. P. Lawson for his multivolume set *A History of the Uniforms of the British Army*, published between 1940 and 1960. The colours do not conform to the later Warrant of 1768. At the center of each colour is a foliated cartouche with crown above. The cartouche has a red interior and is divided into two sections on which are the King's cypher above, and the Roman numerals IV below, to indicate the Fourth battalion. Lawson's sketch is not very precise, but it does not appear that the gold frame of the cartouche is meant to be a Union wreath of roses and thistles. The Royal motto *DIEU ET MON DROIT* is in a two-part scroll beneath. The inclusion of the battalion number on both flags clearly indicates that the battalions were not identified, as some modern sources suppose, by one, two, or three golden rays issuing from the upper corner as might have been done in the seventeenth century, although the second battalion may have been designated by a single golden ray. The regimental number, in a small, foliated cartouche in the upper corner near the staff on the King's Colour only, had the numerals LXII, indicating the colours were made before the regiment was renumbered. Lawson shows the regimental colour with no numerals in the Union canton. Terence Wise, in *Military Flags of the World, 1618–1900*, published in 1978, stated that "the colours survive and show that they were different to any established pattern." He describes the regimental colour with the number of the regiment in the center of the small union. Both authors seem to be describing the colours from life; perhaps the numerals in the canton of the regimental were almost completely faded and one viewer saw them, and one did not? It seems probable that the colours did in fact have the rank designation on all four regimentals. The regimental colours did not, however, have corner badges. The colours as reconstructed here are probably the pattern carried by all four battalions through their various campaigns 1757–1763. The colours of some battalions may have been altered by picking out the two Roman numerals "II" from the designation LXII if the colours were embroidered, or simply overpainting them if the colours were painted (this was obviously not done by the Fourth Battalion).

The third and fourth battalions of the Sixtieth were disbanded at the end of active hostilities in 1763. When the Warrant of 1768 was published, it described the colours as: "The Sixtieth, or Royal Americans. In the centre of their colours the King's cypher within the garter, and crown over it and in the three corners of the second colour the King's cypher and crown. The colours of the second battalion to be distinguished by a flaming ray of gold, descending from the upper corner of each colour toward the center." The Union wreath was conspicuously ruled out, corner badges were authorized and described, and as the regiment only had two battalions at the time, the traditional flaming ray of gold was described as the distinguishing mark of the second battalion. This regiment also served in the American War of Independence.

King's Colour, Sixtieth Royal American Regiment. A version of this colour, made by the author, was used in movie *The Last of the Mohicans*, 1992. This representation has a more correct interpretation of the central motif.

Regimental Colour, Sixtieth Royal American Regiment. A version of this colour, made by the author, was used in movie *The Last of the Mohicans*, 1992. This representation has a more correct interpretation of the central motif.

Seventy-Seventh Regiment of Foot, Montgomery's Highlanders

The Seventy-Seventh Regiment of Foot, known after its first colonel as Montgomery's Highlanders, was raised in 1756–1757 by Archibald Montgomery as the First Highland Battalion. Joined with Simon Fraser's Second Highland Battalion, the two were numbered together as a single regiment on the British establishment as the Sixty-Second Regiment of Foot. Shortly thereafter, however, Fraser's Battalion was renumbered as a separate regiment—the Sixty-Third—and Montgomery's remained the Sixty-Second. The regimental facings and regimental colour were green. These were probably painted, with the regimental numerals directly on the silk field. The regiment embarked for America in June 1757. In 1758, fifteen second battalions from old regiments were renumbered as separate regiments, and the brand new Sixty-Second took its place in seniority after those regiments, becoming the Seventy-Seventh Highland Regiment of Foot, though still generally referred to as Montgomery's Highlanders. The regiment had continued to recruit in Scotland, and the second contingent arrived in America at about the same time as the regiment received its new rank. Possibly new colours accompanied—it would have been difficult to alter the old colours already in service in America. Based on the regiment's redesignation in mid-1758, it may have received one of the interim embroidered patterns known to have been issued around that time, and with the regimental rank "on crimson" per the requirement issued that year. The Seventy-Seventh was disbanded in 1763.

King's Colour, Sixty-Second Regiment, Montgomery's Highlanders, 1756.

Regimental Color, Sixty-Second Regiment, Montgomery's Highlanders, 1756.

King's Colour, Seventy-Seventh Regiment, Montgomery's Highlanders, 1758.

Regimental Colour, Seventy-Seventh Regiment, Montgomery's Highlanders, 1758. Flag reproduction by author, currently on display at Fort Ligonier Museum, Fort Ligonier, Pennsylvania.

Seventy-Eighth Regiment of Foot, Fraser's Highlanders

The Seventy-Eighth Regiment of Foot (Fraser's Highlanders) was raised in Scotland in 1757 by Simon Fraser of Lovat, as the Second Highland Battalion. The new Highland Battalions, First and Second, were placed on the British establishment as a single regiment, the Sixty-Second Regiment of Foot. Later the same year, the battalions were separated, and Fraser's battalion became the Sixty-Third Regiment. As the Sixty-Third, Fraser's Highlanders departed for America in July 1757. The regimental facings were buff, and the regimental colour was buff. Both colours were probably painted, embroidered colours still being fairly rare. Less than a year later, in 1758, fifteen second battalions of older regiments were renumbered as separate regiments, and the two new Highland regiments were pushed back fifteen places in seniority, with the Sixty-Third becoming the Seventy-Eighth (Highland) Regiment of Foot, still generally known as Fraser's Highlanders. New colours were probably procured and sent to the regiment in America; it seems unlikely that the regiment would have served several more years under colours with the wrong unit designation. It also seems improbable that the original colours could have been altered in America, as the gold Roman numerals LXIII would have been painted directly on the silk. The new colours may have been one of the interim embroidered styles being introduced at the time, although with the regimental rank "on crimson" per the letter of 1758 so specifying. The Seventy-Eighth was in America through the rest of the war and was disbanded in December 1763.

Colonel Fraser raised another regiment in 1776, numbered Seventy-First Highland Regiment (which see), which fought in the American War of Independence, and was also known as Fraser's Highlanders.

King's Colour, Sixty-Third Regiment, Fraser's Highlanders, 1756.

Regimental Colour, Sixty-Third Regiment, Fraser's Highlanders, 1756.

King's Colour, Seventy-Eighth Regiment, Fraser's Highlanders, 1758.

Regimental Colour, Seventy-Eighth Regiment, Fraser's Highlanders, 1758.

Eightieth Regiment of Foot

The Eightieth Regiment of Foot, Gage's Light Infantry, was raised in May 1758 as an experimental unit to be trained in woodland fighting and reconnaissance based on individual and small unit tactics, modeled on Rogers' Rangers. Per the circular letter of 1758, the Eightieth Regiment did not carry colours.

Ninety-Fourth Regiment of Foot

The Ninety-Fourth Regiment of Foot was raised in Wales in January 1760 as the Royal Welsh Volunteers. As a Royal regiment, its uniforms were faced in blue and its regimental color was blue. The colours were probably embroidered in one of the new patterns known to have been made for other regiments raised in 1760 for the then-current war, but with the addition of the crown. No other Royal devices are recorded as authorized. The lettering "R. W. V." for Royal Welsh Volunteers is entirely conjectural. The regiment served in North America, France, and the West Indies. It was disbanded in 1763.

King's Colour, Ninety-Fourth Regiment of Foot.

Regimental Colour, Ninety-Fourth Regiment of Foot.

Ninety-Fifth Regiment of Foot

The Ninety-Fifth Regiment of Foot was created in South Carolina from several independent companies originally raised in New York. The uniforms were faced in light gray, and presumably the regimental colour was also of a light gray. The colours were probably one of the interim embroidered patterns known to have been made for other regiments raised during the same period. This regiment only existed from 1760–1763 and should not be confused with the Ninety-Fifth Regiment of 1779–1783, whose colours feature prominently in John Singleton Copley's monumental painting *The Death of Major Peirson*.

King's Colour, Ninety-Fifth Regiment of Foot.

Regimental Colour, Ninety-Fifth Regiment of Foot.

Marines

Battalions of Marines, organized and trained as battalions of infantry, were deployed in several theaters and campaigns during the Seven Years' War, including Louisbourg and Quebec in North America.

Prior to 1747, British Marines had been organized as regiments within the Army. Each carried a King's Colour and a regimental colour in the facing colors of the uniforms. The central device was a man-of-war with its sails furled, with the rank in Roman numerals below. In 1747 the then-serving regiments of Marines were transferred to the Admiralty. The ten numbered positions that had been assigned to the Marine regiments were dropped from the Army rolls in 1748, causing a reshuffling of the seniority rankings of an equal number of regiments of foot, as reflected in the entries on many of the regiments covered in this book. In 1755 the Marines were constituted as an organization within the Navy, generally styled as His Majesty's Marine Forces, organized into fifty companies in three divisions, located in Portsmouth, Chatham, and Plymouth. Each division was evidently supplied with one or more pairs of colours. These would have been similar to the regulation infantry colours as laid down in the Warrant of 1751, probably with a newly designed insignia at center (as described below), though there is no clear record of this before 1760. The second colours were probably white, as the uniform facings of all Marines were now white. Navy authorities were certainly as aware as the Army that a white flag could be mistaken for French—a red cross of St.

George had been added to the all-white ships' flags of "white" squadrons beginning in 1702—and it cannot be ruled out that the new second colours for units of Marines were white with a red cross, as prescribed for Army regiments faced with white.

A purchase order paid in March 1761 lists one King's Colour and one second colour. The King's Colour was embroidered with the "Arms of the Lords High Admirals [the fouled anchor] within a large ornament of thistles and roses," the second colour was a "plain sheet with a small union," with the central device painted "as the above." This is the only known instance of a pair of colours with the central device embroidered on one colour but painted on the other. As the savings was only £2.5.0, it may have been thought (not unreasonably) that the embroidery might be too heavy for the unseamed silk of the "plain sheet." The color of the plain field is not stated, but was probably white, the same as the uniform facings. There is no mention of a red cross. There is no evidence that any Marine colours during this period had either crown or motto as in some later periods.

For unknown reasons, the second colour has been shown in some secondary sources as red. So far as is known, there is no contemporary authority for red. Perhaps each of the three divisions had a different color, but again, there are no contemporary sources for such an assertion.

King's Colour, Marine Battalions, circa 1760.

Battalion Colour, Marine Battalions, 1760. While evidence seems to suggest that the Marine "division" or battalion colours were white, it is possible that each of the three divisions—Chatham, Portsmouth, and Plymouth—had a different color field for its flag, to differentiate it from the others.

BRITISH COLOURS IN THE AMERICAN WAR OF INDEPENDENCE, 1775–1783

Whole or partial remains of at least ten colours carried by British regiments in the American War of Independence still exist, including one on display at the US Military Academy at West Point. The Americans claimed to have captured as many as twenty-seven, but accountability was so poor both during and after the war, that only the one at West Point has survived. Some in that total were never surrendered in the first place, though claimed in official reports. Nine colours carried by British regiments in America 1776–1783 are in British museums or cathedrals, and there are several identified colours of the same period that were never in America but are examples of the same patterns.

The reconstructions in this section are again guided by the principles set out in the introduction, mainly that the many examples which exist from the period clearly suggest that there were standard models used for most regiments. Unlike the colours used in the French and Indian War, virtually all the colours used in the American War of Independence were embroidered. How brightly colored the embroideries might have been when new is unknown. As with the earlier painted colours, this undoubtedly had a lot to do with the taste and expertise of the embroiderers, as well as what color yarns might have been available, and what colors of silk were being embroidered on. Natural colors would simply show better on light colored fields such as yellow or buff, whereas subtle shades of gold would make a striking effect on red, green, or blue. It is also difficult to tell how much the original silk embroidery may have faded—white silk naturally turns to a soft gold as it ages, some red dyes fade while others remain vibrant for decades, greens and blues tend to soften and turn toward gray. The colours shown for most units, when not based on extant originals, therefore, are based on the color of the uniform facings, inspection returns noting presentation of colours at specific dates, the dates the regiments arrived in America, and standard patterns that can be reliably associated with particular time spans. If a regiment arrived in America in 1775 and has an inspection notation of receiving colours in 1767, for example, I have not suggested their colours were of a pattern that has been authenticated no earlier than belonging to a regiment raised and fielded in 1778.

The colours of the five regiments on the American Establishment have their own inherent problems, not the least of which is whether at least two of the five carried colours at all. The American Establishment only came into being mid-1779, so possibly no regiment carried colours with their American rank on them. The First Regiment on the establishment, the Queens Rangers, was consciously modeled on the ranger and light infantry regiments of the previous war, and probably carried no colours at all. The Second and Third Regiments had problems procuring even proper uniforms; colours made in Britain were probably not their principal worry. There were no warrants or regulations to fall back on for regiments in green uniforms. When uniforms arrived mid-1777 for loyalist troops, they were mostly green with white facings. Should the regimental colours be white with a red cross? There are no records to be found. The green uniforms were in some cases replaced by regulation British red, some with buff facings and some with blue. Would the colours reflect any of this? An original King's Colour attributed to the Fourth, the King's American Regiment, still exists. The Fifth regiment on the American Establishment was Tarleton's British Legion. For this we have Joshua Reynold's monumental painting of Tarleton with the Legion colours flying above.

Third Regiment of Foot

The Third Regiment of Foot, or the Buffs, was one of the few regiments that had a motto at the time of the Warrants of 1751 and 1768. The regimental facings, as implied by their traditional title, were buff. Both warrants gave the same description of the colours: "In the centre of their colours the Dragon, being their ancient badge, and the Rose and Crown in the three corners of their second colour." While not mentioned in the text of either warrant, the plates prepared by Adjutant General Napier to accompany the Warrant of 1751 show both colours with the motto *VETERI FRONDESCIT HONORE*, roughly "[Their] Ancient Honor Flourishes," in the label or scroll above the dragon.

According to inspection returns, the Buffs received new colours in 1780, probably in preparation for their deployment to America in the following year. These colours were almost certainly embroidered, the established standard by that time. The regiment arrived in Charleston, South Carolina, in June 1781.

King's Colour, Third Regiment of Foot.

Regimental Colour, Third Regiment of Foot.

Fourth Regiment of Foot, the King's Own Royal Regiment

The Fourth Regiment of Foot, the King's Own Royal Regiment, arrived in Boston in June of 1774. As a Royal regiment, the uniform facings and the regimental colour were blue. The colours, as described in the Warrant of 1751: "Fourth, or the King's Own Royal Regiment. In the centre of their colours the King's cypher on a red ground with garter, and crown over it; in the three corners of their second colour the lion of England, being their ancient badge." The exact meaning of the warrant admitted to some ambiguity in the case of regiments allowed Royal or ancient badges, and the second battalion of the Fourth had been presented in 1756 with an embroidered set of colours with the King's cypher and garter at center surrounded by the Union wreath of roses and thistles. This was not the only regiment to interpret the warrant as meaning the Royal or other badges were to be within the wreath simply in place of the regimental rank in gold Roman numerals, rather than replacing both numerals and wreath. In fact, the practice became general in later periods.

By 1756, the King's cypher had assumed a fancy script-like appearance, with the letters overlapped or entwined. The garter was portrayed as a circular blue band buckled to itself like a belt, the tongue wrapped over the belt and hanging down in the style of the knights of centuries past. On it was the Royal motto of the Order of the Garter, *HONI SOIT QUI MAL Y PENCE*, roughly translated as "Shame on him who thinks evil of it." The "Lion of England" was a lion statant, that is, simply standing with all four feet on the ground, wearing a crown. The lion by this period was generally portrayed quite naturalistically, rather than in an exaggerated heraldic rendering. Neither of the existing colours has a motto scroll, as the regiment did not have an established motto at the time.

Inspection returns show that the Fourth received new colours in England in 1765. These were probably much like those of 1756, but without the wreath surrounding the King's cypher and crown at center, and without the golden ray denoting Second Battalion.

King's Colour, Fourth Regiment of Foot, the King's Own Royal Regiment.

Regimental Colour, Fourth Regiment of Foot, the King's Own Royal Regiment.

Fifth Regiment of Foot

The Fifth Regiment of Foot was one of the regiments enumerated in 1743 as "distinguished by particular devices, and therefore not subject to the preceding articles for colours," referring to the requirement to have at center a Union wreath with the rank of the regiment within. The colours for the Fifth were described in 1751 and again in 1768: "In the centre of their colours St. George killing the Dragon, being their ancient badge, in the three corners of their second colour the Rose and Crown." On both colours the numerical rank of the regiment was in the upper corner near the pike. The regiment's facing colour was gosling green, which Milne described in 1893 as "that peculiar lightish shade of green, which has become so identified with this regiment."[3] Writing 190 years after the fact in 1941, C. C. P. Lawson described Adjutant General Napier's watercolor plates from the Windsor book accompanying the 1751 warrant as "Pale yellow, St. George in white armour on a brown horse, and green dragon. In the three corners a crown and rose proper. The facings are given as gosling green but unless the tone has changed with time a yellow colour was meant."[4] Traditional renderings of St. George and the dragon tend to depict the horse as white, and later colours of Regiment have white horses. The Windsor drawings also included a scroll for motto, left blank, and although the regiment had informally adopted *QUO FATA VOCANT* (Wherever the fates call) as early as 1767, it appears that this motto was not added to the colours until much later.

According to inspection records, the Fifth was presented new colours in 1773 while in Ireland. In the following year the regiment was sent to America, arriving in Boston in July 1774.

King's Colour, Fifth Regiment of Foot.

Regimental Colour, Fifth Regiment of Foot. Flag reproduction by author.

Sixth Regiment of Foot

The Sixth Regiment of Foot arrived in New York in October 1776; however, its personnel were drafted to fill other regiments and the Sixth was never fielded nor engaged as a unit. The regiment's uniform facings and regimental colour were deep yellow. The Warrants of 1751 and 1768 described the colours: "In the centre of their colours the Antelope, being their ancient badge, and in the three corners of their second colour the Rose and Crown." Lawson describes the Windsor drawing as "a white antelope on a green mount, . . . The antelope, as in all the early representations, is more like a goat."[5] The antelope by 1768 was probably being represented somewhat more realistically, in the spirit of the age, rather than as a static white heraldic charge. It is traditionally shown "ducally gorged and chained," that is, with a ducal coronet (a crown that is a simple ring to encircle the head and does not include arches over the top) around its neck like a collar, with a long trailing chain attached. The rank of the regiment, VI, would have been in the upper corner near the pike on both colours, possibly embroidered so as to read correctly from either side. Inspection returns show that the regiment received new colours in 1769, which would undoubtedly have conformed to the Warrant of 1768 just published.

King's Colour, Sixth Regiment of Foot.

Regimental Colour, Sixth Regiment of Foot.

Seventh Regiment of Foot

The colours of the Seventh Regiment of Foot were described in the Warrants of 1751 and 1768: "Seventh, or the Royal Fuziliers. In the centre of their colours the rose within the garter, and the crown over it; the 'White Horse' in the corners of the second colour." The appearance of the crown and garter can be seen on a surviving King's Colour of the Seventh at the US Military Academy at West Point. It is heavily embroidered, with the garter being double-appliquéd so as to read correctly on both sides of the flag. The regimental rank VII is painted on the reverse side of the flag and overpainted as IIV on the front. In addition, as the buckle of the garter appears on the viewer's right—the correct display would show it on the left—it is clear that the whole flag was made backward, with the pole to the right. If the flag were displayed with the pole to the right, both the garter and the numerals VII would appear correctly. (An extant regimental colour of the Seventh probably dating from the mid 1780s or 1790s now at the Church of the Holy Sepulchre in London, obviates this problem by having "VII" embroidered on a small red silk oval appliquéd on both sides of the canton.) Black shading on the gold numerals was added at the time the colours were conserved and would not have been so pronounced originally. The colour is approximately five feet six inches on the pike, and six feet four inches to the fly. Different scholars identify this colour both as one captured at Fort Chambly in 1775, or as one lost at the Cowpens in 1781. The "White Horse" on the regimental colour was the white horse of Hanover, traditionally depicted as "courant," or running, with the rear feet on a green mound, the front feet raised and roughly parallel. Hanover was the original homeland of British King George II.

The Seventh was the only British regiment to suffer the misfortune of losing colours at two different times during the war. As only one of these colours is still in existence, however, it is unclear which colours, and how many, were lost where. The records are also confused by the tendency to use "colours," "stand of colours," "regimental colours," and occasionally "set" of colours to mean either one or both flags belonging to a regiment. The two colours that arrived with the regiment in Canada in 1773 had been made in 1771. It is agreed by all sources that one or both colours of the Seventh were taken at Fort Chambly in 1775; American General Montgomery reported in a letter to Congress, dated October 20, 1775, "Major Brown has brought the Colours of the Seventh Regiment, which I now have the honor to transmit to you."[6] The King's Colour at West Point is usually identified as the one taken at Chambly. Davis described this colour in 1907, as well as the "regimental colours of this regiment, also captured by us."[7] Only a single company of the regiment had been at Chambly, the regiment having been parceled out to several posts to defend Canada from the American invasion of 1775. Much of the rest of the regiment was also captured piecemeal during the campaign.

The Seventh was reconstituted in New York in 1776–1777. New colours were ordered by the regimental colonel in June of that year, the order being received in Britain early in 1778. It is not known how long it might have taken for the new colours to be embroidered and sent to the regiment in America. As the maker of the new colours was the same firm that had made the colours in 1771, there is little doubt that the second set was virtually identical to the first. The requests for both of these pairs of colours, along with a list of the necessary materials and their costs, are in the papers of Lord Robert Bertie.

The second colour, or stand of colours, or set of colours, of the Seventh was captured at Cowpens on January 17, 1781. At least one of these colours was in the thick of the fight. Major James Jackson of the Georgia Militia was apparently commended on the spot by Morgan for his part in the action, but feeling slighted in later years, wrote to Morgan reminding him of "the utmost risque of my life in attempting to seize the colors of the Seventy-First Regiment in the midst of it, on their attempt to form after they were broken."[8] The Seventy-First probably carried no colours into the action, certainly none was captured even though the regiment was taken almost entirely, only those left to guard the baggage escaping. But the units were greatly mixed up in the fighting, and Jackson did not claim he had had the colour in hand nor time to inspect the name embroidered on it. From what is known of Jackson, there is little reason to doubt his retelling of his personal actions.

Again, however, contemporary reports are imprecise as to just what was captured. American General Morgan reported "two standards" along with the prisoners, supplies, and equipment captured.[9] General Greene sent a courier to Morgan in March to "wait upon you to get the colors taken at the Cowpens, to convey them to Congress," not saying whether he meant one or two.[10] Samuel Huntington, president of the Continental Congress at the time, wrote to Morgan on April 11, 1781, "Your letter of the 28th ult. hath been duly received, with the standard of the Seventh British regiment which fell into your hands in the battle of the 17th of January. This will be deposited with other trophies in the War Office."[11] Huntington clearly refers to a single flag.

The post-war history of any colours captured by American forces during the war is hazy at best. The King's Colour of the Seventh now at West Point might just as likely have been captured at Cowpens as at Fort Chambly. It is known that one British and one German colour were gifted by Congress to General Washington in December of 1781. It was generally supposed that these were colours taken by Washington at Yorktown. They remained in Washington's family until about 1858. They were visited and sketched by two different observers in the 1850s. What had traditionally been supposed as flags captured at Yorktown and Trenton turned out to be a flag of the Anspach Regiment from Yorktown—not a Hessian color from Trenton—and a King's Colour of the Royal Fusiliers—which had, of course, been present at neither, nor captured at any battle in which Washington was directly involved. What became of the other one, two, or three colours captured from the Seventh Regiment is unknown.

King's Colour, Seventh Regiment of Foot, the Royal Fusiliers. Flag reproduction by author.

Regimental Colour, Seventh Regiment of Foot, the Royal Fusiliers. Flag reproduction by author.

Eighth Regiment of Foot, the King's Regiment

The colours of the Eighth Regiment of Foot were described in the Warrants of 1751 and again in 1768: "Eighth, or the King's Regiment. In the centre of their colours the 'White horse' on a red ground within the garter, and crown over it; in the three corners of the second colour the King's cipher and crown." The second, or regimental, colour was blue. The "White horse" was the traditional white horse of Hanover, King George's original homeland, depicted "courant," or running, the rear feet on a green mound, the fore feet extended and roughly parallel. The garter was a circular blue band buckled to itself like a belt, the buckle appearing on the viewer's left, with the tongue wrapped over the belt and hanging down in the style of the knights of centuries past. The Royal motto, *HONI SOIT QUI MAL Y PENCE*, roughly translates as "Shame on him who thinks evil of it." The colours of the Eighth were among the few that carried a scroll with motto. Although not in the wording of the warrant itself, the AG's painting of the colour in the Windsor book accompanying the Warrant of 1751 included in the white scroll the motto *NEC ASPERA TERRENT*, variously (and loosely) translated, but basically meaning "Not even adversity deters [us]." According to inspection returns, the regiment received new colours in 1766. By this period, they were likely embroidered, and the "GR" cyphers in the three corners of the regimental colour would have been entwined, in gold foliated script. Both colours had the rank of the regiment in gold Roman numerals in the upper corner near the staff. Some extant colours of the period (see Seventh and Sixtieth Regiments) have the Roman numerals painted on the reverse of the colour, basically the whole flag made with the pole to the right, and as the paint soaks through to the front, the numerals appear backward on the obverse of the flag. In this case the garter is displayed correctly, so the designating Roman numerals would be in the same orientation.

About one hundred men of the Eighth were involved in the siege of Fort Stanwix, July to August 1777, and the Battle of Oriskany. On August 6, while the bulk of the British forces were engaged in the main battle, a smaller American force sallied out of the nearby Fort Stanwix and surprised the British camps. The narrative of Colonel Marinus Willett, second in command of the Americans, listed five colours among

King's Colour, Eighth Regiment of Foot, The King's Regiment.

Regimental Colour, Eighth Regiment of Foot, The King's Regiment.

the equipment and provisions captured.[12] Lieutenant William Colbraith, of the Third New York Regiment, wrote in his journal under August 6, "Four colours were also taken and immediately hoisted on our flag-staff under the Continental flag, as trophies of victory."[13] Some writers have suggested that these would have been the regimental colours of the Eighth and Thirty-Fourth Regiments, plus maybe a camp colour or other flag. But neither unit reported any such loss, and it seems unlikely that a relatively small detachment of regular troops engaged in a siege and camped in the woods would have had the regimental colours with them, rather than being left with one of the larger elements of the regiment in garrison at stationary forti-fications. The colours taken may have belonged to some of the five hundred Canadian or Loyalist troops also engaged in the campaign. No other records from either side confirm (or deny) the loss—nothing from higher up the chain of command, no records of captured colours received by Congress nor the state gov-ernments of the regiments involved, no admissions on the part of either British regiment, or record of new colours being requested or issued.

Ninth Regiment of Foot

The colours of the Ninth Regiment are among the few carried in the American War of Independence that are still in existence. The yellow regimental colour is also one of the very oldest British colours to survive at all, though this is only partially true. New colours were procured for the regiment in 1772, but only the King's Colour was entirely new—the regimental made use of the handsome and apparently fully intact embroidered wreath from an earlier colour of about 1757. The regimental number IX is embroidered di-rectly on the yellow silk; as of 1758 colours were expected to have their rank "on crimson." It has also been speculated that this wreath is even older. This is unlikely, however, as embroidery was not authorized until the Warrant of 1751, and certainly did not replace traditional painted colours immediately.

The King's Colour of the regiment is the pattern that became standard about the end of the previous war and was used by most British regiments during the War of Independence. It is somewhat unusual in that the lettering "REGt" and the Roman numeral IX are so poorly aligned, perhaps partially from age and inexpert repairs, that many later drawings show the regimental name as if on a shield tilted to one side or angled away from the viewer. It is also generally shown as if the tilt were to the right, and the tendrils at the bottom of the cartouche leading off to the left, but that is because the best available photograph, from Milne, actually shows the reverse of this colour. The oldest photographs of the whole colour show the cartouche fairly level, the tendrils leading off toward the fly, and the lettering, though irregular, relatively vertical. The wreath is of the sub-pattern (the Sixty-Second Regiment is another example) on which one of the roses is replaced by an additional twig with leaves, so that there are only three roses where in most cases there would be four. The regimental colour, as mentioned above, had the wreath of an older colour sewn into the center of a new silk colour. The wreath is quite small, only eleven inches at its extreme widest point, even smaller than Napier's 1751 drawing, which in scale was about seventeen to eighteen inches in diameter, so as to fill the center of the thirteen-inch-wide red cross of a King's Colour without overlapping into the white. Gherardi Davis and others have routinely drawn the wreath of the Ninth Regiment at about four times its actual size, making it bigger even than the Union canton. The pole sleeve of this colour is the same yellow silk as the field, not red as usually portrayed.

The Ninth Regiment arrived in Canada in 1776 and took part in the northern campaigns that culmi-nated in the surrender at Saratoga on October 17, 1777. The British regiments were allowed to march out with the honors of war, which included music playing, bayonets fixed, and colours flying. However, the terms of the capitulation, styled a "Convention" rather than a surrender, had been argued and worried over by both sides to such an extent that in the final march into captivity, no colours of either the British nor the German regiments were surrendered. It was reported to the Americans that the colours had not been brought on the expedition, but also, apparently, that they had been burned by the soldiers prior to the capitulation. The story of the German Fahnen being sewn into a mattress and smuggled out in the baggage of Madame Riedesel is well known. It seems the British colours were also hidden by common consent, but without any special coordination. British General G. Surtees, in an article published in 1967, pointed out that by the terms of the Convention, no British officers' baggage was "to be molested nor searched, Lieut.-General Burgoyne giving his Honour that there are no public stores secreted therein."[14] This was considered a pretty neat trick by General Surtees, as regimental colours, being paid for by the colonels of each regiment, were not "public stores," but private property.

When American General Gates had to explain his too-lenient terms to Washington and Congress, he declared in December 1777, "Respecting the Standards, General Burgoyne declared upon his Honor, that the Colours of the Regiments were left in Canada."[15] This was untrue, but whether the lie was on the part of Burgoyne or Gates is not clear. Congress (correctly) did not believe it, and the non-surrender of the colours was one of the reasons given for refusing to ratify and abide by the terms of the Convention. Instead of being sent to Europe on parole, as the Convention stipulated, the surrendered troops were kept in America until 1781.

Lieutenant-Colonel Hill of the Ninth was one of the few who openly gloried in hiding and saving his regiment's colours. After keeping them hidden during his internment, on his return to England he presented the colours to King George III, who graciously returned them, and they remained in the Hill family until late in the next century. Eventually they were donated to the British military academy at Sandhurst, where they were at the time that Milne and Davis were doing their research. They are now at the Royal Norfolk Regimental Museum in Norwich, United Kingdom.

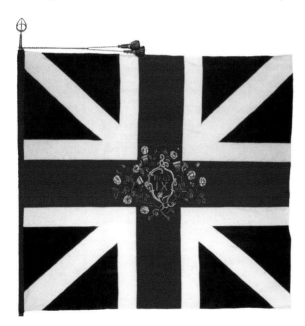

King's Colour, Ninth Regiment of Foot.

Regimental Colour, Ninth Regiment of Foot.
Flag reproduction by author, currently on
display at US National Guard Memorial
Museum, Washington, DC.

Remains of original colour, Ninth Regiment, from Gherardi Davis, *Regimental Colors.* Note that central wreath—not in its original position—is only about one quarter the size of the Union canton.

Gherardi Davis's original watercolor of regimental colour of Ninth Regiment, 1906. Why Davis painted the wreath so large is unknown, as he had photos of the original. More curiously, both versions were published in the same book. Nevertheless, this painting, re-published since the 1950s in many versions of American Heritage histories, and online, has led many researchers astray over the past century plus. Gherardi Davis papers, Manuscripts and Archives Division, The New York Public Library.

Tenth Regiment of Foot

The Tenth Regiment of Foot was already in Canada at the beginning of the American War of Independence, having arrived in 1767. The regimental facings and the regimental colour were bright yellow. The regiment probably carried colours of the standard embroidered rococo pattern that had become common at the end of the French and Indian War. Inspection returns show that the regiment received new colours on its return to England in 1780.

King's Colour, Tenth Regiment of Foot.

Regimental Colour, Tenth Regiment of Foot.

Fourteenth Regiment of Foot

The Fourteenth Regiment of Foot received colours in 1764, probably of the newly introduced embroidered rococo pattern. Its regimental facings and regimental colour were buff. From 1768 to 1770, the regiment was garrisoned in Boston, where its colours would have been an everyday sight to the growing discontent of the inhabitants. Immediately after the Boston Massacre in March 1770, the Fourteenth was removed to Castle Island, in Boston Harbor, well away from the civilians. After final removal from Boston and a period of years in the West Indies, the regiment returned to New York in 1776. There the bulk of the regiment was drafted into other units and the remainder sent back to England.

King's Colour, Fourteenth Regiment of Foot.

Regimental Colour, Fourteenth Regiment of Foot.

Fifteenth Regiment of Foot

The Fifteenth Regiment of Foot received new colours in 1770, presumably of the embroidered rococo pattern introduced at the end of the previous war, and the same as other documented colours issued at about the same time. The regimental facings and regimental colour were yellow. The Fifteenth served in North America 1776–1778, when it was transferred to the West Indies. Its colours were captured by the French at Saint Eustatius in 1781. This regiment had also served in the French and Indian War.

King's Colour, Fifteenth Regiment of Foot.

Regimental Colour, Fifteenth Regiment of Foot.

Sixteenth Regiment of Foot

The Sixteenth Regiment of Foot served primarily in Florida and Georgia, first arriving in 1767. The regimental facings and the regimental colour were yellow. There is no record of colours received while in America, so the colours carried during service in the American War of Independence were probably those of the mid-1760s, of the embroidered rococo pattern carried by most regiments of the period. After a brief remove to New York in 1776, the regiment returned south and was parceled out to various forts and garrisons. The colours of the Sixteenth Regiment were captured by Spanish troops at the surrender of Baton Rouge on September 21, 1779. Most of the remainder of the regiment was garrisoned at Pensacola and captured when the Spanish took that post in 1781. In 1783 the captured colours were sent to Spain along with those of the Waldeck Regiment taken at Pensacola and were displayed in four cathedrals in

King's Colour, Sixteenth Regiment of Foot. Flag reproduction by author. Currently on display at Museum and Education Center, Mount Vernon, Virginia.

different part of the country. A painting mounted in the frame of a British colour also taken to Spain in 1783 shows Spanish General Gálvez on horseback astride two British regimental colours, identified by the small Union canton on each. One of these may represent a color of the Sixteenth Regiment, captured at Baton Rouge, the other a colour of the Sixtieth. Though many researchers British, American, and Spanish have tried, nothing concrete has been found on the ultimate fate of the captured colours.

Regimental Colour, Sixteenth Regiment of Foot.

Seventeenth Regiment of Foot

The Seventeenth Regiment of Foot had uniform facings of white, described in the 1768 warrant in the column "Distinction in the same Colour," as "Greyish White." The regimental colour was white (not grayish) with the red cross of St. George throughout. According to the regimental historian, new colours were received in New York in 1766.[16] These would probably have been the embroidered rococo pattern common at the time. Both colours were captured at the storming and surrender of Stony Point on the night of July 15, 1779. General Washington reported to Congress a few days later that the "two standards of the Seventeenth Regiment" were in his possession and that he would forward them to Congress. No letters or reports have survived to document whether this was ever done, but in any case, as with most other captured colours, those of the Seventeenth simply disappeared sometime after the end of the war. The regiment did not receive new colours in the two years between Stony Point and Yorktown, indeed they received no new colours before 1787, so had none to surrender there.[17] This regiment had also served in the French and Indian War.

King's Colour, Seventeenth Regiment of Foot.

Regimental Colour, Seventeenth Regiment of Foot.

Eighteenth Regiment of Foot, the Royal Irish Regiment

The Eighteenth Regiment of Foot, the Royal Irish, arrived in America in 1767. As a Royal regiment, the uniform facings and regimental colour were blue. The colours of the regiment were described in the Warrant of 1751: "Eighteenth Regiment, or the Royal Irish. In the centre of their colours the 'Harp' in a blue field, and the crown over it, and in the three corners of their second colour, the Lion of Nassau, King William the Third's arms." In the original drawing accompanying the warrant, the traditional Irish harp is placed directly on the blue field of the regimental colour, but also portrayed directly on the red cross of the King's Colour, not "on blue" as described in the warrant. (An extant pair of colours belonging to the Third Battalion of the First Regiment, and carried at Waterloo, similarly has the central device painted directly on the silk field of each colour, blue on the regimental and red on the King's Colour, rather than on the "correct" background color.) Both colours of the Eighteenth had the crown above the harp, as per the warrant, and in a scroll below, the motto, *VIRTUTIS NAMURCENCIS PRAEMIUM*, meaning "The reward of Valor at Namur." The motto and the privilege of bearing the King's arms were granted by William III for the regiment's actions at the siege of Namur in 1695. The "Lion of Nassau" always portrayed the lion on a blue field with gold "billets," but why AG Napier drew it on a circular field rather than a traditional heraldic shield is unknown. The colours carried by the Eighteenth in America were probably painted, and probably the first they had received since the Warrant of 1751. The regiment was in Boston at the opening of the war and was engaged in the battles around that city. In December 1775 the enlisted soldiers were drafted into other regiments and the officers sent back to Britain. New colours were presented in 1776 or 1777, but both of these dates were after the regiment as an organization was home to recruit. It did not return to North America.

King's Colour, Eighteenth Regiment of Foot, the Royal Irish.

Regimental Colour, Eighteenth Regiment of Foot, the Royal Irish.

Nineteenth Regiment of Foot

The Nineteenth Regiment of Foot served in the American War of Independence only during its final year, arriving in Charleston, South Carolina, in June 1781. The regimental facings were deep green, and the regiment was unofficially referred to as the "Green Howards." This dated back to the period when regiments were known by the names of their colonels, and there had been another regiment also known as Howard's Regiment, so the two Howards were distinguished by the color of their uniform facings. The Nineteenth Regiment received new colours in Ireland in 1780, shortly before embarking for America. These would undoubtedly have been of the new pattern introduced in about 1778 and known to have been carried by other regiments raised, mustered, and presented colours at about the same time.

King's Colour, Nineteenth Regiment of Foot.

Regimental Colour, Nineteenth Regiment of Foot.

Twentieth Regiment of Foot

The Twentieth Regiment of Foot received new colours in 1769. These would likely have been of the common embroidered rococo pattern known to have been issued to other regiments at about the same time. The regimental facings and the regimental colour were pale yellow. The Twentieth was one of the six regiments surrendered with Burgoyne's Army at Saratoga. According to the terms of capitulation, the British were allowed the honors of war, meaning they could march out with drums playing, bayonets fixed, and colours flying. No colours were actually surrendered, however, apparently being removed from their pikes and smuggled out in the officers' baggage. Inspection returns remark that the Twentieth received new colours in 1782. It is not known whether the colours hidden away after Saratoga were lost during the regiment's internment in America or returned to England and simply lost to history sometime after.

For further details on the Saratoga Convention, how and why the colours were not surrendered, see entry for Ninth Regiment of Foot.

King's Colour, Twentieth Regiment of Foot.

Regimental Colour, Twentieth Regiment of Foot.

Twenty-First Regiment of Foot, Royal North British Fusiliers

The Twenty-First Regiment of Foot was one of the regiments exempted from the standardization of colours mandated in the Warrants of 1743, 1751, and 1768. As a Royal regiment, the uniform facings were blue. From Warrant of 1751, repeated in the Warrant of 1768: "Twenty-first, or the Royal North British Fusiliers. In the centre of their colours the 'Thistle' within the circle of St. Andrew, and crown over it; and in the three corners of the second colour, the King's cipher and crown." Napier's detail drawing in the Windsor book shows the thistle and crown on blue on the regimental. This suggests that whether painted or embroidered—as the colours received in 1774 almost certainly were—the thistle would have been simply placed on the silk field of the flag within the circle of St. Andrew, with the background being red on the King's Colour and blue on the regimental.

The Twenty-First received new colours in 1774 while stationed in Ireland, so they were relatively new when the regiment arrived in Quebec in May 1776. The Fusiliers were one of the six regiments surrendered with Burgoyne's Army at Saratoga. According to the terms of capitulation, the British were allowed the honors of war, meaning they could march out with drums playing, bayonets fixed, and colours flying. No colours were actually surrendered, however, apparently being removed from their pikes and smuggled out in the officers' baggage. Inspection returns remark that the Twenty-First received new colours in England in 1782. It is not known whether the colours hidden away after Saratoga were lost during the regiment's internment in America or returned to England and simply lost to history sometime after. Such records as there may have been to help clarify this were lost in a fire at the regimental museum in 1985.

For further details on the Saratoga Convention, how and why the colours were not surrendered, see entry for Ninth Regiment of Foot.

King's Colours, Twenty-First Regiment of Foot, Royal North British Fusiliers.

Regimental Colour, Twenty-First Regiment of Foot, Royal North British Fusiliers.

Twenty-Second Regiment of Foot

The Twenty-Second Regiment of Foot received new colours in 1774 while stationed in Ireland. They were almost certainly of the standard embroidered rococo pattern known to have been presented to other regiments during the same period. The regimental facings were pale buff; the regimental colour would have been pale buff as well. The colours were still relatively new when the regiment arrived in Boston in July 1775. A framed fragment of one of the colours of the Twenty-Second is in a private collection. It is mounted on a backing that reads, "[illegible] of the regimental flag carried by the British Regiment 'Twenty-Second Fusileers' at the battle of Bunker Hill, now hanging in the cathedral at Chester. Chester, Eng – Sept 10 -1884." There is no reason to doubt the authenticity of the piece, though the colour of the Twenty-Second probably was not carried at Bunker Hill, as only picked companies from the several regiments in Boston made the assault, rather than whole regiments under their own officers and colours. The

King's Colour, Twenty-Second Regiment of Foot.

Regimental Colour, Twenty-Second Regiment of Foot.

framed red and blue silk pieces are so small that they could have come from either of the flags belonging to the regiment. The colours hanging in Chester Cathedral have long since disappeared; correspondence with the archivists there yield no information on their final disposition.

Twenty-Third Regiment of Foot, Royal Welch Fusiliers

The Twenty-Third Regiment of Foot, the Royal Welch Fusiliers, was one of the Royal regiments exempted from the new rules imposed on regimental colours in 1743. As a Royal regiment, the uniform facings were blue. The colours carried by the regiment during the American War of Independence were as described in the Warrants of 1751 and 1768: "Twenty-third, or the Royal Welsh Fusileers. In the center of their colours, the device of the Prince of Wales, viz., three feathers issuing out of the Prince's coronet; in the three corners of the second colour, the badges of Edward the Black Prince, viz., the Rising Sun, Red Dragon, and the Three Feathers in the coronet; motto *ICH DIEN*" (German for "I serve"). As these colours have not survived, it is unknown whether they were embroidered of painted. Painting seems reasonable, however, based on the complexity of the design, plus a realistic concern that having heavily embroidered roundels in the outer corners might limit how freely the flag would float on the wind while posing the threat of simply breaking out of the silk field at the weakest points of any flag. AG Napier's 1751 drawing from the Windsor pattern book shows the motto in a scroll above the central device of the coronet and feathers, but all contemporary depictions of the Prince of Wales's arms depict the motto issuing out from the underside of the coronet. The motto in effect was part of the arms, rather than an addition to them.

No specific year of issue is known for the colours carried by the regiment in America 1773–1781. Inspection returns of 1764 state the colours at that time were in good condition, and lacking any other reports, it seems likely these are the same ones carried through the American war. The Twenty-Third was captured with Cornwallis's Army at Yorktown in 1781. The colours were not surrendered, however, being pulled off their pikes and smuggled out by Captain Thomas Peter and an ensign, with the flags wrapped around their bodies. It was undoubtedly these same two colours that were described as being in bad condition in an inspection in 1788.[18]

King's Colour, Twenty-Third Regiment of Foot, Royal Welch Fusiliers. Flag reproduction by author.

Regimental Colour, Twenty-Third Regiment, Royal Welch Fusiliers. Flag reproduction by author.

Twenty-Fourth Regiment of Foot

The Twenty-Fourth Regiment of Foot received new colours in 1769. The regimental facings were willow green. The new colours were probably of the standard pattern of the time, with embroidered rococo wreath. The regiment was one of the six captured at Saratoga, but as the Twenty-Fourth had been in the "Avant-Corps" or forward unit deployed as scouts and light infantry, it was probably the one regiment that really had left its colours at Ticonderoga and was without colours at the time of the surrender.

King's Colour, Twenty-Fourth Regiment of Foot.

Regimental Colour, Twenty-Fourth Regiment of Foot.

Twenty-Sixth Regiment of Foot

The Twenty-Sixth was posted to Canada from Ireland in 1767 and was there at the beginning of the American War of Independence. The regiment's uniform facings were pale yellow; the regimental colour would also have been pale yellow. The colours were most likely the standard embroidered rococo pattern presented to other regiments in Ireland at the same period.

Like the Seventh, the Twenty-Sixth was parceled out to several posts in Canada and was captured piecemeal in the American invasion of 1775. The colours were with the detachment at Montreal. When that town was evacuated by bateaux down the St. Lawrence, the Americans gave chase, and the Twenty-Sixth lost its colours. As American vessels closed in, the colours were stripped from their pikes and "carried by an officer round his body; but finding escape impossible, they were wrapped round a cannon-ball and sunk in the river."[19] The regiment was reconstituted through reinforcements and prisoner exchange in 1776, but in 1779 its enlisted men were drafted into other regiments and the officers returned to England to rebuild the regiment. It is not known when new colours may have been sent to the regiment in America, but when the regiment was back in Canada after the war and inspected in 1792, its colours were reported as "entirely worn out."[20]

King's Colour, Twenty-Sixth Regiment of Foot.

Regimental Colour, Twenty-Sixth Regiment of Foot.

Twenty-Seventh, Inniskilling Regiment of Foot

The Inniskilling Regiment of Foot was originally raised in Enniskillen,* County Fermanagh, Northern Ireland, and maintained its strength primarily with new recruits from the same area. Its uniforms were faced in buff. In the Warrant of 1743, the Twenty-Seventh was one of the few singled out as "distinguished by particular devices, and therefore not subject to the preceding articles for colours." This was clarified by the Warrant of 1751 and repeated in 1768: "Twenty-seventh, or the Inniskilling regiment. Allowed to wear in the center of their colours a castle with three turrets, St. George's colours in a blue field, and the name 'Inniskilling' over it." The actual Enniskillin Castle had only two prominent turrets, which were high on

---

*Enniskillin/Inniskilling is variously spelled throughout documents of the period, but "Inniskilling" is always used in warrants referring to uniforms and colours.

the walls; apparently AG Napier's design used a standardized heraldic castle, but with the English flag of St. George added. Unlike other regiments with an associated Royal or ancient badge, the regimental colour of the Inniskillings did not have corner devices. Napier's watercolor of the authorized pattern of 1751 included the regimental number in Roman numerals in the upper corner near the pike on both colours. It also included a scroll for motto, but as mentioned in the introduction, there is no reason to believe that regiments that had no motto at the time carried colours with a blank scroll. Milne's drawing of this colour in 1893 omits the scroll.

According to inspection returns, the regiment received new colours in 1769. These were probably embroidered, as was becoming more common among all British regiments. Later colours of the regiment are known to have had the castle embroidered in white on a blue silk panel. The Inniskillings were sent to America in 1775. They were transferred to the West Indies in 1779 and received new colours there in 1784. This regiment had also served in the French and Indian War.

King's Colour, Twenty-Seventh Regiment of Foot, the Inniskilling Regiment.

Regimental Colour, Twenty-Seventh Regiment of Foot, the Inniskilling Regiment.

Previously unpublished watercolor of the regimental colour, Twenty-Seventh Inniskilling, by Gherardi Davis, 1906. Gherardi Davis papers, Manuscripts and Archives Division, The New York Public Library.

Twenty-Eighth Regiment of Foot

The Twenty-Eighth Regiment of Foot received new colours in 1768 while stationed in Ireland. These would undoubtedly have been the same embroidered rococo pattern presented to other regiments in Ireland at about the same time. The uniform facings and the regimental colour were bright yellow. The regiment arrived in America in May 1776 and was withdrawn and sent to the West Indies in 1778, where it was captured by the French in 1782. When inspected after the war in 1784, it was noted, "Colours—1 pair wanting."[21] This regiment had also served in the French and Indian War.

King's Colour, Twenty-Eighth Regiment of Foot.

Regimental Colour, Twenty-Eighth Regiment of Foot.

Twenty-Ninth Regiment of Foot

The Twenty-Ninth Regiment of Foot received new colours in 1761. These would have been of the embroidered rococo pattern newly introduced and becoming the standard at that time. The uniform facings and regimental colour were yellow. The Twenty-Ninth was posted to Boston in 1768 to help keep the peace, marching up Long Wharf on October 1, "Drums beating, Fifes playing, and Colours flying."[22] Their colours would have been a common sight about the rebellious town. In March 1770 eight grenadiers of the Twenty-Ninth were involved in the Boston Massacre, one of the signal events on the road to revolution and war. Five colonists were killed in the affair and six more wounded, earning the Twenty-Ninth the nickname "Vein Openers." The regiment was immediately withdrawn from the city proper to Castle Island in Boston Harbor, and soon removed from the colony completely. Back in England, the Twenty-Ninth was inspected

King's Colour, Twenty-Ninth Regiment of Foot.

Regimental Colour, Twenty-Ninth Regiment of Foot.

in December 1773, identifying the colours as having been in use since 1761. The regiment was sent to Quebec in 1776 and remained in Canada after the war until 1787. When the colours were next inspected in England in 1789, they were listed as "nearly worn out."[23]

Thirtieth Regiment of Foot

The Thirtieth Regiment of Foot spent the first years of the American War of Independence in Ireland, arriving in Charleston, in 1781. The regimental facings and regimental colour were pale yellow. Inspection returns from 1785 report that the regiment had received colours in 1780. These would likely have been of the new pattern presented to other regiments in 1778–1780.

King's Colour, Thirtieth Regiment of Foot.

Regimental Colour, Thirtieth Regiment of Foot.

Thirty-First Regiment of Foot

The Thirty-First Regiment of Foot arrived in Canada from Ireland in 1776. The regimental uniform facings and the regimental colour were buff. There are no records at all of presentation, use, or later disposition of the regimental colours, so it is assumed that they were of the embroidered rococo pattern often presented in Ireland and used throughout the 1760s and 1770s by other regiments.

King's Colour, Thirty-First Regiment of Foot.

Regimental Colour, Thirty-First Regiment of Foot.

Thirty-Third Regiment of Foot

The Thirty-Third Regiment of Foot had uniform facings of red, so the regimental colour was white with the red cross of St. George. The regiment received new colours in 1761 and 1771. The 1761 colours still exist, framed and mounted high on the walls of Halifax Parish Church (now Halifax Minster) in West Yorkshire, United Kingdom. They are of the embroidered rococo pattern newly introduced about 1760 and may be the oldest surviving example of the type. The new colours presented to the regiment in 1771 in Ireland were probably near identical, as the rococo pattern was being given to other regiments, both old and new, at about the same time. The 1771 colours were carried in the battles and campaigns in America.

The Thirty-Third was one of the regiments captured at Yorktown, but their colours were not surrendered to the Americans. Unlike Saratoga, there is no contemporary documentation that could explain why some regimental colours were surrendered and some not. In any event, the colours of the Thirty-Third returned to England with the regiment after the war and were laid up in the Church of Saint Mary Magdalene, Taunton. In 1832 there was a disagreement over who should get which colours, but eventually the 1771 colours were returned to Mary Magdalene's and last seen there about 1864. It is unknown what became of them thereafter. The 1761 colours went to the family of one of the early colonels of the Thirty-Third. There they simply moldered away for many years, were re-discovered in 1882, and the remnants—mostly the heavily embroidered rococo wreaths—were set into new silks of the proper design and dimensions and put on display in the Halifax Church. An interesting detail is that the colours were still on their original poles in 1882, and these had the "X" type finial. The colours on display in Halifax were long thought to be the colours carried in the American War of Independence, and Milne identified them as such in *Standards and Colours* in 1893. Gherardi Davis did a painting of the regimental colour in 1906, also identifying it as a colour carried in the American revolution, which has been published in popular American histories since the 1950s. The correct identities of the two sets of colours was sorted out by Major A. C. S. Savory of the Duke of Wellington's Regiment and Museum, in Halifax, and privately published circa 1950 as *Regimental Colours, 33rd Regiment and 76th Regiment*.

King's Colour, Thirty-Third Regiment of Foot.

Regimental Colour, Thirty-Third Regiment of Foot.

Gherardi Davis's original watercolor of regimental colour of Thirty-Third Regiment, 1906. One of the few accurate representations of British colours that has been reproduced in popular histories of the war. Davis wrongly attributed this color to the War of American Independence, but the two colours presented to the regiment in 1761 and 1771 were probably identical. Gherardi Davis papers, Manuscripts and Archives Division, The New York Public Library.

Thirty-Fourth Regiment of Foot

The Thirty-Fourth Regiment of Foot had bright yellow uniform facings and a bright yellow regimental colour. New colours had been received in 1771 and presumably were much like those presented to other regiments during the same period. The regiment was sent to Canada in May 1776, where it was parceled out in detachments to several forts and composite units. The grenadier and light companied were captured at Saratoga. The unit never served as a single battalion in a line of battle fight.

A detachment of one hundred men of the Thirty-Fourth with a like number of the Eighth King's Regiment were involved in the siege of Fort Stanwix, July to August 1777, and the Battle of Oriskany. On August 6, while the bulk of the British troops were engaged in the main battle, a smaller American force sallied out of the nearby Fort Stanwix and surprised the British camps. The narrative of Colonel Marinus Willett, second in command of the Americans, listed five colours among the equipment and provisions captured. Lieutenant William Colbrath, of the Third New York Regiment, wrote in his journal under August 6, "Four colours were also taken and immediately hoisted on our flagstaff under the Continental flag, as trophies of victory." Some writers have suggested that these would have been the regimental colours of the Thirty-Fourth and Eighth Regiments, plus maybe a camp colour or other flag. But neither unit reported any such loss, and it seems unlikely that the relatively small detachments of regular troops engaged in a siege and camped in the woods would have had the regimental colours with them. The flags taken may have belonged to some of the five hundred Canadian or Loyalist troops also engaged in the campaign. No other records from either side confirm (or deny) the loss—nothing from higher up the chain of command, no records of captured colours received by Congress nor the state governments of the New York or Massachusetts regiments involved, no admissions on the part of either British regiment, or record of new colours being requested or issued.

King's Colour, Thirty-Fourth Regiment of Foot.

Regimental Colour, Thirty-Fourth Regiment of Foot.

Thirty-Fifth Regiment of Foot

The Thirty-Fifth Regiment of Foot was the only regiment in the British Army with orange as the color of its regimental facings. Originally raised in Belfast and maintained and recruited entirely in Ireland, the regiment was strongly Protestant, at least in its early years, and had been rewarded by King William III with special permission to adopt orange for its uniform facings and regimental colour. New colours were presented to the regiment in 1767, probably of the embroidered rococo pattern used throughout the 1760s and 1770s by most regiments. Contemporary paintings of officers of the regiment suggest that the orange was very light, almost a deep ochre, rather than the deep burnt orange or bright pumpkin orange often associated with William and the Protestant cause.

The Thirty-Fifth arrived in Boston in 1775 and transferred to the West Indies in 1778. This regiment had also served in the French and Indian War. One or more colours of the regiment were at one time in the Governor's Palace in Malta, but it is unknown what became of them, or whether they really dated from the American war as reported.

King's Colour, Thirty-Fifth Regiment of Foot.

Regimental Colour, Thirty-Fifth Regiment of Foot.

Thirty-Seventh Regiment of Foot

The Thirty-Seventh Regiment of Foot was one of very few regiments that carried two different pairs of colours during the War of American Independence. The regimental facings and regimental colour were yellow. The regiment surely had colours on its arrival at Cape Fear from Ireland in 1776. These would have been the standard rococo pattern used by most regiments throughout the 1760s and 1770s. Inspection returns of November 1784, however, report that the colours were new in 1780, when the regiment was still in America. There is no record of what may have happened to the first pair; perhaps they were just worn out. The new colours probably were of the pattern introduced about 1778 and known to have been presented to several other regiments raised and equipped at about that time.

King's Colour, Thirty-Seventh Regiment of Foot, 1776.

Regimental Colour, Thirty-Seventh Regiment of Foot, 1776.

King's Colour, Thirty-Seventh Regiment of Foot, 1780.

Regimental Colour, Thirty-Seventh Regiment of Foot, 1780.

Thirty-Eighth Regiment of Foot

The Thirty-Eighth Regiment of Foot received new colours in Ireland in 1768, probably of the embroidered rococo pattern introduced early in the 1760s. The regimental facings and regimental colour were yellow. The Thirty-Eighth arrived in Boston in 1774 and remained in America through 1783.

King's Colour, Thirty-Eighth Regiment of Foot.

Regimental Colour, Thirty-Eighth Regiment of Foot.

Fortieth Regiment of Foot

The Fortieth Regiment of Foot had only returned to Britain in 1767, after forty-eight years in America and the Caribbean. The regiment received new colours in Ireland in April 1767 and again in 1770, presumably on the appointment of its new colonel. The regimental facings were buff and the regimental colour was buff. Either or both of these new sets of colours would likely have been of the standard embroidered rococo pattern introduced in the early 1760s. The Fortieth arrived in Boston in June 1775 and was transferred to the West Indies in 1778. This regiment had also served in the French and Indian War.

King's Colour, Fortieth Regiment of Foot.

Regimental Colour, Fortieth Regiment of Foot.

Forty-Second Regiment of Foot, the Royal Highland Regiment

The Forty-Second Regiment of Foot, the Royal Highland Regiment, received new colours in 1768, perhaps to better conform to the warrant issued in that year, and again in 1774 while in Ireland. As a Royal regiment, the uniform facings were blue, and the regimental colour was blue. The regiment had not existed at the time of the original warrants pertaining to colours in 1743 and 1751, so the Warrant of 1768 was the first to address the colours officially: "The 42nd, or Royal Highlanders. In the centre of their colours the King's cipher within the garter, and crown over it; under it, St. Andrew, with the motto, *NEMO ME IMPUNE LACESSIT*, in the three corners of the second colour the King's cypher and crown." While the earlier colours of the regiment may have had a wreath surrounding the central devices, the wording of the 1768 warrant does not seem to allow for it on the now carefully defined colours for the Forty-Second. The oldest identified colours of the reg-

King's Colour, Forty-Second Regiment of Foot, the Royal Highlanders. Flag reproduction by author, currently on display at Fort Ligonier, Pennsylvania. Later research suggests that the colour carried by the regiment in the French and Indian War (which Ft. Ligonier commemorates) had a wreath around the central device.

iment, presented to the Second Battalion in 1780, have all the general characteristics of other colours made during the period and do not include the Union wreath. The 1774 colours carried by the regiment during the American War of Independence would have been embroidered, much like the colour of the Seventh Fusiliers on display at West Point, and no doubt like that prepared for the Second Battalion in 1780. The cypher, gold on a red background within the garter, by this period was in foliated script-like letters, overlapped and entwined. The Royal motto *HONI SOIT QUI MAL Y PENSE* (Shame on him who

Regimental Colour, Forty-Second Regiment of Foot, the Royal Highlanders.

thinks evil of it) was in gold letters on the garter. St. Andrew, with the motto, was a small round badge portraying the holy man holding the traditional X-shaped cross; the motto, traditionally translated as "No one harms me with impunity," in a circle around him. All of these would be on silk panels appliquéd to the flag so that they would read correctly on both sides. The King's cyphers in the three corners of the regimental colour were also in fancy foliated script letters. By the time of the 1774 presentation the cypher was usually doubled, reversed, and entwined, so a single embroidery would read the same on both sides of the flag. Remnants of the colours of the second battalion, raised in 1780 for service in India, clearly show the cyphers doubled. It is also clear that these colours were made back-to-front, such that with the pole on the left the Roman numerals LXII in the upper corner near the pole are backward and the buckle of the garter appears on the viewer's right—the correct heraldic display would show it on the left. Colours made for the Forty-Second in 1787 and 1802 were also made back-to-front, and as they all appear to have come from the same source, it is likely that the colours carried by the regiment in America were made that way.

The Forty-Second arrived in New York in 1776 and served in America through 1783. This regiment also served in the French and Indian War.

Forty-Third Regiment of Foot

The Forty-Third Regiment of Foot arrived in Boston in 1774. Its regimental uniform facings were white, the regimental colour white with the red cross of St. George superimposed. The regiment had received new colours in 1763 and again in March 1774, no doubt of the standard embroidered rococo pattern, just before embarking for America. The Forty-Third remained in America for the entire war. In April 1781 the regiment marched south to reinforce British forces in Virginia, and in October was captured with Cornwallis's Army at Yorktown. The colours of the Forty-Third are listed in General Knox's report to Congress as among the six British colours captured. It was later claimed that they were not surrendered, as they had been left in New York. American records of captured colours were so poorly kept, and the colours themselves simply lost in the years after the war, that is impossible to ascertain whether the colours of the Forty-Third were or were not surrendered. When the regiment was inspected in England in 1785, however, it had on hand "6 colours, good," suggesting that the colours at Yorktown had indeed been somehow spirited away.[24] This regiment had also served in the French and Indian War.

King's Colour, Forty-Third Regiment of Foot. Flag reproduction by author.

Regimental Colour, Forty-Third Regiment of Foot. Flag reproduction by author.

Forty-Fourth Regiment of Foot

The Forty-Fourth Regiment of Foot arrived in Boston in 1775. The regimental uniform facings and the regimental colour were yellow. This regiment had earlier served in the French and Indian War, where their original colours had figured prominently in the Battle of the Monongahela, or Braddock's Defeat, in 1755. There are no records of when the regiment received new colours, but those carried during the American War of Independence were probably of the standard embroidered rococo pattern carried by most regiments throughout the 1760s and 1770s.

King's Colour, Forty-Fourth Regiment of Foot.

Regimental Colour, Forty-Fourth Regiment of Foot.

Forty-Fifth Regiment of Foot

The Forty-Fifth Regiment of Foot arrived in Boston from Ireland in July 1776. The uniform facings and regimental colour were deep green. No records have been found to verify the dates of receipt of colours prior to American War of Independence; the colours carried in America were probably the standard embroidered rococo pattern used by other regiments throughout 1760s and 1770s. In 1778 the regiment was so reduced that the enlisted men were drafted into other regiments and the officers sent back to England to rebuild. New colours were received by the regiment in 1779 or 1780, but the regiment never returned to America. This regiment had also served in the French and Indian War.

King's Colour, Forty-Fifth Regiment of Foot.

Regimental Colour, Forty-Fifth Regiment of Foot.

Forty-Sixth Regiment of Foot

The Forty-Sixth Regiment of Foot arrived in America in May 1776. Regimental uniform facings and the regimental colour were yellow. The regiment had received new colours in Ireland in 1774. These would likely have been the standard embroidered rococo pattern known to have been given to other units at about the same time. Spearpoints from colour pikes in the regimental museum in Cornwall are of the "X" pattern. In 1778 the Forty-Sixth was transferred to the West Indies. Inspection returns made in 1784 note the regiment also received colours in 1778. What became of the relatively new colours of 1774 is not known, but it seems probable that the 1778 pair was in preparation for the change of station and not carried in North America.

This regiment had also served in the French and Indian War.

King's Colour, Forty-Sixth Regiment of Foot.

Regimental Colour, Forty-Sixth Regiment of Foot.

Forty-Seventh Regiment of Foot

The Forty-Seventh Regiment of Foot received new colours in Ireland in 1770, probably of the common rococo pattern known to be presented to other regiments at about the same time. The regimental facings were white; the regimental colour was white with red cross of St. George. The Forty-Seventh arrived in New Jersey before the war, in 1773. In 1777 it was one of the six regiments surrendered with Burgoyne's Army at Saratoga. According to the terms of capitulation, the British were allowed the honors of war, meaning they could march out with drums playing, bayonets fixed, and colours flying. No colours were actually surrendered, however, apparently being removed from their pikes and smuggled out in the officers' baggage. It is not known whether the colours hidden away after Saratoga were lost during the regiment's internment in America or returned to England and simply lost to history sometime after.

For further details on the Saratoga Convention, how and why the colours were not surrendered, see entry for Ninth Regiment of Foot. This regiment had also served in the French and Indian War.

King's Colour, Forty-Seventh Regiment of Foot. Flag reproduction by author.

Regimental Colour, Forty-Seventh Regiment of Foot. Flag reproduction by author.

Forty-Ninth Regiment of Foot

The Forty-Ninth Regiment of Foot received colours in 1772, the same year it was posted to Newfoundland. The regimental uniform facings were full green. A regimental coat at the National Army Museum in London, dated circa 1770 and attributed to an officer of the Forty-Ninth, shows this to be a somewhat olive color. Lawson, writing in the 1950s, inspected the official pattern books and described full green as very dark blue green.[25] Both of these samples were wool, however, which takes dyes and retains its color somewhat differently than silk. The original silk regimental colour of the Forty-Ninth was probably a very dark green with a bluish or grayish cast, certainly not a clear bright primary green. Both colours were probably of the embroidered rococo pattern given to other regiments at about the same time. The Forty-Ninth arrived in Boston in 1775 and transferred to the West Indies in 1778.

King's Colour, Forty-Ninth Regiment of Foot.

Regimental Colour, Forty-Ninth Regiment of Foot.

Fifty-Second Regiment of Foot

The Fifty-Second Regiment of Foot was raised in 1755 as the Fifty-Fourth but renumbered in 1757 with the capture and disestablishment of the Fiftieth and Fifty-First Regiments at Oswego. Possibly the regimental rank LIV was merely overpainted on the colours as LII, but it is just as likely that new colours were procured and may have been of one of the interim patterns with the regimental number directly on the silk field before the letter of 1758 specified the rank "on crimson in the center." As the regiment took no active part in the Seven Years' War either in Europe or America, it probably still carried the original colours when transferred to Canada in 1765. The regimental facings and the regimental colour were buff. The Fifty-Second was transferred to Boston in 1774 and lost heavily at Bunker Hill. The remnants were moved to New York, where in 1778 the enlisted men were drafted to other regiments and the officers sent back to England to recruit.

King's Colour, Fifty-Second Regiment of Foot.

Regimental Colour, Fifty-Second Regiment of Foot.

Fifty-Third Regiment of Foot

The colours of the Fifty-Third Regiment of Foot carried in America during the American War of Independence still exist. The regimental uniform facings were red, and the regimental colour white with the red cross of St. George throughout. The ragged remnants of both colours, including the cords and tassels and spearheads of the pikes, are carefully framed and preserved at the Shropshire Regimental Museum in Shrewsbury, United Kingdom. Both colours are embroidered and clearly came from the same maker but are of a pattern unknown in any other regiment. They appear most like the colour prepared for the Thirty-Ninth regiment in 1759, with more or less diamond shaped wreath and a blue-tinged bow below the central cartouche. These colours, however, are unique in having only Tudor-style roses, rather than the naturalistic garden roses of all other known colours of the period. The lettering appears to have been embroidered in silver, which quickly tarnishes and appears as black. The tassels are also non-standard, being bottle-shaped rather than straight-sided, and gold with silver netting, while the cords, though much discolored, appear to be red and gold. A perhaps trivial, but interesting, detail is that both colours are constructed with the upright section of the red cross of St. George in one piece running from top to bottom of the flag, with the horizontal arms of the cross as the separate pieces of silk, rather than the single long piece being horizontal as on almost every other known British colour from the period.

The history of these colours is fairly complete. They were presented to the regiment in 1774 while stationed in Ireland. In May 1776 the Fifty-Third was sent to Canada. The following year the regiment was part of Burgoyne's northern campaign, but in August the battalion companies of the Fifty-Third were detailed to remain at Ticonderoga and thus the bulk of the regiment, along with the colours, were not surrendered at Saratoga in October of 1777. One tradition claims that the colours were stripped from the pikes during the regiment's retreat back to Canada after Saratoga. On the regiment's return to England and the presentation of new colours, the old colours were given to the Colonel of the regiment, Sir Dalrymple Elphinstone. They remained in the Elphinstone family until 1903.

King's Colour, Fifty-Third Regiment of Foot.

Regimental Colour, Fifty-Third Regiment of Foot.

Fifty-Fourth Regiment of Foot

The Fifty-Fourth Regiment of Foot was raised in 1755 as the Fifty-Sixth regiment but was renumbered Fifty-Four in 1757 on the disestablishment of the Fiftieth and Fifty-First Regiments captured at Oswego. The regimental uniform facings were popinjay green, a very bright and slightly olive-green color becoming popular during the period. The regimental colour would also have been popinjay green. Inspection returns dated June 1769 indicate the regiment was still carrying colours presented in 1755. As the change in regimental ranking had occurred two years after that date, the colours had probably been altered to reflect the change in title, LVI being easily overpainted to read LIV. (There are several extant colours that were altered rather than replaced when the Act of Union required colours after 1801 to include the red cross and shamrocks of Ireland, and the Ninth Regiment, covered in this book, had used a section of its old colors in making new ones in 1772.) Additional returns from inspections of the Fifty-Fourth in 1772, 1773, and 1775 do not list colours at all; presumably the regiment still had its original colours and these were in good enough condition to be in continued use. These colours would likely have been of the same pattern most regiments had carried in the previous war, very like AG Napier's 1751 drawing, and painted rather than embroidered, as embroidered colours from such an early date are rare. The following year the regiment was sent to America, landing in North Carolina in May 1776. The final record of inspection that has survived for this regiment, dated 1781 and made while the regiment was still in America, again makes no mention of the colours, suggesting the same colours were still in use and presentable enough to merit no special remark.

King's Colour, Fifty-Fourth Regiment of Foot. Note that this colour is of the older pattern with wide St. Andrew's cross; the original designation LVI has been overpainted to read LIV.

Regimental Colour, Fifty-Fourth Regiment of Foot. The original LVI has been overpainted to read LIV.

Fifty-Fifth Regiment of Foot

The Fifty-Fifth Regiment of Foot arrived in Boston in 1775. Its uniform facings and regimental colour were dark green. Colours were received in 1767 and probably were the standard embroidered rococo pattern common to most regiments of the period. In 1778 the Fifty-Fifth was reassigned to the West Indies, where the regiment and its colours were captured by the French in 1782. This regiment had also served in the French and Indian War.

King's Colour, Fifty-Fifth Regiment of Foot.

Regimental Colour, Fifty-Fifth Regiment of Foot.

Fifty-Seventh Regiment of Foot

The Fifty-Seventh Regiment of Foot received new colours in 1770. These likely were the standard embroidered rococo pattern known to have been presented to other regiments at about the same time. The uniform facings and regimental colour were yellow. The Fifty-Seventh arrived in America in 1776 and remained until 1783.

<table>
<tr><td>King's Colour, Fifty-Seventh Regiment of Foot.</td><td>Regimental Colour, Fifty-Seventh Regiment of Foot.</td></tr>
</table>

Fifty-Ninth Regiment of Foot

The Fifty-Ninth Regiment of Foot arrived in Canada at the end of the previous war, in 1763. It had been raised in 1756 as the Sixty-First Regiment but was renumbered soon after when the Fiftieth and Fifty-First were disestablished after their capture at Oswego. The regimental facings were described in 1756 as "pompadour," a newly invented deep rose or reddish-purple color, just then coming into popularity.[26] Unfortunately, the fashionable new color, made from a common form of lichen, could vary considerably, and apparently was not very consistent from one batch to the next. In the Warrant of 1768, the color of the Fifty-Ninth's uniform facings was listed as purple, in the column "Distinctions in the same Colour" for regiments faced in red. Purple at the time generally meant a dark red or violet, not the blueish or indigo color we might now picture. The 1768 warrant used the same language as those of 1743 and 1751, that all regiments with facings of either white or red were to have a regimental colour with the red cross of St. George in a white field. In the same warrant, the Thirty-Fifth had its own category as the only regiment with orange facings and an orange regimental colour, but the Fifty-Ninth—whether considered pompadour or purple—was listed among the reds. Only Guards regiments were to have colors with a red/crimson field, and these were considered the King's Colours of the three Guards regiments, so it is unlikely that the Fifty-Ninth carried an all-red regimental colour, regardless of which word was used to describe the precise shade. Likewise, the traditional red cross of St. George and England could hardly be made a unique pompadour or purple shade to reflect a single regiment's uniforms.

The Fifty-Ninth transferred to Boston in 1772. Both colours of the regiment at that time would likely have been of the embroidered rococo pattern introduced about 1760. In 1775 the grenadier and light companies of the regiment were part of the composite British force at the Battle of Bunker Hill, but as the regiment as a whole was not engaged, the colours would not have been involved. Soon after, the remainder of the enlisted men were drafted into other regiments and the officers sent back to England to rebuild the regiment. In February of the following year, possibly due to the difficulty of getting a consistent pompadour/ purple, "His Majesty has given directions relative to the clothing of the Fifty-Ninth Regiment of Foot. The facings to be white instead of purple."[27] The regiment later sported the nickname "the Lily Whites." New colours were received in England in 1776, and again in 1781, but the regiment did not return to America.

King's Colour, Fifty-Ninth Regiment of Foot.

Regimental Colour, Fifty-Ninth Regiment of Foot.

Sixtieth Regiment of Foot, the Royal Americans

Two battalions of the Sixtieth Regiment, the Royal Americans, were in North America when the war began in 1775. Both were soon shipped to other theaters, however, and did not serve on the continent during the War of American Independence. The original third and fourth battalions had been disbanded in 1763, but to meet the new emergency, a new third and fourth battalion were quickly raised and arrived in Florida in 1776. The Warrant of 1768 described the colours for a two-battalion regiment: "The Sixtieth, or Royal Americans. In the centre of their colours the King's cypher within the garter, and crown over it and in the three corners of the second colour the King's cypher and crown. The colours of the second battalion to be distinguished by a flaming ray of gold, descending from the upper corner of each colour toward the center."

A regimental colour of the Fourth Battalion of the Sixtieth photographed at the National Army Museum in London in the 1980s suggests that the newly raised Third and Fourth Battalions received colours generally in conformity with the Warrant of 1768. The surviving colour has an embroidered cypher, garter, and crown at center, and in each corner the King's cypher entwined and reversed, with crown. The Roman numerals LX are painted in the Union canton. A small circlet below the garter with the numerals IV indicate the battalion number; the new Third and Fourth battalions were identified much as they had been in

1756–1763, and not as some modern sources suppose, by two or three golden rays issuing from the upper corner as might have been done in the seventeenth century. (The Second battalion had probably been designated by a single golden ray as per the warrant.) Like the colours of several other regiments with the Royal cypher at center, the flag was made back-to-front; the garter at center is in the correct orientation on the reverse of the colour, and the numerals LX are painted going toward the pole. From the front of the colour, with pole to the left, both garter and Roman numerals are reversed. The cypher and all lettering are on double layers of silk appliquéd onto the flag, so read correctly on both sides. The colours of both new battalions would have been alike except for the small secondary badges with the appropriate number in Roman numerals. Some sources suggest one or more of the colours of the Third Battalion Sixtieth Regiment were taken by the Spanish at Pensacola. However, there is no specific record of it from either Army. A painting in the frame of one of the captured British flags taken to Spain in 1783 shows Spanish General Gálvez on horseback astride two British regimental colours, identified by the small Union canton on each. One of these may represent a color of the Sixteenth Regiment, captured at Baton Rouge, the other a colour of the Sixtieth.

King's Colour, Sixtieth Regiment of Foot, the Royal Americans.

Regimental Colour, Sixtieth Regiment of Foot, the Royal Americans. Flag reproduction by author, currently on display at Fort Ligonier, Pennsylvania. Later research suggests that the colour carried by the regiment in the French and Indian War (which Fort Ligonier commemorates) had a different central device.

Sixty-Second Regiment of Foot

One original colour of the Sixty-Second Regiment of Foot still exists. It is a King's Colour embroidered in the rococo pattern with tendrils wrapping around the lower stems of the wreath. It is the same type as that of the Ninth Regiment—the wreath is missing one rose on the right side, having instead extra leaves where the rose ought to be. According to inspection returns the regiment received new colours in 1770 or 1771 while stationed in Ireland. The regimental facings were light yellowish buff; the new regimental colour would have been roughly the same yellowish buff with the same rococo wreath as the King's Colour. The Sixty-Second was one of the six regiments surrendered with Burgoyne's Army at Saratoga. According to the terms of capitulation, the British were allowed the honors of war, meaning they could march out with drums playing, bayonets fixed, and colours flying. No colours were actually surrendered, however, apparently being removed from their pikes and smuggled out in the officers' baggage. The King's Colour of the Sixty-Second was one of these colours. Presumably the regimental colour was saved as well, but what became of it after the war is unknown. The original King's Colour is at The Wardrobe: The Rifles, Berkshire and Wiltshire Museum, in Salisbury, United Kingdom.

For further details on the Saratoga Convention, how and why the colours were not surrendered, see entry for Ninth Regiment of Foot.

King's Colour, Sixty-Second Regiment of Foot.

Regimental Colour, Sixty-Second Regiment of Foot.

Sixty-Third Regiment of Foot

The Sixty-Third Regiment of Foot received new colours in 1774 while stationed in Ireland. These would likely have been the standard embroidered rococo pattern common among regiments receiving colours at about the same time and in the same place. The regimental facings were very deep green, the regimental colour the same. The Sixty-Third arrived in America in 1775 and remained until 1782.

King's Colour, Sixty-Third Regiment of Foot.

Regimental Colour, Sixty-Third Regiment of Foot.

Sixty-Fourth Regiment of Foot

The Sixty-Fourth Regiment of Foot had black uniform facings; it was listed in the circular letter of 1758 describing for the first time colours for those regiments faced in black. The regiment received new colours in 1766, probably of the common embroidered rococo pattern presented to most regiments throughout the 1760s and 1770s. The Sixty-Fourth arrived in Boston in November 1768 as part of the British show of force in the rebellious town. As such, its colours would have been an everyday sight for the Boston inhabitants. The Sixty-Fourth and Sixty-Fifth were withdrawn to Halifax the following summer. The Sixty-Fourth returned to Boston in 1772 and remained in America for the rest of the war. At the Battle of Eutaw Springs, September 8, 1781, the Sixty-Fourth briefly broke the American lines but was driven back in a fierce struggle, only to rally and advance again and assist in driving the Americans from the field. It was probably here that the King's Colour of the regiment was lost, possibly in the first repulse in the thick wooded terrain. The colour was never found by either Army; it was not reported as captured by the Americans, nor as lost by the British, but when the Sixty-Fourth was inspected in Jamaica in 1782, it had only one colour. The regimental colour which returned with the regiment to England is currently held by the Staffordshire Regiment Museum in Lichfield, United Kingdom.

King's Colour, Sixty-Fourth Regiment of Foot.

Regimental Colour, Sixty-Fourth Regiment of Foot. Flag reproduction by author.

Sixty-Fifth Regiment of Foot

The Sixty-Fifth Regiment of Foot had white uniform facings; its regimental colour was white with the red cross of St. George superimposed. The regiment had been created in 1758 when the newly raised second battalions of fifteen regiments were designated as separate regiments. The colours presented in that year may have been one of the intermediate patterns before the embroidered rococo pattern which cannot be verified any earlier than 1760. There are no records of new colours before the regiment was sent to Boston in November 1768. As part of the British show of force, the colours of the Sixty-Fifth would have been an everyday sight for the Boston inhabitants. The regiment was withdrawn to Halifax in 1769 but returned

King's Colour, Sixty-Fifth Regiment of Foot.

Regimental Colour, Sixty-Fifth Regiment of Foot.

to Boston in 1772. The Sixty-Fifth lost badly at the Battle of Bunker Hill in 1775 and recruitment proved so futile that rather than try to rebuild the regiment in America, in 1776 its enlisted men were drafted into other regiments and the officers sent back to England. Inspection returns cite new colours in 1776, but the regiment did not return to America.

Sixty-Ninth Regiment of Foot

The Sixty-Ninth Regiment of Foot served primarily as Marines aboard ships in the British fleet. It may have been in New York for a short time in 1781, but quickly departed in the same year for the West Indies. The regimental uniform facings and regimental colour were willow green, a somewhat grayish green that could be either dark or light. Colours were presented to the regiment in England in 1779, probably of the new embroidered pattern known to have been received by several other regiments beginning in 1778.

King's Colour, Sixty-Ninth Regiment of Foot.

Regimental Colour, Sixty-Ninth Regiment of Foot.

Seventieth Regiment of Foot, Glasgow Lowland Regiment

The Seventieth (Glasgow Lowland) Regiment of Foot was created in 1758 when the newly raised second battalions of fifteen regiments were redesignated as separate independent regiments. The regimental facings of the Seventieth were set in 1758 as deep gray, but the Warrant of 1768 listed them as simply black. There are no inspection returns or other records specifically mentioning regimental colours. Assuming at some point new colours were procured that put the regiment in line with the Warrant of 1768—whether this was to make the regiment reflect what was in the warrant, or conversely, that the warrant was describing what was already in place—the regimental colour would have been black with the red cross of St. George when the regiment arrived in America in 1776. If these colours were procured at any time after 1760 they were likely the standard embroidered rococo pattern first identified with that year.

King's Colour, Seventieth (Glasgow Lowland)
Regiment of Foot.

Regimental Colour, Seventieth (Glasgow Lowland)
Regiment of Foot.

Seventy-First Regiment of Foot, Fraser's Highlanders

The Seventy-First Regiment of Foot is one of the few regiments whose colours from the American War of Independence have survived to the present day, being carefully preserved in the National Museum of Scotland in Edinburgh. The regiment was raised in 1775–1776 for service in America by Simon Fraser of Lovat, who had raised and led the Seventy-Eighth Highland Regiment in the French and Indian War. Both regiments were generally referred to as Fraser's Highlanders. Recruitment for the new regiment in 1776 went so well that the Seventy-First departed for America as two battalions. It appears that only one set of colours was ever presented to the regiment, however, as it was not originally planned as more than a single battalion. In addition, a large number of the regiment was captured soon after landing in America, and most historical records seem to suggest that the remainder of the regiment was generally fielded as a single unit, the individual battalions being separated only later and in special situations.

The regimental facings were white and the regimental colour was white with a small Union canton, but without the required red cross of St. George. The pole sleeve was also white. The central cartouche and wreath were embroidered directly on the white silk field; the interior of the cartouche (also white) being double layered to allow the numerals and lettering to read correctly on both sides. Much of the original embroidery still exists, though greatly broken up and not in its original position around the cartouche. It is faded to an almost uniform soft golden hue with deeper brown shading, though it is clear the roses were originally at least somewhat pink, and the thistles (rather surprisingly) having their thistledown a light grayish green rather than the usual pink color. The roses are very unusually portrayed in the embroidery, being neither traditional heraldic roses nor the realistically portrayed "garden" roses on most other colours of the period. Instead, they appear like chrysanthemums or some other blossom with innumerable tiny petals. The central design on the King's Colour is completely missing. It was probably identical to that on the regimental, this being how all other pairs of colours were made, and there being no remnants of a larger wreath in what remains of the original red silk. The interior of the cartouche would be the red silk of the St. George's cross, with a second panel sewn on the reverse so that the lettering would be correct on both sides. The King's Colour has a blue pole sleeve, and from the angle of the remaining portion of the St. Andrew's cross, it appears that the flag was longer and more rectangular than most.

The first battalion of the Seventy-First was attached to Tarleton's command during the southern campaign of 1780–1781 and was virtually destroyed at the Battle of the Cowpens on January 17, 1781. Major James Jackson of the Georgia Militia wrote years later of "attempting to seize the colors of the Seventy-First Regiment in the midst of it, on their attempt to form after they were broken."[28] One King's Colour was indeed captured at Cowpens, but it belonged to the Seventh Fusiliers (which see). Like many British regiments on the uneven, wooded battlefields of America, the Seventy-First probably carried no colours into the fight. Possibly they were left with the second battalion in Georgia. In any event, no colour of the Seventy-First was reported or alleged by either side to have been captured there. Units were greatly mixed up in the fighting, and Jackson never claimed he had any British colour actually in hand nor time to inspect the name embroidered on it, only that he had seen a colour among the Highlanders and attempted to seize it. The Seventy-First returned to Britain with two colours after the end of the war and was disbanded.

King's Colour, Seventy-First Regiment of Foot, Fraser's Highlanders. Note that the widths of the white cross and fimbriations are more in line with the original pattern of 1751 than other King's Colours of this period.

Regimental Colour, Seventy-First Regiment of Foot, Fraser's Highlanders.

Seventy-Fourth (Highland) Regiment of Foot

The Seventy-Fourth (Highland) Regiment of Foot was raised in Argyll County, Scotland, in 1777–1778 to serve in the war in America. The Seventy-Fourth's regimental facings were yellow, and the regimental colour yellow. Both colours were probably of the embroidered symmetric wreath pattern known to have been presented to other newly raised regiments during the same period. There is no evidence that any Highland regiment besides those with special Royal authorization had a thistle in place of the standard cartouche at the center of the wreath at this time. Whether the regimental number was in standard Arabic numbers rather than Roman numerals is unknown, as both styles were used with this pattern. The Seventy-Fourth arrived in America in 1778 and was disbanded in 1784.

King's Colour, Seventy-Fourth (Highland) Regiment of Foot.

Regimental Colour, Seventy-Fourth (Highland) Regiment of Foot.

Seventy-Sixth Regiment of Foot, MacDonald's Highlanders

The Seventy-Sixth Regiment of Foot (MacDonald's Highlanders) was raised in Scotland in 1777–1778 for service in the American war. Its uniform facings and regimental colour were deep green. The regiment landed in America in 1779. Both colours of the regiment were captured at Yorktown in 1781 and are pictured in James Peale's portrait, *Washington at Yorktown*. The painting is based very closely on the large portraits of Washington done by the artist's brother Charles Willson Peale, except that the flags at Washington's feet are those taken at Yorktown rather than Trenton. So far as is known, James Peale, like his brother, had the original captured colours to work from. Both colours appear to be the embroidered pattern received by other regiments raised in Scotland at about the same time. The King's Colour clearly shows the regimental rank in Arabic numerals. As with other colours captured by the Americans during the war, neither of these colours has survived and nothing of their post-war history is known. The Seventy-Sixth was disbanded in 1784.

King's Color, Seventy-Sixth (Highland) Regiment of Foot. This colour can be seen at Washington's feet in James Peale's *Washington at Yorktown*, 1782. Peale had the original captured colours to work with.

Regimental Colour, Seventy-Sixth (Highland) Regiment of Foot. This colour can be seen partially furled and leaning on the cannon just above the white Ansbach flags in James Peale's *Washington at Yorktown*, 1782. Peale had the original captured colours to work with.

James Peale, *Washington at Yorktown*, 1782. Original at the Metropolitan Museum of Art, New York.

Eightieth Regiment of Foot, Royal Edinburgh Volunteers

The Eightieth Regiment of Foot, Royal Edinburgh Volunteers, was raised by the city of Edinburgh in 1778 specifically for service in America. It arrived in New York in 1779. Some sources list the regimental facings as yellow, and perhaps they were at first, but the title "Royal" would suggest blue, as every other Royal regiment, and only Royal regiments, had blue facings. A portrait of the regiment's colonel in a private collection shows that officer in a uniform with blue facings. The regimental colour would also be blue. Regiments with the word "Royal," or a Royal personage in their title, with only one known exception, had crowns, cyphers, or other Royal badges on the colours. (The exception was the 103rd Regiment, the King's Irish Infantry, 1780–1783, whose colours were the standard rococo pattern, embroidered on a blue field.) The city of Edinburgh may have procured colours for the Eightieth Regiment based on various Royal motifs, perhaps similar to those of the Eighty-Fourth Royal Highland Emigrants (which see). The colours of the Eightieth were captured at Yorktown in 1781, along with the Seventy-Sixth and Forty-Third Regiments. James Peale, brother of Charles Willson Peale, did a painting of Washington at Yorktown, based on his brother's more famous work, with captured German and British colours at Washington's feet. It is believed that Peale had the actual colours to work from. The colours of the Seventy-Sixth are clearly visible in the painting, while there is some question as to whether the Forty-Third actually surrendered its colours. An unidentified King's Colour also appears in the painting, partially covered by one of the white Ansbach flags. This is probably the King's Colour of the Eightieth. As with all but a very few of the many flags captured by the Americans during the war, nothing is known of what became of colours of the Eightieth. The regiment was disbanded in 1783.

King's Colour, Eightieth Regiment of Foot, Royal Edinburgh Volunteers.

Regimental Colour, Eightieth Regiment of Foot, Royal Edinburgh Volunteers.

Eighty-Second Regiment of Foot, Duke of Hamilton's Regiment

The Eighty-Second Regiment of Foot (Duke of Hamilton's) was raised in Scotland in 1777–1778 to serve in the war in America. Its regimental facings were black and the regimental colour black with the red cross of St. George. Both colours were still extant in the 1880s and are pictured in Andrew Ross, *Old Scottish Regimental Colours,* published in 1885 (see plate in introduction to British colours). Both were of the embroidered symmetric wreath pattern, in this case with the regimental rank in Arabic rather than Roman numerals. The lettering may have been originally silver, which tends to tarnish black fairly quickly. The Eighty-Second arrived in America in 1778 and was disbanded in 1784.

King's Colour, Eighty-Second Regiment of Foot.

Regimental Colour, Eighty-Second Regiment of Foot.

Eighty-Third Regiment of Foot, Royal Glasgow Volunteers

The Eighty-Third Regiment of Foot (Royal Glasgow Volunteers) was raised in Scotland in 1778 for the war in America. As a Royal regiment, its uniform facings were blue, as was the regimental colour. Although it is possible that the city of Glasgow presented the regiment with a made-to-order set of colours, perhaps something similar to those presented to the Eighty-Fourth Royal Highland Regiment, there is no documentation to support this. It is just as likely the regiment was presented colours of the new symmetric wreath pattern known to have been given other new regiments raised at about the same time. As a Royal regiment, however, the crown would probably have been included—at least one extant colour of this pattern shows that the basic design could have elements added for a particular regiment. The Eighty-Third arrived in New York in 1783 but very soon returned to Scotland and was disbanded late in the same year.

King's Colour, Eighty-Third Regiment of Foot (Royal Glasgow Volunteers).

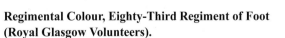

Regimental Colour, Eighty-Third Regiment of Foot (Royal Glasgow Volunteers).

Eighty-Fourth Regiment of Foot, Royal Highland Emigrants

The Eighty-Fourth Regiment of Foot was raised in Canada in 1775, as the Royal Highland Emigrants, largely from veterans of earlier Highland regiments mustered out at the end of the previous war. The regiment was originally classed as a provincial unit; it was not officially placed on the British establishment until December 1778 when it was ranked as the Eighty-Fourth. The regiment comprised two battalions, which were fielded separately. The original organization was overseen by Allan Maclean of Torloisk. When a second battalion was added, Maclean continued as the commander of the first battalion. A well-preserved pair of colours of the regiment is on display at Torloisk House in Scotland. Neither colour has numerals to indicate the rank of the regiment, only the Royal Highland Emigrants title. Both appear to have been made with blue silk much darker than the usual British royal blue. Nothing is known of the colours of the second battalion, but it seems likely that they were from the same maker as the first, identical except with the addition of a "flaming ray of gold" to identify the second battalion. The regiment was disbanded in 1784.

King's Colour, Eighty-Fourth Regiment of Foot, Royal Highland Emigrants.

Regimental Colour, Eighty-Fourth Regiment of Foot, Royal Highland Emigrants.

Queen's American Rangers, First American Regiment

The Queen's American Rangers, also known as Simcoe's Rangers, was a loyalist regiment raised in 1775–1776 by Robert Rogers, who had gained fame in the French and Indian War as the creator and leader of Rogers' Rangers. The new regiment was primarily light infantry or rangers but included a number of light cavalry troops. The unit did not fare well under Rogers and in 1777 the command was passed to John Graves Simcoe, at which time it began to be listed simply as Simcoe's Rangers. With the creation of an American establishment in 1779, Simcoe's Rangers became the First American Regiment, Queen's Rangers. As a mixed force of infantry rangers and light cavalry, consciously modeled on the Rangers of the previous war, the Queen's Rangers most likely did not carry any colours. There certainly is no mention of colours anywhere in Simcoe's very complete history of the unit published shortly after the war. The regiment was disbanded in 1783.

In 1791 the Queen's Rangers were re-established as a regiment in York, Upper Canada, again under John Graves Simcoe, then lieutenant governor of the province. A very handsome pair of colours, which still exist, was presented to the regiment. These colours have sometimes been claimed to have belonged to the Queen's Rangers of 1776–1783. However, they are painted in the style associated with numerous well-documented colours procured for both regular and fencible units in the 1790s, and not like any colours reliably associated with either of the wars fought in North America in the eighteenth century.

Volunteers of Ireland, Second American Regiment

The Volunteers of Ireland was a loyalist regiment raised in Philadelphia in 1777. In 1779 the regiment was placed on the newly created American establishment as the Second American Regiment, Volunteers of Ireland. Very little is known about this regiment. Its uniforms were red without turnbacks or standard facings, but with green brandenburgs—fancy cable buttonhole trim. The regimental colours were probably green, embroidered with the standard rococo wreath, as illustrated by Milne from another short-lived regiment of the same period. The lettering of the central cartouche is entirely open to conjecture, though probably not V. I., which would have appeared to observers of the time as Roman numerals for "6." That the regiment did indeed have colours, and that at least one was carried into battle, is attested by an article in *The Royal (New York) Gazette*, September 20, 1780, which identified Ensign Thomas Flynn as carrying one of the colours of the Volunteers of Ireland at the Battle of Camden.[29] The regiment was placed on the Irish (British) Establishment in December 1782 as the 105th Regiment of Foot. If colours were procured with the new designation, they were never carried in America. The regiment was disbanded in 1784.

King's Colour, Volunteers of Ireland, Second American Regiment.

Regimental Colour, Volunteers of Ireland, Second American Regiment.

New York Volunteers, Third American Regiment

The New York Volunteers was a loyalist regiment raised in Halifax early in 1776. Its early uniforms were green, probably with white facings. The regiment later received red coats with buff and blue facings. There is no specific information on the regiment's colours; possibly they carried none until the regiment was placed on the American establishment as the Third American Regiment in 1779. A letter from the regimental commander entitled "Memorial of the Officers of the Corps of New York Volunteers" written in 1783 to the British Commander in Chief in North America, reminded that officer, "That we had the Honor of a Standard and Thanks for the Repulse at Rocky Mount 30th July (1780)." If the colonel was speaking literally, then perhaps the regiment only received its first colours after becoming the Third American Regiment. The colours carried by the regiment, whenever received, were likely of the same embroidered pattern given other short-lived units raised at about the same period.

King's Colour, New York Volunteers, Third American Regiment.

Regimental Colour, New York Volunteers, Third American Regiment.

King's American Regiment, Fourth American Regiment

The King's American Regiment was raised in December 1776 as "The Associated Refugees." It recruited primarily in New York and was soon renamed King's American Regiment. The uniforms were red, like British regulars, with blue facings. A King's Colour carried by the regiment has survived and is currently in the Alejandro M. de Quesada Jr. Collection in Tampa, Florida. It is close to the regulation size, though somewhat narrower on the pole than most: approximately sixty-four by eighty inches rather than seventy-two by seventy-eight. All other details of this flag point to local manufacture rather than a professional maker in Britain. The silks are of a very coarse weave compared to the taffeta used for most colours throughout the period, and the whites have faint decorative bands of yellow woven in, both points suggesting silk repurposed from something else—draperies, upholstery, winter-weight garments. The red cross of St. George is overly wide, and the white silk pieces of the St. Andrew's cross are not properly placed to make an accurate corner-to-corner white cross. There was originally a small device of approximately six by eight inches appliquéd on both sides of the red silk at the center of the St. George's cross. A shadow of where it kept the silk from fading, and several cut stitches, remain where it was cut away, probably as a souvenir. A separate emblem appliquéd on both sides is virtually unique among flags of the period, generally if anything were appliquéd to one side, the opposite side would be cut out, but in this case the red silk of the cross was sandwiched between the two separate emblems. A fairly complete outline now remains, and an unusual spiral row of stitching, suggesting it may have originally been a representation of the eye of Providence, a popular motif of the period. An obvious example is the all-seeing eye at the top of a pyramid on the reverse of the Great Seal of the United States, proposed in 1776 and adopted in 1782, and still on the reverse of one-dollar bills. Overlays made from woodcuts and printer's blocks of the period show an almost perfect match. The finial is a tall iron pike, triangular in cross section. A bit of red cord tied just below appears to be the remnants of cord and tassels. The pole sleeve and the pole beneath it have been shot through and subsequently repaired.

If there was an accompanying regimental colour, nothing is known of it. If one were purchased and received from Britain, it would have been blue, possibly of the embroidered rococo pattern known to have been presented to at least one other short-lived and blue-faced unit raised at about the same period (the 103rd King's Irish Regiment). The lettering at the center of the reconstructed colour is entirely conjectural as the regiment had no rank on the British establishment, but "K.A.R." could be read as either "King's Associated Refugees" or "King's American Regiment." When an American establishment was created in 1779, the unit became the Fourth American Regiment, but it is unlikely that new colours with this designation were obtained. The regiment was transferred to the British establishment in December 1782 and disbanded in 1783.

King's Colour, King's American Regiment, Fourth American Regiment.

Regimental Colour, King's American Regiment, Fourth American Regiment.

British Legion, Fifth American Regiment

The British Legion was one of the most famous British-Loyalist regiments to emerge from the American War of Independence. It was created in New York in 1778 from several small loyalist units as a mixed force of light infantry, mounted cavalry, and a section of "flying" artillery—light guns that could keep up with the other mounted troops. The Legion was placed under the field command of Lieutenant Colonel Banastre Tarleton, and for much of the war was known simply as Tarleton's Legion. In May 1779 the British Legion became the Fifth American Regiment on the newly created American establishment. In 1782, after Yorktown, the Legion was transferred to the British establishment. It was disbanded in 1783.

It is unknown with any certainty what, if any, colours, standards, or guidons were carried by the British Legion. American colors captured by Tarleton were kept in the Tarleton family for generations, but no original colour carried by the Legion itself has survived. General Morgan's report to General Green on the outcome of the battle of Cowpens, dated January 24, 1781, lists "the standards of the legion and the Seventh regiments" among the personnel and equipment captured. It is likely that the five foot companies of the Legion, as light infantry, had no colours at any time during the war. The mounted companies probably had at least one standard or guidon, which may be the "standard of the legion" referred to by Morgan. Additional records show that two "standards" were forwarded to Congress after the battle, though the response of the then-President of Congress implies that only one was received, and only the King's Colours of the Seventh Fusiliers have survived to the present.[30]

Joshua Reynold's monumental painting of Tarleton done in 1782 prominently shows what is generally considered a reasonable depiction of the standard of the British Legion. It is clearly an "artist's impression," with nothing approaching the realistic detail given to the horses in the painting, or Tarleton's face and uniform. Nevertheless, it gives a reasonable depiction of the main features of the flag. An engraved print of this painting was made for sale by J. R. Smith, also in 1782. Smith had worked closely with Reynolds since 1774, reproducing at least thirty-three of his paintings in mezzotint. The print accentuates some of the flag details otherwise close to invisible on the original oil painting. It is unknown whether Reynolds worked from an original flag, now lost, or from a description. Nor is it known what became of this standard, whether captured in America or brought home and actually posed for Reynolds; in either case it has not survived.

The standard—as the designating flag of the Legion, it would be considered a standard, whether rectangular or swallow-tailed, and the fly end of the flag is not clearly shown—has been much discussed and interpreted. It is clearly not per British warrants; in fact, in size and shape it is similar to standards and guidons made for American mounted units. It also features a canton, common on American standards for mounted troops, but unknown on British. Its color seems to be a deep crimson, on which the red script letter "L," presumably for "Legion," barely shows against the background. Like some other colours of the period, it is made back-to-front—the letter at center reads correctly when looked at with the pole to the right. An American-made, non-regulation flag was probably painted, but painted or embroidered, the entire design would appear backward on the opposite side of the flag. The "L" is surrounded by a wreath which appears to depict roses and thistles, as described for British colours since 1751. The wreath is surmounted by a crown. There are two cannons in the lower quadrant next to the pole, which has led some to posit that there were other elements in the two corners near the fly—perhaps two infantrymen in one corner and a mounted man in the other, representing altogether the three arms of the Legion—but though Reynolds suggests various details on other flags in the painting, he gives no hint of anything at all at the outer ends of the Tarleton standard. The flag has no fringe. The most prominent feature of the colour is the white canton in the upper corner next to the staff, with what appears to be an eagle and lightning bolts. Some have claimed that the bird is meant to represent a swan, possibly the swan of the House of Lancaster. But besides the fact that Tarleton was from Liverpool, in Lancashire, there seems to be no reason for it to be a swan, and there is nothing in the painting or print to suggest the crown and chain that modify an everyday heraldic swan into the Lancastrian swan. Add to this the clear prohibition in every warrant from 1743 onward, that "No colonel is to put his Arms, Device, Livery, on any part of the Appointments of the Regiment under his Command." In any event, Tarleton was neither the proprietary nor appointed colonel of the regiment; that was William, Lord Cathcart, a Scottish nobleman. The bird on the Legion standard also resembles many heraldic drawings of a phoenix, but while the feet cannot be seen on the flag in the painting, even less does there appear to be any indication of the flames that a phoenix must be rising from. The eagle on the other hand, is an ancient heraldic device with military connotations, often depicted since Roman times with lightning in its talons. Granted the bird here has an unusually long neck and its head is almost touching its wing, but though perhaps wretchedly drawn by modern standards, it strongly resembles the drawings of eagles used in both the New York arms adopted in 1778 (same state and same year the Legion was established) and the great seal of the United States adopted in 1782. Smith's print of Reynold's painting closely mimics all details in the painting. It shows no crown or chain on the bird and shows an eagle's head with slight crest at the back and a hooked beak rather than a swan's bill.

The size of the standard can only be estimated. Judging from the horse and uniformed soldier depicted just below the lower edge of the flag, it would appear to be about the width of both British and American standards and guidons of the time, perhaps twenty-five to twenty-seven inches, while somewhat longer on the fly than British guidons with their rounded ends. Some of this is simply artistic convention; no flags refold themselves at the fly the way they were drawn in flag sheets or other depictions throughout much of the period. In fact, the Tarleton standard as depicted by Reynolds appears very like the American-made standard of the Second Continental Light Dragoons, which still exists. Keeping in mind that the sizes of available silks were limited, and that ease of manufacture would always be a consideration, especially where there were no specific regulations to govern the product, a reasonable case can be made that the length of the standard was two widths of approximately nineteen inches, sewn selvage to selvage, like the flag of the Second Continental Dragoons. With proportions of twenty-six by thirty-eight inches, or approximately one to one-and-a-half, the flag would appear much as Reynolds has painted it, dismissing the artistically elongated tail. Whether the Tarleton standard was attached to its lance by a British style pole sleeve or an American style cord running through several eyelets in the leading edge cannot be seen in the painting. On the assumption the standard is of American manufacture it is reproduced here with eyelets and a cord to attach it to the lance, American style. Also invisible in the painting, the cord and tassels, as well as the spear, would likewise be from what was available in America.

Standard, Tarleton's British Legion, Fifth American Regiment. Flag reproduction by author.

Brigade of Guards

This unit was a composite created by draft of individual soldiers from each company of the three Guards Regiments then on the English establishment. On arrival in America in August 1776, the unit was designated Brigade of Guards, comprising two battalions of five companies each. In 1781 the "Brigade" was reorganized as a single battalion. This reduced battalion was surrendered at Yorktown. There is no evidence that any colours were carried by the Guards in America. None are mentioned in existing reports of the Brigade's actions; none were listed among the inventories of persons and equipment captured at Yorktown. This was not a unique situation, however; composite battalions of grenadiers traditionally carried no colours even when formed and engaged in line of battle. As both officers and men of the Brigade of Guards had come from all companies—each of which had its own unique colour—of all three Guards regiments, it is hard to see how any colours could have been agreed on without much squabbling over honor, seniority, and rank, not to mention that any taken to America would necessarily have left some units without colours back in England.

Sixteenth (the Queen's) Regiment of Light Dragoons

The Sixteenth (the Queen's) Regiment of Light Dragoons arrived in New York in October 1776 and served in most of the northern battles through 1778. In 1779 the enlisted troopers were drafted into other units and the regiment returned to England. The regimental facings were royal blue. According to the Warrant of 1768, all three guidons of the Sixteenth had gold fringe and were painted. The King's guidon was red, the same pattern for all units, with the numerals XVI on blue in the upper right and lower left compartments. The second and third guidons were blue, at the center the Queen's cypher—"CR" for Charlotte Regina—within the Garter, and the motto *AUT CURSU, AUT COMINUS ARMIS*, roughly, "Either the charge, or in hand-to-hand." The white horse of Hanover was in a compartment in the upper left and lower right corners, the same as the King's guidon, the numerals XVI on a red ground in a wreath of roses and thistles in the opposite positions. The third squadron was designated by a small circle with the numeral 3, below the motto scroll.

Inspection returns dated 1771 list six standards, probably three as described in the Warrant of 1768, which would have been carried in North America, and three from the brief period 1766–1768 when the regiment had been titled Second, or the Queen's, before traditional seniority rankings were reinstated and standardized in the warrant.

King's Guidon, Sixteenth Regiment of Light Dragoons.

Squadron Guidon, Sixteenth Regiment of Light Dragoons. The guidon of the Second Squadron would be identical except without the small roundel below the motto scroll.

Seventeenth Regiment of Light Dragoons

The Seventeenth Regiment of Light Dragoons arrived in Boston in 1775 and remained in America until nearly the end of 1783. It had been raised in November 1759 as the Eighteenth Light Dragoons, one of five newly authorized regiments of that designation. All sources agree that Lieutenant-Colonel John Hale, upon receiving the authorization to raise such a regiment, immediately proposed and had accepted by the King, the death's head badge and the "Or Glory" motto, as a commemoration of General James Wolfe who had died at the moment of victory on the Plains of Abraham at Quebec only weeks earlier. When the regiment originally numbered Seventeenth was disbanded in 1763, the Eighteenth moved up one spot on the seniority list. Then for a brief period in the mid-1760s all light dragoon regiments were renumbered First through Fifth, with Hale's regiment becoming the Third. This scheme was soon reversed and the original rankings that included all dragoon regiments regardless of type were reinstated in 1768.

Inspection returns from 1769 note that the Seventeenth had received standards in 1759—these would undoubtedly have had Hale's death's head badge and motto at center. This inspection report was a year after the new Warrant of 1768 described standards and guidons of all regiments, so it seems clear that the regiment had not received new guidons after the warrant but was making do with those received ten years earlier. As the guidons were painted, the original XVIII may have simply been overpainted to XVII, then possibly to III, then back to XVII as the regiment was serially redesignated. Early variations of the regiment's badge show the crossed bones above the skull. This was quite unusual even at the time; the usual display of skull and crossbones as seen on contemporary gravestones, monuments, and broadsides had the bones below. David Morier, considered the most conscientious and accurate chronicler of the time, portrayed the Seventeenth Light Dragoon helmets and saddlecloths with the crossed bones above. An original helmet of the style portrayed by Morier, with the bones above, is preserved by The Royal Lancers & Nottinghamshire Yeomanry Museum in Britain. The helmet believed to have been worn by the regiment during service in America has the crossed bones below the skull, and no motto scroll, but this obviously would not affect guidons painted some fifteen years earlier. In the 1790s the regiment received new uniforms with a different type of helmet, which again featured the crossed bones above the skull. Descriptions of the guidons in the nineteenth century do not address such details, and unfortunately, the regiment lost its guidons and many regimental records on its return voyage at the end of its American service in 1783. According to the Royal Lancers Museum, the regimental badge did not show the bones below the skull until probably late 1790s.

Also at the museum, however, is a signet ring with the regimental arms and a wax seal (as used to verify important documents or to seal such a document closed) with the signet's impression. At least one additional wax seal made from this ring has survived and can be seen on various pages online. The design of the seal shows the badge of the regiment, the death's head as portrayed by Morier with the bones above, supported by a display of arms and flags. One of these is a swallow-tailed guidon, with the skull and crossed bones, with the bones *below*. The regimental name on the seal is shown as III Reg. Light Dragoons, which dates it to 1766–1768, the brief period the regiment was so designated. It seems reasonable to suppose that whoever cut the original die for the signet and wax seal for the newly redesignated Third Light Dragoons saw not only the regiment's original badge and accoutrements, but its original 1759 guidons as well—otherwise why not make all the same? For whatever reason, it appears that the guidons did indeed carry the death's head in its traditional form, with the crossed bones below. The motto scroll throughout this period was still depicted as a separate element—the current design with motto scroll draped over the bones did not come into use until much later when a one-piece regimental cap-badge was introduced. Finally, there is nothing in the Warrant of 1768 to suggest that the flags described for the Seventeenth in that document were not indeed the same guidons first presented in 1759, and there is no reason to think that these guidons were not what was carried in America from 1775–1783. If new guidons were presented between 1769 and 1775, there is no mention of it in any extant records; if there were, it is unlikely they would have been very different in design from the originals.

The Warrant of 1751 had not addressed Light Dragoons, as there were no regiments of that type at the time. The Warrant of 1768 apparently described not just what was authorized for the Seventeenth, but what was actually on hand, as it noted that the guidons of the Seventeenth were painted (as were also the guidons of the Twelfth, Fifteenth, Sixteenth, and Eighteenth). The King's, or First guidon, was presumably exactly as described in the warrant—similar in all respects to all other King's guidons, but with the prescribed silver and red fringe. The second and third squadron guidons were white—the color of the regimental facings—with silver and red fringe. In the center was the regimental badge described above and scroll with the motto "Or Glory" below, thus the nickname, "Death or Glory Boys." The official regimental history compiled by Richard Cannon in 1841 describes the second and third guidons as having the badge on a red field surrounded by a wreath of roses and thistles, but Cannon referred to the Warrant of 1768 rather than original regimental documents—which had been lost years earlier along with the original guidons—for all details of uniform and accoutrements, simply copying the wording of the warrant and replacing all generic references with the specifics of the Seventeenth. This, however, did not take into account the various ambiguities built into a warrant, which was trying to describe different types of guidons in long rambling sentences to cover every eventuality. Judging from other guidons of the period, the death's head badge of the Seventeenth was placed directly on the white silk, not on a crimson ground—the red ground and Union wreath only applied to regiments that did not have a "particular badge." (In fact, there is not a single surviving British guidon that has an authorized badge on a crimson ground, even though there are a few that have the badge surrounded by a wreath.) The first and fourth corners (upper left and lower right) of the squadron guidons had a cartouche with the white horse on a red ground, same as the King's guidon. In the other two corners was a small wreath of roses and thistles with XVII and LD on a red ground within. This wreath was specified in both the Warrants of 1751 and 1768 for regiments that had a particular badge at center. Cannon—taking his description from the wrong part of the warrant—says there were compartments with rose and thistle conjoined upon a red ground in these two corners, but this would leave the guidons of the Seventeenth without the regimental rank anywhere on them. The third squadron was designated by a small circle with the numeral 3, on a red ground, below the motto scroll.

King's Guidon, Seventeenth Regiment of Light Dragoons.

Squadron Guidon, Seventeenth Regiment of Light Dragoons. The guidon of the Third Squadron would be identical except with addition of a small roundel with numeral "3" below the motto scroll. Flag reproduction by author.

Marines

Two battalions of British Marines were posted to Boston in 1774, with more arriving in May 1775. They were organized and trained like infantry battalions of the Army. In February 1775, the Marine divisional headquarters at Portsmouth and Plymouth were ordered to send their divisional colours "with the Marines" to Boston, with assurances that they would be replaced with new ones. Colours from both divisions presumably arrived in Boston with the additional contingents in May. At the Battle of Bunker Hill, June 17, 1775, it is likely that the only British colours on the field were those of the Marine Battalion, as the first two assaults had been made by picked grenadier and light infantry companies of several different regiments.

The Royal Marines Museum in Britain has the remnants of an original colour said to have been carried at Bunker Hill. Though two versions of its provenance both seem reasonable, the physical details of the remnant bring the supposed date into question. It is a section of the red silk cross of St. George, with the embroidered device beautifully done in shades of gold, highlighted with touches of red and green. There is no way to know for certain whether this was saved from a King's Colour or a white colour with red cross, though evidence suggests that Marine battalion colours had a plain white field. Besides the wreath surrounding the fouled anchor as described in 1761, the central design includes a crown above and a scroll with the motto *PER MARE ET TERRAM* (By sea and by land) surrounding the anchor but within the wreath. The motto scroll is a double layer so that the lettering reads correctly on both sides. In response to an inquiry made to the Royal Marines Museum in 1986, it was stated that this form and spelling of the motto was used from 1775 (when it also shows up on a Marine Light Infantry cap) to 1803.[31] As mentioned above, colours were sent to the Marine battalions in Boston in May 1775.

There are several problems with the dating of this remnant, all of which might reasonably be explained away, but certainly must be addressed. The first is the crown; the Marines did not become a Royal regiment until 1802. The inclusion of a crown a quarter century before it was appropriate seems questionable, yet both the design and embroidery are virtually identical to the crowns on colours reliably dated to 1760–1780. (The shape of the crowns on Army colours changed considerably after about 1790.) On the other hand, though the regiment was not technically listed as Royal, it was routinely characterized as "His Majesty's Marine Forces." The second problem is the wreath of roses and thistles, which includes a shamrock, which could not have been added before the union with Ireland in 1801. The wreath is almost perfectly symmetric, with the left and right being mirror images of each other, except for the shamrock, placed on one side only, and not really integrated into the otherwise symmetric design. It was not unusual, however, to add shamrocks and the cross of St. Patrick to existing colours to update them to the new specifications in 1801 rather than purchasing entirely new ones. Personnel at the Marine Museum have inspected the fragment and agree that the shamrock appears to have been added later, based at least in part on the awkward positioning. But the corresponding parts of the design on the other side of the wreath are missing entirely, so it appears likely that a second shamrock was in fact there, regardless of when it was added. Nevertheless, the provenance records that this colour was carried at Bunker Hill would not rule out having the shamrocks added later. That the whole design fits entirely into the red cross is also typical of an earlier date—the wreath on colours made after about 1780 and well into the nineteenth century spill out of the red cross and onto the white silk around it.

A third point of contention is the inclusion of the motto. This was clearly not mentioned in the invoice of 1761 (detailing work done on one of first set of colours for Marines; see Marines entry in section on French and Indian War), and if it only came to be used beginning in 1775, would it have appeared on the colours sent to Boston in May of that year? Perhaps this fragment belonged rather to one of the replacement colours promised by the Admiralty when the Portsmouth and Plymouth Divisions were ordered to send their on-hand colors to Boston.

King's Colour, His Majesty's Marine Forces.

Battalion Colour, His Majesty's Marine Forces, 1775. While evidence seems to suggest that the Marine "division" or battalion colours were white, it is possible that each of the three divisions—Chatham, Portsmouth, and Plymouth—had a different color field for its flag to differentiate it from the others.

French Regimental Drapeaux in North America

INTRODUCTION: FRENCH REGIMENTAL DRAPEAUX IN THE EIGHTEENTH CENTURY

It must be pointed out from the very beginning, that unlike sources of study of British colours, German Fahnen, and Spanish banderas carried in North America, not a single French drapeau from the period under study has survived. All conclusions are based on contemporary documents and illustrations, and a few surviving similar drapeaux from periods just before, and in some cases, just after the wars in North America in the eighteenth century. French regimental names during that time span also went through a confusing series of redesignations of existing regiments and reuse of older territorial names for regiments that had traditionally been known by the names of their colonels. This makes it sometimes difficult to follow the evolution of the drapeaux of individual regiments and pin down just what would have been carried when. Also because of this, the entries for individual French regiments are generally far longer and more detailed than the brief entries used for British, German, or Spanish units.

All French regimental colors (singular *drapeau* and plural *drapeaux* in French) carried in North America were descended from the reforms of Louis XIV in the late seventeenth and early eighteenth centuries, when all French regiments were taken away from hereditary or mercenary colonels and made to respond directly to the crown. Colonels commanding regiments now held commissions directly on authority of the King and commanded their regiments in the King's name. Uniforms and weapons were standardized. The regimental drapeaux were standardized as well.

By the early years of the eighteenth century virtually all French forces were represented by drapeaux based on the white cross of France. Although blue was then the color of the Royal House of France, white was considered a traditional French color, and a white cross had been used to identify French troops at least since the time of Joan of Arc. The white cross neatly separated the flag into four quadrants, and these quadrants, rather than being of a single color or pattern with the cross superimposed, were made of different colors, designs, and patterns. The colors and devices in some cases derived from the livery or arms of the hereditary colonel at the time the regiment was first raised, and some were based on traditional symbols and devices related to the territory or province the regiment was associated with, but there was no hard and fast rule to this effect. In most cases it appears that colors or designs were entirely random or assigned simply to distinguish one regiment from another in the smoke and turmoil of battle. Unlike British and to some extent German military flags, there is no particular relation between the colors used in the drapeaux of a French regiment and the colors of the uniform facings of that regiment. While the designs of some drapeaux certainly had history and symbolism behind them, at this point it would be difficult to identify much of it.

Detail, "*Ticonderoga, 1758,*" by Don Troiani, 2022, oil on canvas. Photo courtesy of the artist.

Regiments of different nationalities in French service were less constrained by the French Army's rules of standardization and tended to have drapeaux that mirrored their native imagery and could include armorial devices of the current colonel or noble proprietor. Thus, the Irish regiments had red rather than white crosses, with harps and British-style crowns as their salient features. Swiss regiments were easily distinguished by their drapeaux with rays or flames of many colors radiating from the innermost corners, like the colorful raiment of the famed Swiss mercenaries of centuries before. Allemand, or German, regiments tended to display the standard white cross, though the well-known *Deux-Ponts* or *Zweibrucken*, "Two Bridges," in French and German, respectively, Regiment, which served in North America during the War of Independence, had a white saltire, or corner to corner cross, and the Regiment la Marck featured a blue and white checkered border taken from the arms of Bavaria. Scottish regiments carried drapeaux with painted thistles and the white corner-to corner cross of St. Andrew. (Although the white cross on French drapeaux is simply called the *croix blanc*, and not "the cross of St. Denis" or "cross of St. Joan," or some other name, the corner-to-corner cross, which would be a *saltire blanc* in heraldic terms, is routinely identified as a *croix de Ste Andre*.) The Regiment Bourgogne (Burgundy), which served at Fortress Louisbourg in 1758, had drapeaux with the barbed red saltire of Burgundy, which is the Burgundian interpretation of the cross on which St. Andrew was martyred: two crossed tree limbs, their smaller branches trimmed short, rather than two flat-sided beams.

French Royal regiments, and certain others for various now-unknown reasons, had additional designs on them. Generally, these were either in the four quadrants, or on the white cross, only sometimes on both. The fleur-de-lis was the most common embellishment, but crowns, the rising sun, mottoes, and other devices were also found. Throughout the period of this study these devices were always painted, the only exception being the embroidered *etendard* (standard) of the mounted portion of Lauzun's Legion in the War of Independence.

The *Compagnies franches de la Marine* were the garrison and security forces in New France throughout most of the eighteenth century. These independent companies were administered by the French Navy and should not be confused with two ancient French infantry regiments of the line, both created in the previous century, with "Marine" in their titles. As independent companies, the Compagnies franches did not carry colors, but the overall organization had been presented drapeaux in 1737. When several companies were formed as a battalion, as for the defense of Louisbourg in 1759, they may have carried drapeaux as did other infantry battalions.

At the beginning of the eighteenth century, each company in a French battalion or regiment carried one drapeau. Sometime after about 1713 this number was reduced, generally to three per battalion. In 1749 this was further reduced to two per battalion, and in 1765, after the French and Indian War, to two per regiment—one per battalion, with each regiment having two permanent battalions. Among these flags, each regiment had one colonel's color, called in French the *drapeau colonel*, carried by the colonel's company, the first company of the first battalion. In most regiments this was a white flag with a white cross. To set off the cross from the field, the seams were embellished with white stitching. As no example of such a white-on-white flag has survived, it is not known exactly what this implied. The cross itself was made of three pieces, so the seams holding the arms of the cross to the upright would always be somewhat visible. The additional "white stitching" was probably heavy embroidery thread rather than thin silk sewing thread, stitched over the seams between the cross and the cantons, but not across the seams holding the cross together. In addition, during some periods at least, particularly during the American War of Independence, the four white quarters of each drapeau colonel mimicked the colored quarters of the *drapeaux d'ordonnance* of the regiment, with any piecing of the silk panels also highlighted in white stitching. Many secondary works do not mention or illustrate this—the white colonel's color is now generally portrayed with a white cross and four plain white quarters. Prints from 1721 show the drapeaux colonel as simply white with a white cross and plain white cantons, and *Troupes du Roi, Infanterie française et étrangère, année*

1757 (*Troops of the King, French and Foreign Infantry, in the year 1757*), which shows the uniforms and drapeaux of the French infantry regiments then in service, also shows the drapeaux colonel as very plain. But the *Tableaux Militaire* produced in 1771, clearly shows each drapeau colonel with the quarters seamed the same as the drapeaux d'ordonnance, and it seems highly dubious that such an odd or unlikely detail was invented by the artist. Gustav Desjardins's *Recherches sur les Drapeaux francais*, published in 1874, cites this tableau and points out, in case it was not clear from the illustrations, "They [the drapeaux colonel] are marked like the flags of color: crosses, flames, and fess, drawn in white on white by seams." A series of uniform plates made in 1772 by Claude-Antoine Littret de Montigny (who later did many of the engravings for Diderot's *Encyclopédie*) also show the drapeaux colonel with the cantons sectioned the same as the drapeaux d'ordonnance. American researcher Gherardi Davis, after corresponding with French archivists, stated in his 1907 study on regimental colors in the American War of Independence, "The white crosses or other patterns on the colored flags were reproduced on the white flags in white stitching." As the number of flags carried by a regiment was reduced to only one per battalion after 1765, it is possible that the piecing of the quarters on the drapeaux colonel was begun at that time to better distinguish to which regiment the white drapeau belonged, since it was no longer carried in close company to the colored drapeau d'ordonnance. Van Blarenberghe's paintings of the siege and surrender at Yorktown, done in 1785, seem to show white-on-white details on the drapeaux colonel, though with the small size of the flags in the paintings, this may just be the artist's way of showing the shadows on flags flowing in the breeze.

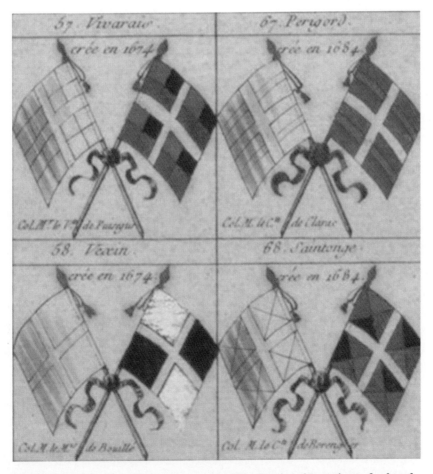

Small section of the *Tableau Militaire* of 1771, showing the sections of colored silk on the drapeaux d'ordonnance mimicked in white on the white drapeaux colonel.

Painted embellishments on drapeaux of the French regiments, such as fleur-de-lis, rising sun, mottoes, or other devices, were generally identical on the drapeau colonel to those on the drapeau d'ordonnance of the same regiment. Foreign regiments in French service had more leeway in this respect and the drapeau colonel could be significantly different from the drapeaux d'ordonnance. Virtually all French regiments in North America 1755–1763 were only the second battalions of their regiments; the first battalion of each of these regiments remained on active service in Europe as part of the French establishment engaged in the Seven Years' War against Britain and Prussia—presumably their drapeaux colonel remained with them. René Chartrand, a historian with Parks Canada, stated in 1984 that only the Regiment Angoumois, with its single battalion stationed in New Orleans in 1762–1763, carried the white drapeau in America.

Between the French and Indian War and the American War of Independence, French infantry regiments and battalions were reorganized. Regiments sent to America in 1779 and 1780 each had two battalions fielded together as a single unit. Each battalion was composed of five companies, four line companies of fusiliers and one elite company—grenadiers in the first battalion, chasseurs in the second. French regiments at Yorktown carried two drapeaux per two-battalion regiment, one white drapeau colonel, and one of the regiment's traditional drapeaux d'ordonnance. Many of these can be seen dotting the French line in Louis-Nicolas van Blarenberghe's painting *Surrender at Yorktown*, produced in 1785 by the official

Section of Louis-Nicolas van Blarenberghe's painting "Surrender at Yorktown," clearly showing a single drapeau at the center of each French battalion. In the original painting, the details are great enough that individual regiments can be identified. Photo by author from original, from the collection of the Hon. Nicholas F. Taubman, on loan and displayed at National Museum of American History, Washington, DC.

military painter to the French court. French tactical guides of the period show each two-battalion regiment being treated as a single tactical unit, unlike the earlier period, during which each battalion was considered a separate tactical unit and routinely separated from its parent regiment. The two drapeaux of each two-battalion regiment were separated, however—the white drapeau colonel at the center of the first battalion, the colored drapeau d'ordonnance at the center of the second. As in the tactical manuals, van Blarenberghe shows the drapeaux during the surrender ceremonies stationed individually at the centers of each of the two battalions of each regiment.

The French siege force at Savannah, however, used composite regiments made up of detached companies from several regiments stationed in the French West Indies or on ships of the French fleet. There is no direct evidence of the drapeaux of these regiments being present at the siege, but various listings of the troops present suggest that entire battalions of the contributing regiments were dispatched and it seems reasonable to suppose that these would have been accompanied by their battalion drapeaux—white drapeau colonel for those regiments sending their first battalions, colored drapeaux d'ordonnance for those regiments sending their second battalions.

Johann Conrad Dohla, of the German Bayreuth regiment in service with the British at Yorktown, stated that each French regiment carried at the surrender ceremonies a "white silk, with three silver fleur-de-lis embroidered upon it." Several paintings and map cartouches done shortly after the war depict white French flags with three fleur-de-lis more or less in the upper quadrant near the staff. From this it has been suggested that the French drapeaux colonel during this period had three large fleur-de-lis in the upper canton near the staff, above the horizontal arm of the white cross. However, not a single French source shows such a flag, and those in paintings and maps seem to have the fleur-de-lis added only to make clear the nationality of the flag or troops, just as many paintings have entirely conjectural versions of the stars and stripes to indicate American troops, or very badly drawn Union colours for the British. What Dohla probably saw at Yorktown was the three fleur-de-lis in the upper corner of the white drapeau colonel of the Royal Deux-Ponts, and simply generalized his observation.

At the end of the seventeenth century French drapeaux had been outlandishly large, some eight-by-eight feet. By mid-eighteenth century they had become reasonably standardized at perhaps sixty-six to sixty-nine inches per side. Several sources suggest that by 1768 the size was approximately sixty-four to sixty-five inches, but no specific orders or regulations have been found to substantiate this, and to specifically aim for this exact size would require extra cutting, hemming, and wastage of silk from the standard widths generally available. Pierre Charrie, in his groundbreaking work published in 1989, *Drapeaux et Etandards du Roi*, attributed the sixty-four-inch standard to Denis Diderot's *Encyclopédie*, which listed the size of the French drapeaux as 165 cm (64 inches) with cross of 32 cm (12.5 inches) in 1785. But this was Charrie's calculation in metric units based on whatever unit the encyclopedists had used at the time of publication. Since the metric system had not yet been introduced in 1785, the units used to define the drapeaux in that year would have been subject to the same vagaries of measurement that impelled the desire for a new system of measurement in the first place. Gherardi Davis said the drapeaux were even smaller, 130 cm (51 inches) square, but gives no source. Drapeaux carried in Canada in the French and Indian War were either captured and lost or burned at the time of the final surrender in 1760, and those carried in the American War of Independence were burned or otherwise lost during the French Revolution. The few surviving flags more or less contemporary to the period under study are on the larger end of the range. In any event, as outlined below, ease of manufacture probably overrode meeting precise targeted sizes if there ever were any.

Unlike British or German colors of the same period, the French drapeaux were, with few exceptions, actually square. The flags were nailed to their staffs with brass or gilt-headed nails about one inch apart along the entire length of the leading edge. Drawings and photos suggest that there was usually not a sleeve; rather the leading edge of the flag was simply wrapped around the pole and nailed down. One row

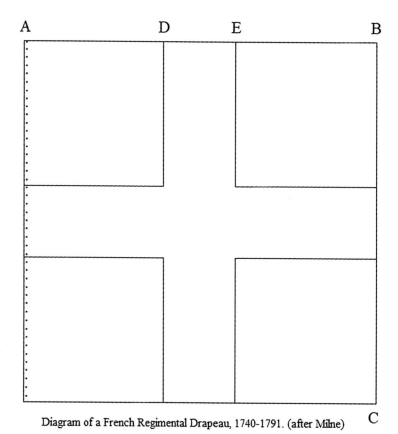

Diagram of a French Regimental Drapeau, 1740-1791. (after Milne)

A B. 65-69 standard inches. B C. 65-69 standard inches. D E. 13-14 standard inches.

Length of staff (*pique* and *talon* included), 8 ½ to 9 ½ feet. Diameter of staff, 1 inch, untapered.

Length of cord and tassels, approx. 4 ½ feet overall, hangs 2+ feet when tied to staff.

Each tassel 4 inches. Length of spear, including ferrule 6-9 inches, several different patterns.

Drawing by author, after Milne.

of closely spaced nails would obviously be sufficient to hold the flag tightly on the pole, but there appear to have been sometimes two or even three rows of nails simply for the decorative effect. Without a separate sleeve, the color or design of the leading edge of the flag simply continued around the pole. For this reason, French flags of the period often appear awkward to modern eyes. We are used to picturing a flag as being from the pole to the outer fly only. Whether the flag is secured to the pole by nails, or ties, or a pole sleeve, we tend to see that as a separate element, not part of the flag proper. The French concept, on the other hand—based on virtually all contemporary drawings as well as a few extant flags from near periods—show that the flag was mentally pictured as reaching from the extreme outer or far side of the staff to the hemmed fly at the opposite end. A row of nails, or an attached sleeve, or the bulge of the staff where the flag was wrapped around it, was simply not seen as separate.

Thus, while British, German, Spanish, or American flags have their designs more or less centered on the field of the flag, not counting the pole or pole sleeve, French flags have their design centered on the whole visible face of the flag *including* where it wraps around the pole. In practice this means that the center of the design is actually a little off-center—closer to the pole edge—since about one and a half inch of the originally square flag wraps around to the back. It also means that designs near the leading edge of the flag—fleur-de-lis, crowns, or coats of arms, will sometimes lie right on the pole. On the reverse of the flag, some of this detail will be covered by the pole itself and the silk wrapped around from the front.

In some cases, it appears that the edge to be wrapped around the pole was made somewhat longer to account for the wrap. At least one drapeau of a Swiss regiment in French service, for which we have photographs both on its original pole and after it had been removed, clearly shows this. A few extant flags show that there were also exceptions in which a separate sleeve was sewn to the leading edge of the flag. This was probably more common on flags that had either complex designs in the quadrants, making it awkward for the design to wrap around the pole, or had devices or lettering on the central cross that would have been interrupted or too visibly off-center if wrapped around the pole. Not a single contemporary drawing or painting, however, shows either a separately attached sleeve, nor a drawn line or tick-marks to suggest the leading edge of the flag was rolled over and stitched into a sleeve. Some do not even show the rows of nails. Existing flags show that even some with fairly complex designs were originally made perfectly square, and some of the design details wound up partially or completely wrapped around the pole. It is possible that a narrow filler piece in appropriate colors and possibly even painted details, was sometimes sewn in to compensate for too much of a painted design being obscured on the flag's reverse, but there are no drawings, paintings, or surviving flags of the period that explicitly show this. There are, however, several flags that exhibit a very awkward appearance on one side of the flag where the silk had been wrapped around the pole and the designs do not line up.

As the flags were all based on the premise that the cross was symmetric and the four corner quadrants were square and equal, and as the poles were quite slender, the proportions of the drapeaux were generally not much compromised by wrapping around the pole. This made for both ease of manufacture and correct appearance. It may also have led to mistakes in which the flags were sometimes attached with the wrong edge to the pole, either back-to-front or sideways. Apparently so long as the flags had the correct combination of colors and/or designs, it was not especially important which end was up—even if one arrangement was statistically more common throughout the period of the regiment's existence—or which side was against the staff. This could account for the many discrepancies in sources which have flags shown with either of their opposing colors in the upper left next to the staff. A sheet showing drapeaux captured in Holland in 1713 includes three French regiments where at least one of the flags from each regiment has the "wrong" color in the upper left quarter. A French compilation of the state of the King's troops published in 1748[1] lists drapeaux details for all French regiments then in service, describing them by their primary colors "*par opposition*," but without regard to which color is in which quadrant. As just one example, a 1757 print of the drapeaux of the Regiment la Reine, which served in Canada in the French and Indian War, shows the "wrong" color in the upper left canton and the fleur-de-lis all pointing toward the pole rather than straight up. Was the artist doubly wrong, or was the flag actually attached to the pole sideways?

The width of the cross on French drapeaux has been a cause of debate and varies greatly among both contemporary and modern drawings. The correct width—very regular among the few original colors that still exist—is one-fifth the overall width (or height) of the flag. While this may sound arbitrary, it is actually simple and straightforward, and probably has more to do with ease of manufacture than with some arbitrary decision of heraldic design. The correct width of any side of the flag is simply made in proportions of 2:1:2, that is, color/cross/color.

As mentioned in the general introduction, silk in the seventeenth and eighteenth centuries was made in a few fairly standard widths. In France, silk was nominally twenty-seven French inches wide, approximately twenty-eight modern US or English inches. (Of course, even this could vary somewhat—an important genesis of the creation and adoption of the metric system during the French revolutionary period a generation later was a response to an outcry for standardization of measurements.) Based on a few reports of costs incurred by the makers, it is known that an all-white drapeaux colonel required four *aunes*. An aune, again taking into account the vagaries of period measurements, was forty-five French inches or approximately forty-six and a half modern inches. This is generally described as one and a quarter yards (thirty-six plus nine inches) but is also exactly one-and-two-thirds the standard width of silk (twenty-eight plus eighteen-and-two-thirds inches). Silk for a colored drapeau d'ordonnance required one-and-a-half aune for the cross and two-and-a-half aune for four quarters, again equaling four aunes total. Assume the maker wants to do no more sewing than necessary (all sewing was of course hand-sewing at this period; in fact, the selvage edge of the cloth was often used where possible to avoid the need for hemming), so the size of the flag is based on that width. Since the French drapeaux were all based on squares, it was relatively easy to tear the twenty-eight-inch-wide silk into twenty-eight by twenty-eight-inch squares for the corner pieces. Two-and-one-half aune would give four such squares with a few inches left over. These squares of silk could then be cut if necessary, and the pieces switched around and reassembled into different designs for different regiments. To make the cross, the flag-maker took a standard twenty-eight-inch-wide piece of white silk and tore it lengthwise down the center. This produced two pieces, each fourteen inches wide, exactly half as wide as the corner pieces. One-and-one-half aune would yield two fourteen-inch-wide stripes approximately sixty-nine to seventy inches long, enough for one upright and two arms of the cross. Laid out and sewn together the flag would be in proportions two-to-one-to-two (twenty-eight inches/fourteen inches/twenty-eight inches). The finished flag would be approximately 67–69 inches square (170–175 cm), taking into account an inch or so where the overlapped pieces were sewn together and the raw ends of the cross pieces hemmed, with the cross approximately one-fifth the total width of the flag. Flags with more piecings of different colors might come out a little smaller due to having more fabric overlapped in the seams. In any event, no mathematics were required and no silk was wasted. In addition, this would work for any width of silk—if the flag-maker were presented with silks a little wider or narrower than the standard, the proportions would still come out the same. There is no reason to doubt that the French encyclopedists accurately measured one or more flags available to them, or that Charrie correctly recalculated their measurements to equal 165 cm, but this could simply suggest that the maker used silks closer to twenty-six modern inches rather than twenty-eight. Very few flags of the period exist, but of those that do, all are in the same proportions of two-to-one-to-two.

An interesting detail in the construction of the French drapeaux is that the cross was usually made with the long piece running from top to bottom of the flag, perhaps in imitation of an actual cross with a single upright, rather than from the pole to the outer edge. Like most flags throughout history, the drapeaux were made of a single thickness. As in other countries, and in heraldic tradition, the flag "reads" from left to right, with the pole on the left, and the fly or outer hem on the right. Descriptions of the individual drapeaux typically follow heraldic tradition as well: reading left to right, the quarters are numbered 1 and 2 above the cross and 3 and 4 below. (Quarters 1 and 4 are diagonal from each other, and 2 and 3 are diagonal from each other.) All descriptions of the colors and designs were based on this understanding (*État général des troupes de France, 1748* being an exception). Since the flags were a single thickness, this meant that the entire flag was reversed on the opposite side—a flag that had the corners say, green at the top and black on the bottom next to the pole, would have green on the top and black on the bottom next to the pole when the flag was looked at from the opposite side, even though now the pole would be to the right (which is how they were presented by Lucien Mouillard in 1882, contributing to modern confusion). In addition, since the paints generally would bleed through the silk and were then overpainted on the reverse of the flag, painted designs and lettering would be reversed on the back. In a few cases, gilt letters applied to a clear sizing compound would allow for correct lettering on both sides of a dark color—the lettering on the red crosses of two surviving Irish regiments in French service, one from the late seventeenth century and one from 1745, have their mottoes correctly lettered on both sides—but any lettering of a motto on white silk, as *PER MARE ET TERRAS* on the drapeaux of the Compagnies franches de la Marine at Louisbourg, would, unless painted on blocks of solid white, read backward on the reverse. Period drawings generally portray the motto reading correctly on both sides, suggesting that in some cases the cross was a double layer of silk, but as this would require the painting to be done before assembling the pieces into a flag, this seems unlikely. A motto on a painted scroll, as on the drapeau colonel of the Royal Deux Ponts, for example, could read correctly on both sides of the flag, because the scroll itself would be painted as a solid panel and the lettering applied as a second layer.

The staffs of French drapeaux throughout this period were un-tapered poles approximately one inch in diameter, indifferent in length from about nine-and-a-half to ten-and-a-half feet, topped by a brass or gilded iron spear or *pique*, and capped at the bottom with a pointed or ball-ended iron or brass *talon* (literally "heel"), or ground point. There was no standard design for the pique; the very earliest were sometimes shaped as fleur-de-lis, but by mid-century most were variations on military pikes or lance points, while some tended to be shaped like an ace of spades (still referred to as *pique* in French). Some used during the period 1770–1785, which of course includes the American War of Independence, were leaf or teardrop-shaped and pierced with a fleur-de-lis. All military drapeaux were accompanied by cord and tassels; for the drapeau colonel all white silk or white with silver or gold highlights, for the drapeaux d'ordonnance white silk intermixed with colors to match the colored silks of the flags. French tassels tended to be short and barrel-shaped, with flat top surmounted by a small round bead. The cords were fairly short and served no function other than decoration. Each drapeau was also adorned with a white silk *cravate* tied around the staff just below the pique. Technically, it was these silk cravats, and not the white drapeau colonel, that represented the King and identified the troops as French. The cravat was approximately ninety-three inches in length (two aunes) and seven to eight inches wide. It is often shown as tied in a bow and hung down about one third the length of the flag.

The exact appearance of any individual French drapeau as actually carried in North America in the French and Indian War (1754–1763) or the American War of Independence (1777–1783) is difficult to accurately establish. Several near-contemporary sources and many secondary historically researched sources are available, but there are numerous disagreements among them on details of the drapeaux of individual regiments as well as very different artistic interpretations based on the biases, artistic conventions, and technical processes of the periods during which these sources were produced. Listings made at different times often portray regiments of the same name, some of which were not in fact the same regiment, but completely different organizations re-titled with older, traditional names, thus contributing to the confusion. There is also a tendency to want to change some details of contemporary documents to mirror what seems to be "correct" to the modern eye. For example, the drapeaux of Regiment Angoumois have the lower outside quarter at a ninety degree turn from the others. This may well have been a mistake on the part of the makers sewing new flags at some point—the earliest representation of the regiment's drapeaux in 1721 does not show this—yet it is repeated in both the white drapeau colonel as well as the colored drapeaux d'ordonnance in the tableaus printed in 1771 and 1773 and redrawn with this same unlikely detail by Desjardins in 1874. Nevertheless, they were portrayed in 1856 and 1882—long after the originals had been lost—with this defect "corrected" so that all four quarters of the flag are symmetric and in line with other French drapeaux of similar style, and this "corrected" version has been favored by books and websites published in the twentieth century.

In addition, modern readers, and many researchers as well it would seem, expect there to be one right answer. If three pictures of the same flag show three variants, then two of them must be wrong and we simply have to work harder to find out which one is correct. But this may not be so. As already mentioned, it does not seem to have been uncommon for a flag to have been sideways or reversed from what we would like to think was the one and only correct orientation. For a regiment in service for decades it is highly unlikely that the same flags were carried without damage, simple wear-out, and replacement. And while heraldry can seem very precise in description, it can be surprisingly malleable in execution. As in the example above, the drapeaux of the Regiment Angoumois may have been replaced many times, and during one span of years at least, the lower right quadrant was turned ninety degrees from the others. Each time new flags were made, the indentations of the two pieces of colored silk in each quarter could also have been cut and pieced together somewhat differently and still be heraldically described as "indented." Each of the four quarters of the drapeaux of Regiment Saintonge, which served in the American War of Independence, was made of four triangles—red, blue, yellow, green. One would be hard pressed to find many drawings that show all four corners in the same arrangement of the triangles. But this need not mean that all but one of the drawings is wrong—at the time the flags were made and in use there may not have been any single "correct" arrangement. Gherardi Davis commented in 1907, "The sequence of these colors does not seem to be determined . . ." So long as each corner had four triangles red, green, yellow, blue, the flag would be perfectly identifiable as belonging to Saintonge. There may even have been flags with different arrangements of the colored panels in use at the same time.

Painted details on the flags also left a good deal of leeway for variation. As noted in the general introduction, different artists would paint fleur-de-lis, crowns, lettering, or other devices very much to their own taste and talents, and in the changing fashions of the times. Fleur-de-lis in the eighteenth century

Example of fleur-de-lis semé on the drapeau d'ordonnance of Regiment Bourgogne, as drawn by Montigny in 1772. Note that the pattern is perfectly regular and where other elements are added—in this case the barbed cross of Burgundy—some fleurs are crowded or deleted, yet the overall diagonal pattern remains unbroken. Montigny drew his flags as if they were made with fabrics that already had the fleur-de-lis on them prior to being cut and sewn into flags. The "tail" of the flag was a contemporary artistic device to indicate a flag flapping in the breeze, while still allowing the entire square or rectangular face of the flag to be shown. Bibliothèque Nationale Française.

tended to display the middle petal as much more bulbous than in later periods, and the side petals often far away; overall not at all a natural looking flower. Styles of shading and highlighting changed as ideas of beauty and elegance shifted and drifted in the society at large. A drapeau painted in 1757 might look quite different from its replacement painted in 1777 just before shipping out to America. We also do not know for certain how many fleur-de-lis would have been on any one flag (those that had them at all). Many contemporary drawings are too small to give an accurate depiction of individual fleurs. In heraldic descriptions of drapeaux, the fleur-de-lis were simply described as *semé*, that is, evenly distributed over whatever portion of the drapeau they were on. On embroidered textiles the fleurs often ran right off the edge where the fabric was cut and hemmed, as shown in the illustration. On painted drapeaux, the flag itself would have been made first, then the number and placement of fleur-de-lis semé could be calculated so that no partial fleurs were necessary. Pierre Charrie generally gives very exact numbers of fleur-de-lis per flag, but his counts appear to be taken from the 1721 manuscript *Drapeaux de l'Infanterie*, which shows the early very large flags of eight feet per side. The most common distribution on the white cross on the later, somewhat smaller, French drapeaux seems to be forty-eight: three rows of four-three-four on each of the four arms and four in the center such that the pattern appears uninterrupted in all directions. But again, as these flags were made by individual makers at different times, there may have been variation from one to the next.

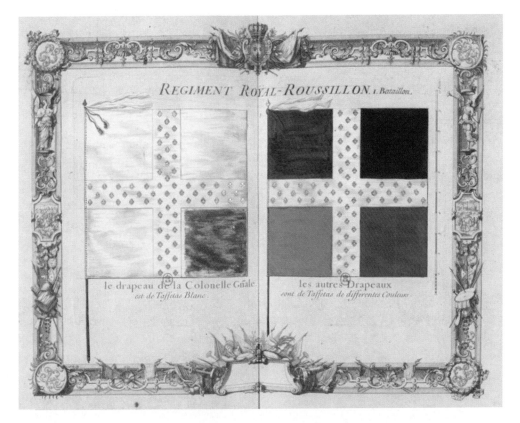

Sample plate from *Drapeaux de l'Infanterie tant Françoise qu'Etrangère au service de la France. En l'année 1721*, the earliest complete set of illustrations of French drapeaux. Note the scale indicating the sizes as eight feet per side, and the fleur-e-lis semé, painted so as to fit within the white cross. (The off-color quarter on the drapeau colonel is from something in the orangish paint on the opposite page discoloring it when book is closed.)

A Note on French Colors

Most of the colors used on French flags are fairly easy to identify and I have used the standard English translations for standard colors red, yellow, blue, green, black, white, violet. All of these tended to be clear and bright primary colors; for example, unless specifically noted, blue would never mean navy, green would not be dark forest green or evergreen. Of course, how light or dark, how intense or how pastel due to fading a particular color looked at a particular time cannot always be known. A few colors bear explanation.

White: Any white silk of this period would actually be a very light cream color, not snowy white or typing paper white—what a catalog or store might call off-white or perhaps antique white. This is partly because silk can only be bleached so much before it loses all strength, and partly because white silk tends to yellow as it ages.

Isabelle: A light yellow-buff-cream color, sometimes shown in old illustrations as light yellow, sometimes as light beige or tan. It is said that the color derives from the chemise worn by Isabella of Castile at the end of the eight months siege of Grenada, the last Moorish town in Spain in 1492. How white her chemise had been at the start of the campaign is unknown, but the story is that Isabella vowed to not change it for as long as it took to finally prevail. (The story is sometimes attached to a later Isabella, and the siege to that of Ostend 1601–1603, but the color was already well known by that time—an inventory made in England of clothing belonging to Elizabeth I used the term "Isabella-colour" in 1600.)

Feuille morte: Literally "dead leaf," though more poetically it might be translated as autumn leaf. A medium yellowish or slightly orangish brown.

Gorge de pigeon: Literally "pigeon throat." A medium dark iridescent color made with warp and weft of red and green yarns. Used in the drapeaux of the Royal Artillery regiments.

Aurora: A deep yellow/orange iridescent made with warp and weft of yellow and red yarns. Used in the drapeaux of several regiments, though sometimes identified by observers as merely yellow, and sometimes painted in illustrations as orange.

Cramoisi/Crimson: A deep dark red, darker than standard red (*rouge*).

A Note on French Regimental Titles

French regiments had both a name, generally from the province or principality from which they drew their recruits or in which they had originally been raised, as well as a number, based on their seniority on the official French establishment. Both of these changed from time to time as regiments were disbanded, reorganized, amalgamated, or new regiments introduced. The gilt or white metal buttons on regimental uniforms sometimes had the regimental number on them. New regiments were often given a historic name of a regiment that had been disestablished earlier. The Regiment Agenois of the French forces in the American War of Independence, for example, was not the same regiment as the original of that name, which existed 1692–1749, with completely different drapeaux. The reorganization in 1765 of all the old regiments to the new standard of two battalions per regiment caused a major reshuffling of regimental seniorities. However, the regimental numbers were not used to identify regiments in correspondence, orders, records, accounts, or other documents in either of the wars in North America. The seniority of the regiments was only invoked in ceremonial occasions; for example, the French regiments can be seen arranged in order of their seniority in van Blarenberghe's painting of *Surrender at Yorktown*.

A Note on Sources

No original French drapeau from either the French and Indian War or the American War of Independence has survived. Therefore, all subsequent studies have had to rely on illustrations and documents predating that period. In general, the drapeaux of the French regiments did not change over time except, as noted above, in size and artistic execution. However, the names of several regiments did change over time, many regiments were discontinued, and sometimes new regiments using the same names were created. Thus, going back to "original sources" is not always as easy or secure as it sounds.

The earliest complete set of illustrations of French drapeaux are the beautiful color plates in *Drapeaux de l'Infanterie tant Françoise qu'Etrangère au service de la France. En l'année 1721* (*Flags of the Infantry both French and Foreign in the Service of France in the Year 1721*) published in that year by M. d'Hermand, illustrations by Jacques-Antoine Delaistre. These plates include both the drapeaux colonels and the drapeaux d'ordonnance (here called *le autre drapeaux*, "the other flags"). At least two copies of this work were made—some plates that can be found online have different collection stamps and marginal notes for duplicate plates of the same regiment. The second useful source is *État général des troupes de France, sur pied en Mai 1748. Avec le traitement qui leur est fait tant en quartier d'hiver qu'en campagne, suivant les ordonnances du Roi* (*General State of the Troops of France, on Foot in May, 1748. With the Treatment Accorded Them in Winter Quarters as Well as on Campaign, According to the Orders of the King*) published in Paris in 1748. (Such reports were published intermittently throughout the period, but few have survived. An article published in *Revue de l'Université d'Ottawa* in 1950 giving a brief overview of French uniforms and drapeaux in Canada during the eighteenth century, has footnote citations from the *État général des troupes* of 1753 and 1758.) The official report of 1748, which can be found online, gave the current uniforms and drapeaux of each of the regiments then in French service. However, this text-only source has two drawbacks when it comes to the drapeaux: first, while it generally corroborates what is illustrated in Hermand/Delaistre, it does not give the different colors of the quarters of the drapeaux in a standardized format; the chronicler simply reported what he saw, saying for instance, that such-and-such flag had green and black "in opposition," not which colors were where. Second, as with Hermand/Delaistre, the modern researcher must be aware that many of the regiments listed were discontinued shortly after the book's publication, and regiments with the same names serving in North America 1755–1763 or 1777–1783 are not the same regiments, and thus the flag descriptions are not relevant to the later period. Another book of color plates, *Troupes du Roi, Infanterie française et* étrangère, *année 1757* (*Troops of the King, French and Foreign Infantry, in the Year 1757*) was formerly held by the Library of the Ministry of War in Paris, now transferred to the Musée de l'Armée. These plates show uniforms and drapeaux of every French regiment then in service. It appears that the plates were made both from contemporary research and from life. Several of the drapeaux appear to be attached to the staff along the "wrong" edge when compared to the 1721 prints. Not only are the colored quarters of some of the flags in different positions, but painted elements such as fleur-de-lis, coats of arms, and other devices are portrayed sideways from what would seem the correct or normal orientation. As these plates are exactly contemporary to the Seven Years' War/French and Indian War, they ought to be trusted as generally accurate for regiments serving at the time. It must be kept in mind, however, that all of the units in North America were second battalions of their regiments. The flags brought to or described to the artist of the plates could have been those which remained in Europe with the First Battalions, and anomalies such as attachment on the wrong side may represent only the flag seen at the time, while those in America may still have been "correct" in their orientation.

One of 125 regimental plates from the manuscript *Troupes du Roi, Infanterie française et* étrangère, *année 1757 (Troops of the King, French and Foreign Infantry, in the Year 1757)*, **Musée de l'Armée, Paris.**

Finally, there exists an unnamed series of watercolors cryptically annotated in their lower left corners with the notation "*Effectif 1740–1775*," some of which are in the archives of Parks Canada (and published in some of the Osprey books on French and Indian War topics), showing drapeaux d'ordonnance of regiments during the French and Indian War. It appears that these were made sometime between 1763 and 1775, just after the French and Indian War and approximately the time period that French regiments were being reorganized. It is unknown how extensive the original series was, as only five prints are known. Four of these are identified by title and marginal information as regiments which served in North America 1755–1762. The fifth plate is missing its title and marginal information. The drapeau illustrated has quarters of green and yellow, suggesting it represents not a regiment that served in North America, but the new Regiment Berry created when the first of that name, which did serve in America, was disestablished at the end of 1762.

Shortly after the disastrous outcome of the Seven Years' War, which included the French and Indian War in North America, French military structure underwent a massive overhaul. Many multi-battalion regiments were split up and new regiments made on the two-battalion model. Three new documents/collections of materials relating to the regimental drapeaux were created during this period. The first was created as a wall-sized "*Tableau Militaire des Drapeaux, Etendards des Troupes au Service de la France*," in 1771. The large format tableau, printed "with the privilege of the king" using thirty or more copper plates, was supervised by Sieur Chaligny, and reproductions taken from this source are often identified by that name. Rather than having to keep in mind too many relatively obscure French names, however, I have used "Tableau of 1771" to identify information taken from it. After printing on the cloth wall-hanging, each flag was hand-colored. So far as is known, only one full-color print and one printed in black, but not colored, exist. This was the first document to show the drapeaux colonel with their plain white cantons detailed with seams to mimic the drapeaux d'ordonnance. The second source produced in this period was a series of plates titled *Uniformes militaires, où se trouvent gravés en taille-douce les uniformes de la Maison militaire du Roi, 1772 (Military Uniforms, with Intaglio Engraving of the Uniforms of the King's Military House, 1772)*, by Claude-Antoine Littret de Montigny (who also did many of the engravings for Diderot's *Encyclopédie*). Montigny's plates also show the drapeaux colonels with seams to mimic the divisions of the silks on the drapeaux d'ordonnance of the same regiment. The third source is another large tableau, "*Tableau Militaire, de tous les Drapeaux, Etendards, et Guidons des Troupes de France leurs Creation les noms des Commandants Colonels, et Pour l'anee, 1773*," in the collection of the Musée de l'Emperi, and reprinted as a color plate in Pierre Charrie's *Drapeaux et Etendards du Roi*, in 1989 and 2012. This tableau shows only tiny figures holding the drapeau d'ordonnance of each regiment, all flying to the left, pole on the right, thus showing the reverse of each flag. The drapeaux colonels are not shown. Finally, a large number of plates made over a thirty-year span and collected under the title *Drapeaux des regiments francais et d'autres troupes 1745–1776*, also at Musée de l'Armée, illustrate many drapeaux that had been changed, introduced, or discontinued during that period of military expansion and reorganization. It does not include the several new regiments created in 1776 just before deployment to America. Charrie made use of this collection for *Drapeaux et Etendards du Roi*, as did Rene Chartrand for his studies published in 1984 and 1995, characterizing them in 1984 as "official pattern book."

Basically, all studies of French drapeaux of any period before the French Revolution have to refer back to these same sources. Gustav Desjardins's study of 1874 redraws the plates of Chaligny's Tableau of 1771. Mouillard's *Armée Francaise,* published 1882, does not cite its sources, and in addition confuses later researchers by illustrating the reverse side of each drapeau. Compared to earlier sources, Mouillard's flags are all backward. But when one sees that on some (not all) pages there is a spearpoint over the *right* edge of the flag, it becomes clear what is going on. There are many other books and documents that bear upon this point or that, and several twentieth century studies of varying value; these are cited where necessary in the descriptions of the individual regiments, and all are listed in the annotated bibliography.

Descriptions of the Drapeaux

The following entries are focused primarily on the drapeaux of each regiment. Details on the history or lineage of a regiment and the battles it participated in are included only insofar as it is relevant to the drapeaux or tend to clarify why one source or conclusion was found preferable to another. For the American War of Independence, I have used the commonly accepted list of regiments involved, noting that in some cases the flags of these regiments may never have been present on mainland North America.

FRENCH DRAPEAUX IN THE FRENCH AND INDIAN WAR, 1754–1763

Descriptions of the Drapeaux

During the period of the French and Indian War, each battalion of a French regiment carried two drapeaux—the first battalion, with the colonel's company, carried the white drapeau colonel and one drapeau d'ordonnance, the second battalion carried two drapeaux d'ordonnance. With few exceptions, all of the French battalions in North America during the period were the second battalions of their regiments, thus each carried two identical drapeaux d'ordonnance.

Regiment Angoumois

The Regiment Angoumois was one of the few regiments in the French army that had only one battalion during this period, thus when it was sent to garrison New Orleans in 1762–1763, it became the only regular French regiment to carry the white drapeau colonel in North America. (The combined battalion of the Compagnies franches de la Marine were the only other possible exception—but the Compagnies were not Army, nor technically a regiment.)

The drapeau d'ordonnance of Angoumois had two colors in each canton, aurora and violet, divided diagonally by a "toothed" line from the inner corners of the white cross to the outer corners of the flag. Although the drapeau colonel is depicted in the Tableaus of 1771 and Montigny in 1772 with the toothed seams of the colored flags reproduced in white, it is shown as perfectly plain in the plates of 1757—the artist not even indicating a white cross on the white field. The regiment was reorganized and augmented in the general reorganization of the army in 1762, however, and it may have been at that time that new drapeaux were acquired, with the drapeau colonel made to resemble the drapeau d'ordonnance by duplicating the zigzag seams in the cantons. The Tableaus of 1771 and 1773 also depict the fourth canton (outer canton, below the cross) set at right angles to the others, so that while the flag ought to have the four quadrants of two colors arranged pinwheel style, like many other French drapeaux, these have one corner out of pattern, on both the colonel's and the ordonnance flags. Such an odd detail would hardly be invented, but rather drawn from life or from a very careful eyewitness account. As the regiment was not present for the surrender of French forces in Canada and the subsequent burning of the drapeaux to avoid surrendering them to an ungracious foe, it is possible that the drapeaux of Angoumois were returned to France at the end of hostilities and were the same ones seen and drawn in the Tableaus of 1771 and 1773, only eight and ten years later.

The unusual arrangement of the cantons is most likely the result of a simple mistake made by whomever manufactured these flags as replacements for a set worn out in service, or of the old too-large size, or perhaps for the reorganized regiment in 1762. The drawing of the drapeaux from 1721 shows them at eight feet to the side, and with the cantons arranged in the standard pinwheel fashion. Apparently when the awkward flags shown in the Tableaus of 1771 and 1773 eventually wore out, they were replaced by new ones of the original or more correct pattern. Drawings made in 1856 and 1882 again show the more usual pinwheel arrangement, and modern reconstructions tend to follow.

The Angoumois drapeaux are difficult to accurately interpret in another detail: each quarter is divided diagonally into two triangles by a sawtooth rather than a simple straight line. In heraldry this would be called "indented," in French it is *dentele*. One source (de Bouille) says the colored pieces are divided by a line like "lightning." But how many indents or teeth should this dividing line have, and how deep? In heraldry "indented" generally means many rather small triangular-shaped teeth; if there are only three or four, the design would be called "dancette" or "dancetty." The 1721 representation shows relatively few "teeth" (as in the present reconstruction) but not so deep as later drawings would make them. Some modern reconstructions show a straight line with a dozen or more very small indentations. As with drapeaux of other regiments, however, it must be kept in mind that they may have been substantially different at different times, reflecting changing artistic norms in the society as a whole, or simply to suit the tastes or skill of the makers.

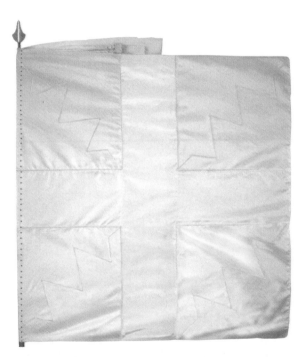

Drapeaux colonel, Regiment Angoumois.

Drapeau d'ordonnance, Regiment Angoumois.

Regiment Artois

The drapeaux d'ordonnance of Regiment Artois were yellow and blue, with yellow in quarters one and four, blue in two and three. This is one of the few regiments for which all the original sources agree.

Artois was one of the four regiments captured and denied the "honors of war" at Louisbourg in 1758. Its drapeaux were among the eleven colours—which presumably would have included any large woolen garrison flags taken—sent to England and displayed at St. Paul's Cathedral until transferred to the Royal Hospital at Chelsea in 1835; possibly they are among the flags, now lost, that were formerly labeled "French flag, date of capture not known."

Drapeaux d'ordonnance, Regiment Artois.

Regiment Bearn

All four quarters of the drapeaux d'ordonnance of Regiment Bearn were isabelle with two red bars. The color isabelle, while generally a very light color, is shown as almost brown in some sources, but certainly the two colors in the original drapeaux were sufficiently different to clearly show the stripes.

Regiment Bearn was disestablished at the end of the French and Indian War in 1762, but its name was transferred in the same year to another very senior regiment that had previously been known only by the names of its colonels. Thus, the name Bearn shows up in post-1762 sources with drapeaux of aurora and violet.

Drapeaux d'ordonnance, Regiment Bearn.

Regiment Berry

Two battalions, the Second and Third, of Regiment Berry served in North America during the French and Indian War, thus there would have been four drapeaux d'ordonnance present. These had four quarters the same, violet with a broad horizontal band of isabelle across the center, dividing each canton into thirds, violet/isabelle/violet. As with other drapeaux in which the color isabelle is used, it is often shown far darker than it ought to be, sometimes appearing so dark as to make the three stripes almost impossible to discern.

Regiment Berry was disestablished at the conclusion of the war in North America in 1762. However, its name was transferred to another regiment which had previously been known only by the names of its colonels, so the name Berry in sources after 1763 will show a flag of yellow and green.

Regiment Bourgogne

The Regiment Bourgogne was one of only two French regiments that had the barbed cross of Burgundy (*Croix de Bourgogne*) on its drapeaux (the other being the Royal Comtois). The drapeaux d'ordonnance of the regiment featured the cross in red on a white field with gold fleur-de-lis semé. The drapeaux colonel was the same except with the cross in white. Charrie says there

Drapeaux d'ordonnance, Regiment Berry.

were twenty-eight fleur-de-lis per triangle on the drapeau colonel (not carried in America; it remained in France with the first battalion) and forty-five per triangle on the drapeaux d'ordonnance. The sources for these numbers are uncertain—for the drapeaux d'ordonnance, the count of forty-five fleurs per triangle seems to come from the 1721 print based on the much larger flags of eight-foot square. However, the drawing of the drapeau colonel in that print actually shows forty-three to forty-five fleurs per triangle. No period source makes any distinction between the two drapeaux, always showing both colonel and d'ordonnance with the same number and layout of the fleur-de-lis. There were probably fewer fleur-de-lis on the smaller flags of the period of the French and Indian War. The important point was that they were uniformly and equally spaced throughout the field (semé). In proper heraldic form, this could mean that some fleurs in the pattern were cut by the Burgundy cross overlaid on it, however painted flags tend to fit the semé pattern to avoid this. The cross itself varied considerably on flags of the period but is portrayed fairly consistently in all French sources as being somewhat narrow with short, wide barbs (originally meant to represent secondary branches cut off the tree trunks used to make the X-shaped cross of St. Andrew) and all pointing the same direction. The 1757 print shows the drapeau d'ordonnance attached to the pole "sideways," such that the barbs of the cross

Drapeaux d'ordonnance, Regiment Bourgogne.

and all the fleurs point toward the pole. The drapeau colonel is portrayed in what we would generally consider "right side up."

The second battalion of Regiment Bourgogne was among the units surrendered at Louisbourg in 1758. The French were not allowed "the honors of war," and their captured drapeaux were among those taken to England and displayed in St. Paul's Cathedral before being transferred to the Royal Hospital at Chelsea in 1835.

Regiment Cambis

Regiment Cambis had been raised in 1676, but unlike most French regiments, had changed both its name and its drapeaux several times while maintaining its identity and lineage. Until 1749 the regiment was called by the name of its current colonel. In 1721, when the Hermand/Delaistre plates were prepared, the regiment's seniority was sixty-three and its title Regiment Laval. The drapeaux d'ordonnance was illustrated as red and green in opposition, with red in cantons one and four, green in cantons two and three. After two more changes in title, the regiment was again called Regiment Laval, from 1743 to 1749. Its drapeaux d'ordonnance were described in 1748 in *État général des troupes de France*, as having white quarters with three wavey lines through each. When the regiment served in North America under its final title of Regiment Cambis, however, it was carrying the original Laval drapeaux of red and green. These can be seen in the *Troupes du Roi* plate of 1757 (reproduced in the introduction to French section) as well as a contemporary watercolor held by Parks Canada.

In the spring of 1758, the second battalion of Regiment Cambis was sent directly from France to be part of the reinforced garrison for an expected attack on the Fortress of Louisbourg. When the post was finally surrendered to the British in July of that year, British General Amherst refused the garrison the usual "honors of war," and the men of Regiment Cambis "filled with indignation, tore up their colors," rather than surrender them.[2]

Drapeaux d'ordonnance, Regiment Cambis.

Compagnies franches de la Marine

The independent companies administered by the Navy and collectively titled Compagnies franches de la Marine were the garrison and security forces in New France throughout most of the eighteenth century. As independent companies, they did not carry flags, but the overall organization was presented drapeaux in 1737. These same drapeaux, or a replacement set, may have been carried during the French and Indian War whenever several of the individual companies were formed together as a battalion. If so, it is still unknown whether a white drapeaux colonel accompanied.

According to research added by Pierre Charrie in his second edition of *Drapeaux et Etandards du Roi*, in 2012, a document from the archives of the Ministry of Finance mentions the blessing of several drapeaux of the Compagnies franches on July 23, 1737, in Brest.

According to Charrie, the flags were described as having a white cross with gold fleur-de-lis semé, the quarters red and blue in opposition, in the center a lightning or thunderbolt (*foudre*) in gold, and on the cross the legend: *PER /MARE ET/ TERRAS*. He then appends: "The lightning is an anachronism; it is more likely two crossed anchors." There is no further explanation for this observation.

This description, however, appears to be Charrie's rewording of the original document into his habitual format for describing the drapeaux, and based on his understanding of common or uniform attributes of French drapeaux. Correspondence with Parks Canada, Fortress of Louisbourg, in 2022, obtained the original wording reporting the blessing of three (not several) drapeaux in 1737: "*Il y en avait un parsemé de fleurs de lys d'or et un foudre au milieu de chacun. Les trois avec ces paroles « Per Mare et Terras » (Par mer et par terre)' Les deux autres avaient une croix blanches écartlée de rouge et de bleu et aussi parsemée de fleurs de lys d'or.*" This might be literally translated as, "There was one strewn with golden fleur-de-lis, and a thunderbolt in the middle of each. All three with these words 'Per Mare et Terras' (By sea and by land). The other two had a white cross quartered with red and blue and also sprinkled with golden fleur-de-lis." This might be re-interpreted into flag terminology as: "There was one (the white drapeau colonel) with gold fleur-de-lis semé, and a gold lightning/thunderbolt at the center of each. All three had the motto *PER MARE ET TERRAS*. The other two (the drapeaux d'ordonnance) had the white cross—quartered with red and blue—also with gold fleur-de-lis semé."

Clearly the original, perhaps archaic, wording in French admits of considerable ambiguity.

None of these descriptions, however, seems to comport with the reconstructed drapeaux popularized in the 1990s, adopted as correct by official Canada, and currently to be found everywhere on the internet. Both the original wording as well as Charrie's paraphrase place the "foudre" device at the center of all three drapeaux, and specify that it is gold, not in the reds or yellows that might be associated with thunder or lightning. Charrie's rewording of the Finance Ministry document clearly places the fleur-de-lis on the cross, not in the quarters, which is in line with most French drapeaux; very few had fleur-de-lis or other embellishments in both the cross and the cantons—it was usually one or the other. But given the lack of clarifying punctuation, the original document could theoretically be construed to allow the fleur-de-lis semé in the red and blue quarters instead, or even in addition to, the cross. It might also at first seem unlikely that the lettering would be on the cross, as Charrie states, if the cross were already covered with fleur-de-lis semé. But this was not unknown; the collection of the Musee de l'Armée has drawings of two drapeaux of the Regiment Royal Corse in 1773 with a motto across the horizontal arms of the fleur-de-lis covered crosses. The motto obscures the middle row of fleurs. Drapeaux of several other French regiments had one or more devices on a cross with fleur-de-lis semé (see Regiment la Reine, for example). The drapeaux of Regiment du Roi had a cross with fleur-de-lis and the same breakdown of words as suggested by Charrie: the first word on the upper arm of the cross, the second on the arm next to the pole, the last word on the cross arm to the right, opposite a central device. On the drapeaux of the Compagnies franches this would appear as *PER* on the upper arm of the cross, *MARE ET* on the left, lightning or anchors in the center, and *TERRAS* on the right.

Drapeau colonel, Compagnies franches de la Marine. A reproduction of this drapeau by the author, in the interpretation with the fleur-de-lis in the quarters, and the flames in color, is currently on display at Fortress of Louisbourg National Historic Site, Nova Scotia.

Drapeaux d'ordonnance, Compagnies franches de la Marine. A reproduction of this drapeau by the author, in the interpretation with the fleur-de-lis in the red and blue quarters, and the flames in color, is currently on display at Fortress of Louisbourg National Historic Site, Nova Scotia.

Regiment Guyenne

The drapeaux d'ordonnance of Regiment Guyenne in the French and Indian War were of isabelle and gray-green. The plates of 1721 and 1757 show isabelle in cantons one and four, green in cantons two and three. As with other drapeaux with isabelle, this color is shown very differently in different sources. A contemporary print owned by Parks Canada shows the colors reversed, with green in the upper left canton. As pointed out in the introduction to the section on French colors, it was not especially unusual or remarkable for a drapeau to be "sideways" on the staff, but as the Parks Canada print was apparently made onsite in 1762, it seems reasonable to believe that the drapeaux actually carried in Canada had gray-green in cantons one and four.

At the end of the French and Indian War, Regiment Guyenne was consolidated with another regiment, retaining the name Guyenne, but adopting the drapeaux of the other. Sources after 1762 show the new drapeaux of red and violet.

Drapeaux d'ordonnance, Regiment Guyenne.

Regiment la Reine

The drapeaux of the Regiment La Reine (Queen's Regiment) included both fleur-de-lis and crowns as symbols of the Royal connection. There are numerous discrepancies in these embellishments in both contemporary as well as later scholarly depictions. The regiment had been created in 1661, and the earliest portrayal of its drapeaux in the plates of 1721 show the usual design of a flag quartered by a white cross, with the four quarters green, black, green, black, without further embellishment. By1748, the regiment was documented in *Troupes de France* as having one white drapeau colonel and eleven drapeaux d'ordonnance green and black in opposition, on the white crosses gold fleur-de-lis semé, and in the center four gold crowns.

The one detail universally agreed on is that the crowns always point outward from the center. It is also usually agreed that at the center of the crowns there were three fleur-de-lis in the traditional arrangement of two above and one below as in the Royal coat of arms. The Tableaus of 1771 and 1773 seem to show these on a shield as from the coat of arms; all other sources show them directly on the white silk. The 1770s depictions would have been a later issue in any event, the flags carried in Canada having been burned in 1760. The earliest drapeaux may have had five fleur-de-lis in each arm of the cross, all pointing away from the center, as if above each of the crowns. By 1748, however, the fleur-de-lis were described as semé, meaning they all faced the same direction and were uniformly spaced out over the entire area containing them. On the drapeaux of the Regiment la Reine, it appears that the arrangement of the fleur-de-lis was identical to other drapeaux that had them (see Regiment Royal Roussillon) but with the innermost of them obliterated by the four outward facing crowns. The three central fleurs are roughly in the same distribution as the others—the entire cross thus adorned semé.

The crowns are the traditional French crown, with fleur-de-lis, jewels, and a red interior. Depictions up to and including 1772 show only the oval at the base of the crown as red; later drawings show the upper part of the crown partially or completely filled by red, as the visible part of the actual red velvet cap within an actual crown. The 1757 print shows the drapeau attached to the staff by the "wrong" edge—the first quarter in the upper left is black rather than green, and all the fleur-de-lis on both drapeaux point toward the staff rather than straight up. As the first battalion of this regiment remained in Europe during the period of the Seven Years' War, the odd orientation may have been drawn from life. The flag shown here represents the two drapeaux d'ordonnance with the second battalion of the regiment in North America since 1755.

Without further description from contemporary documents, it seems certain that the two green quarters were a deep primary green. Charrie described them as light green (*vert clair*) in 1989, but without attribution. They are dark in all contemporary and later drawings through at least the nineteenth century. Charrie also described the drapeaux as having twenty fleur-de-lis semé, five in each arm of the cross, as well as the three at center; but semé, as described above, and as shown on other French flags described with fleur-de-lis semé as early as 1721, implies all available space evenly filled—only five fleur-de-lis per arm would necessarily have been widely or unevenly distributed.

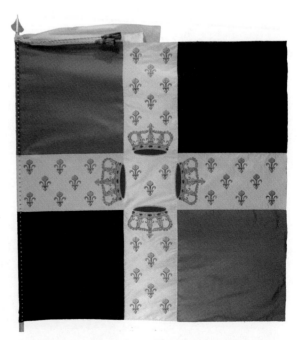

Drapeaux d'ordonnance, Regiment La Reine. Flag reproduction by author. An earlier version of this drapeau, also made by the author, was used in the movie *The Last of the Mohicans* (1992).

Regiment La Sarre

The drapeaux d'ordonnance of Regiment La Sarre during the French and Indian War, as depicted in the plates of 1721 and 1757, were cramoisi (crimson) in cantons one and four, black in cantons two and three. The Tableaus of 1771 and 1773 (the flags actually carried in America had been burned in 1760) show these colors reversed, with black in the upper left.

While there are no serious disagreements on the crimson/black combination among illustrations made over a span of fifty years, two written sources are clearly mistaken. The *État général des troupes de France, 1748* lists La Sarre as having drapeaux with cantons feuilles morte, green, blue, and violet, but this was a mistake of the typesetter, who copied the entry from the regiment directly above for which these colors are correct. More curiously, Montigny's plate for La Sarre in 1772 shows the

Drapeaux d'ordonnance, Regiment La Sarre.

drapeaux as black and crimson, like the tableaus, but at the bottom of the panel has the colors in words as aurora, apple green, royal blue, and violet. Since these plates were not color-printed, it seems likely that the mistaken words were printed on the paper at the same time as the picture, which was later correctly colored by hand.

Drapeaux d'ordonnance, Regiment Languedoc.

Regiment Languadoc

The drapeaux d'ordonnance of Regiment Languedoc were violet and feuille morte (dead leaf) in opposition. They are shown in virtually all original sources 1721 through 1772 with the violet in cantons one and four, feuille morte in two and three. The Tableau of 1773 shows these colors reversed. A watercolor owned by Parks Canada apparently made in 1762 at the end of the French and Indian War, shows the colors as orange—perhaps a poor approximation of the orangish brown of feuille morte—and a violet color that could be better described as blue. The orange/feuille morte is in cantons one and four and the violet/blue in two and three. The Languadoc drapeaux were burned with the others after the final capitulation of French forces at Montreal in 1760. If the drapeaux in the Parks Canada series were indeed drawn from life, the off-colors might indicate how faded the original bright silks had become after years in constant use.

Regiment Royal Roussillon

Regiment Royal Roussillon was created in 1667 as a Royal regiment, thus it had gold fleur-de-lis semé on the white cross of its drapeaux, both colonel and d'ordonnance, from its very beginning. The earliest depictions of the drapeaux of the regiment, made in 1721, were on the older, very large dimensions of eight feet square, and depicted sixty-five fleurs-de-lis. By the time of the French and Indian War, the size of drapeaux had decreased to somewhat less than six feet per side, and the number of fleur-de-lis generally reduced to forty-eight in the standard pattern of eleven on each arm and four in the center, equally spaced in both directions. The colors of the drapeaux d'ordonnance of Royal Roussillon are generally agreed on in all early sources as blue, red, feuille morte, and green in cantons one, two, three, four respectively. Only the shade of the feuille morte in number three canton—lower left against the pole—is varied, appearing closer to orange or aurora in some depictions, a darker brown in others.

Drapeaux d'ordonnance, Regiment Royal Roussillon.

Volontaires Étrangers

The Second Battalion of the Regiment Volontaires Étrangers (Foreign Volunteers) was sent from France directly to Fortress Louisbourg in 1758 as reinforcements against the expected siege. The drapeaux d'ordonnace of this regiment were somewhat unusual in that each canton was bisected vertically; each was half green and half white. According to a drawing in the Musée de l'Armée, these were arranged such that the green half of each canton was against the upright of the central white cross, and the white half of each was against the pole on one side and the fly on the other. As the regiment was raised in 1756 and discontinued only three years later, it was not included in any of the more complete compilations of drapeaux produced during the period.

Drapeaux d'ordonnance, Volontaires Étrangers.

FRENCH DRAPEAUX IN NORTH AMERICA
IN THE AMERICAN WAR OF INDEPENDENCE, 1777–1783

Descriptions of the Drapeaux

Each French regiment during the American War of Independence was composed of two permanent battalions, fielded together as a single tactical unit. Each regiment carried two drapeaux—the first battalion, with the colonel's company, carried the white drapeau colonel, the second battalion carried the drapeaux d'ordonnance. The regiments listed are those commonly accepted by French, British, and American sources as having participated in the war, although as noted in the individual unit entries, some of them, and thus their drapeaux, may have never actually been present on the North American mainland.

Regiment Agenois

The Regiment Agenois, which served in North America, taking part in both the siege of Savannah in 1779 as well as Yorktown in 1781, was created in 1776. It was the second regiment of that name in the French Army. The original Regiment Agenois had been created in 1692 and had entirely different drapeaux from the same-named regiment that served in America. This first Agenois was merged with Regiment Berry in 1749 and its name disappeared from the rolls. Regiment Berry served in the French and Indian War (which see).

The name Agenois was resurrected in 1776, when two of the battalions of Regiment Bearn were detached and reformed as a new two-battalion regiment for service in the expected war with Britain. This was not the same Regiment Bearn as had served in the French and Indian War (which see), however—that regiment had been discontinued in 1762. The new Regiment Bearn had been formed in December 1762 from Regiment La Tour-du-Pic, also sometimes identified as Leuville, one of the oldest in the French Army. Its drapeaux d'ordonnance had cantons of yellow (or aurora) and violet. Because it was formed from battalions

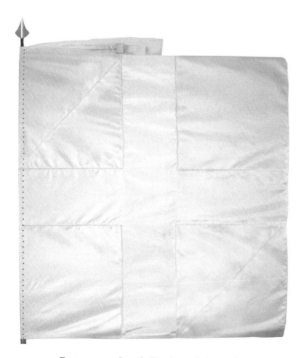

Drapeau colonel, Regiment Agenois.

Drapeau d'ordonnance, Regiment Agenois.

taken from Regiment Bearn, the new Regiment Agenois took its seniority as next in line immediately after Bearn. In 1780 the regimental seniority of Agenois was sixteen. As with other new regiments created from proud older units, the new Regiment Agenois was given drapeaux with the traditional colors of the parent regiment, but in this case with one new color added to avoid confusion. Looking at the new drapeaux, it is quite possible they were made from the now-redundant old drapeaux, by simply cutting off two opposite corners and adding new pieces of a contrasting color. Thus, Regiment Agenois's drapeau d'ordonnance in North America had green split diagonally with the original yellow of cantons one and four, and all-violet in cantons two and three. This flag can be seen, unfortunately with the colors almost completely washed out, in van Blarenberghe's painting of *Surrender at Yorktown*. The drapeau colonel probably had white seams in cantons one and four to mimic the piecing of the silks on the drapeau d'ordonnance.

Regiment Armagnac

Regiment Armagnac was created in 1776 from elements of the historic Regiment Navarre, raised originally in 1563. The drapeaux of Armagnac were in the original colors of the Regiment Navarre: the drapeau colonel was all white with white cross, the drapeaux d'ordonnance with the white cross and four cantons colored *feuille morte*. The drapeaux of Navarre had fleur-de-lis on the cross, as well as five Navarre coats of arms, one at the center and one at each end of the cross, on both the drapeau colonel and drapeaux d'ordonnance. Charrie says the drapeaux of Armagnac were identical to those of Navarre, but without the coats of arms (*armoiries*). As Armagnac was not a Royal regiment, however, it is probable that the crosses on its drapeaux were plain white, not white with fleur-de-lis.

Armagnac was sent to the West Indies in 1777. A battalion of four to six companies including the grenadier and chasseur companies were among the French forces at Savannah in 1779. Probably only one drapeau accompanied; which one would have depended on which battalion companies were sent.

Drapeau colonel, Regiment Armagnac.

Drapeau d'ordonnance, Regiment Armagnac.

Regiment Auxerrois

Regiment Auxerrois in the American War of Independence was the second regiment of that name; the original Auxerrois, with completely different drapeaux, had been disestablished in 1749.

The new Auxerrois was created in 1776 from the Fourth Battalion of the ancient Regiment la Marine and brought to full strength with new levies. The Regiment la Marine had drapeaux with cantons blue and green, for sea and land. Based on its immediate lineage, the new regiment had a drapeau d'ordonnance with the same colors; each quarter divided into blue and green. The diagonals ran from the edges of the flag, rather than pinwheel style from the center, and the colors were alternated from one quarter to the next, with the arrangement of the colors being green in the outer corners in cantons one and four, and in the inner corners next to the cross in cantons two and three. It is unknown but quite possible that the original flags were simply altered, with each of the four corners simply cut off and resewn onto the opposite colors. The drapeau colonel probably mimicked the seams in each quarter of the d'ordonnance with white stitching on white.

Auxerrois contributed a detachment of several companies, including the single grenadier company and some number of fusiliers, to the siege of Savannah in 1779. At least one of the regiment's drapeaux would have accompanied, but which one would have depended on which companies. The presence of the grenadiers suggests that it was the first battalion, which included the colonel's company and the drapeau colonel. According to some sources, the regiment also had detachments involved in the attacks on Gloucester, across the river from Yorktown, in 1781, but unless these were landed as an intact battalion, likely neither drapeau accompanied.

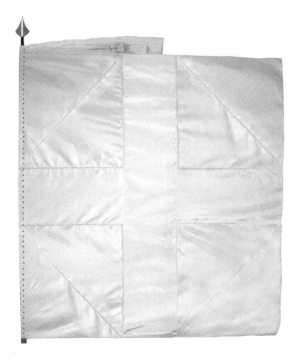

Drapeau colonel, Regiment Auxerrois.

Drapeau d'ordonnance, Regiment Auxerrois.

Artillery Regiment Auxonne

Artillery Regiment Metz

The French Royal Artillery was originally organized as a single regiment or corps of five battalions, each of which was treated as an independent regiment, and which carried one drapeau colonel and two drapeaux d'ordonnance. From 1765, the corps was reorganized along lines similar to the infantry, as seven large regiments of two battalions each. Although there are no specific records to say so, it seems reasonable that at this point, again like the infantry, the number of drapeaux was reduced to two per regiment, one in each battalion, with the first battalion carrying the white drapeau colonel and the second battalion carrying the drapeau d'ordonnance. The drapeaux of the artillery regiments were all very similar. The white crosses on both the drapeaux colonels and drapeaux d'ordonnance were adorned with gold fleur-de-lis semé, probably forty-eight in the common pattern.

The Second Battalion of Regiment Auxonne was a part of Rochambeau's army in North America. The drapeau d'ordonnance of this regiment had quarters one and four of gorge-de-pigeon, and quarters two and three aurora. As a second battalion detached from its parent regiment still in metropolitan France, this unit probably would not have carried a drapeau colonel, but only the drapeau d'ordonnance.

The drapeau of Regiment Metz had the same two colors as Auxonne, but in the opposite corners. Some sources say yellow instead of aurora. While it is generally agreed that Regiment Metz was stationed in the French West Indies from 1777 to 1783, sources are very unclear on the regiment's participation in campaigns on the North American continent. A portion of the regiment, perhaps an entire battalion—which might suggest one or both drapeaux accompanying—was at Savannah in 1779, and two (or maybe four) companies were detached for service at Yorktown, where they were placed along with Auxonne and one company from Grenoble, under a unified artillery command.

Drapeau colonel, Artillery Regiment Auxonne. Flag reproduction by author.

Drapeaux d'ordonnance, Artillery Regiment Auxonne. Flag reproduction by author.

While Artillery technically held a seniority position in the French establishment—all seven regiments of the "Corps d'Artillerie" shared the number Sixty-Four in 1779—the drapeau d'ordonnance of neither Auxonne nor Metz is shown in the line of French troops in van Blarenberghe's paintings of Yorktown. The artillerymen, readily identified by their blue uniforms, stand in position between the Regiments Saintonge (Eight-Five) and Soissonnais (Forty-One), however, and are represented by a single drapeau colonel, white with a white cross, but with no fleur-de-lis apparent.

Regiment Bourbonnais

The drapeaux of Regiment Bourbonnais were first illustrated in 1721: the drapeau colonel as the standard white with white cross, the drapeaux d'ordonnance with quarters one and four blue, quarters two and three violet. While sources since then have generally agreed, the drapeaux d'ordonnance in the period 1771–1773 may have been different—whether by design, or by fading or weathering of the silks cannot be known. The Tableau of 1771 shows the blues in cantons one and four as a bluish purple, and quarters two and three as very reddish. It is difficult to tell whether the inks or paints of the tableau have simply given a more reddish cast to both colors. Montigny's plate of 1772 shows what were almost certainly the same flags and describes the colors in words as violet and crimson (cramoisis). The Tableau of 1773 seems to depict the same thing, though the very tiny illustration shows only a very slight difference between the two colors, with all four quarters appearing quite reddish. By 1781, however, the drapeau d'ordonnance is again depicted as blue and violet.

Both flags of this regiment can be clearly seen in van Blarenberghe's *Surrender at Yorktown*. Probably new drapeaux were presented before deployment to America. Van Blarenberghe paints the drapeau d'ordonnance with cantons one and four a very bright primary blue, while the other two quarters are violet, very faded, but not remotely red or crimson. The faded violet probably reflects the actual appearance of the flag in 1781, as most of the pigments in van Blarenberghe's painting remain fairly bright and crisp to this day.

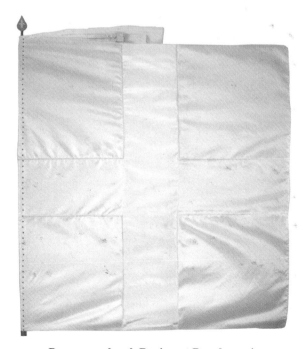

Drapeau colonel, Regiment Bourbonnais.

Drapeau d'ordonnance, Regiment Bourbonnais.

Regiment Champagne

Regiment Champagne was one of the oldest in the French Army, with a seniority of two. Its drapeaux d'ordonnance were green with the white cross. Charrie in 1989 describes the green as *très clair*, or very light, but none of the early sources in either words or illustrations suggest this. Since the drapeaux were first illustrated in 1721, the cross was always displayed as the standard white Latin cross, but apparently, and for reasons unknown, both drapeaux during the period leading up to the American war were made with a corner-to-corner St. Andrew's cross. The Tableaus of 1771 and 1773, as well as Montigny's plate of 1772, show this. Mouillard (1882) implies that the regiment reverted to the traditional design after the war.

Champagne was stationed in Martinique in 1779; the chasseur company took part in the unsuccessful siege of Savannah in October of that year, and detachments of the regiment were with French fleets in 1780 and 1782. However, as the regiment did not commit a full battalion at any time on the mainland, it is unlikely that either of its drapeaux was ever unfurled on American soil.

Drapeau colonel, Regiment Champagne.

Drapeau d'ordonnance, Regiment Champagne.

Regiment Dillon

Regiment Dillon had substantially the same drapeaux throughout its long service, if going by word descriptions of the flags, but the artistic interpretation was considerably different during the war in America than it had been during the regiment's first half century. Most reconstructions of the regiment's drapeaux are based on the original drawing of 1721 and the remnants of an original flag dating to the Battle of Fontenoy in 1745. The three sources closest to the period of the war in America, however—the Tableaus of 1771 and 1773, and Montigny's plate of 1772—give these drapeaux a different overall appearance. While these three sources usually agree with earlier documents, diverging only in relatively minor details in the drawings of the fleur-de-lis and crowns, in the case of the drapeaux of Regiment Dillon (and two other Irish regiments), the changes are more striking—all three sources agree on the crowns being smaller than earlier versions, all have the crowns placed at the corners of the flags rather than centered in each canton, and all show the red English cross as outlined only on the edges, not the ends. As drapeaux carried in 1745 and drawn in 1757 would have been more than twenty-five years old by the time the Tableau of 1771 was prepared, it seems probable that new drapeau had been presented by that time, and that these new flags were recorded in the new documents of 1771, 1772, and 1773. These new drapeaux, incorporating a more up-to-date style, may have been made sometime after 1762 when all regiments in French service were reorganized on the new two-battalion model and the Irish regiments were consolidated. There may also have been practical considerations—very large painted elements tended to crack or tear out of the silk more readily than smaller ones. The flags of the Irish regiments Bulkeley and Clare also reflect the new design in all three sources, as does a plate depicting the drapeau of Regiment Bulkeley circa 1772, published in 1830 by Alfred Marbot.[3] (Apparently in this same period Regiment Walsh lost its Irish-themed drapeaux completely.)

As the original drawings of 1721 and remnants of the drapeaux of 1745 are generally credited as the "correct" flags for Regiment Dillon in America, it may be worthwhile to record some details of them, if only to reinforce the idea that flags may be identical in their word descriptions yet very different in their actual appearance.

The colors of Regiment Dillon were originally red and green, changed to red and blue in 1730, and finally to red and black in 1739. Since that time all illustrations of the drapeau d'ordonnance show quarters one and four red, two and three black. The white cross had a red cross of St. George superimposed, such that it was outlined in white on all sides, including the ends of each arm. This was one of the changes noted in all three of the later references—the white outline no longer includes the ends of the cross. At the center was an Irish harp, illustrated in 1721 with the bust of a young man on the drapeau colonel and a young woman on the drapeaux d'ordonnance, but by 1745 the head of a bearded old man (at least on the d'ordonnance). Later interpretations have sometimes depicted this as a devil's mask, but from the remnants of the original of 1745 there is no indication of horns ever having been part of the design. None of these could really be considered a "traditional" interpretation of the Irish harp, and none of the harps depicted by Montigny or in either of the tableaus show a head or mask of any sort. Above the harp was an English crown, clearly identified by having crosses as well as fleur-de-lis on its rim, and on the arms of the cross on both flags the motto *IN / HOC / SIGNO / VIN/CES* (In this sign [we] conquer). The existing drapeau has the red silk of the cross blocked with red paint or some other sizing so that the lettering was painted to read correctly on both sides of the flag. Centered in each quarter was a very large English crown, oriented on the diagonal with the top pointed toward the corner of the flag. The original 1721 plate shows the crown with red velvet cap within, but by about the middle of the century it became more common to show the crown with red only at the bottom, none showing between the bars above the rim. The 1745 drapeau has only one crown still intact, and it is on a red canton, but while the base of the crown is painted red, the interior shows no paint at all. The prints of 1757 also show no red within the crowns, as does Montigny's drawing of 1772. The drawings on the Tableaus of 1771 and 1773 are too small to know for sure whether a red interior was intended.

The drapeau colonel of the regiment as drawn in 1721 was virtually identical to the drapeau d'ordonnance except for both the cross and the cantons being white, with the painted devices and motto being the same. Charrie wrote in 1989 that this drapeau had a red cross, like the drapeaux d'ordonnance, but surviving illustrations and documents do not support this. It is assumed the white drapeaux colonel had a solution similar to the drapeaux d'ordonnance for the real-world problem of the paint soaking through the silk, though it is possible that rather than having opaque panels of white paint wherever the lettering was applied, the motto was simply backward on the back of the flag. The 1757 print, however, shows the motto reading correctly on the reverse.

The drapeau colonel during the period of the American War was all white without cross, the crowns in the four corners the same as on the drapeaux d'ordonnance, and the motto on a painted scroll over the central design of crown and harp. A painted scroll would obviate the problem of painted lettering showing through both sides of the white silk. Such a flag would still have had to be pieced together from standard widths of silk, so it would have had seams that were simply not included in the drawings, but there is no suggestion of a white cross on white as shown for other regiments in either the Tableau of 1771 or Montigny's plate of 1772. (The Tableau of 1773 does not include the drapeaux colonel for any regiment.) The Tableau of 1771 depicts the space between the strings on the harp as red; Montigny shows the harp directly on the white field, as in all earlier drapeaux of the regiment.

Several companies of Regiment Dillon participated in the siege of Savannah in 1779, including the grenadier company, suggesting it was the first battalion, which included the colonel's company and the drapeau colonel. One of the main composite storming columns was led by Colonel Arthur Dillon himself, which also gives support to the idea that if only one drapeau accompanied, it was probably the drapeau colonel.

Gherardi Davis's 1907 watercolor of the drapeau d'ordonnance of the Regiment Dillon, based on the manuscript of 1721. This pattern is copied very closely in an original drapeau dating from 1745, though probably unknown to Davis. The pattern used in the American War of Independence had smaller crowns placed farther out into the corners. The drapeau behind is Artillery Regiment Metz and was probably not brought to America. Gherardi Davis papers, Manuscripts and Archives Division, The New York Public Library.

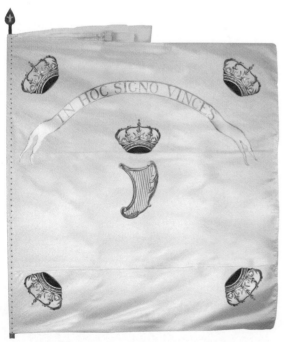

Drapeau colonel, Regiment Dillon.

Drapeau d'ordonnance, Regiment Dillon.

Regiment Foix

Regiment Foix was one of the few regiments involved in the American War with an unbroken history and no change in its drapeaux. From the very earliest sources these are shown as a standard white drapeau colonel and drapeaux d'ordonnance with each canton divided diagonally green and isabelle, displayed pinwheel style with the diagonals radiating from the central cross to the outer corners. The early sources are about equally divided on which color was against the pole in the first canton, but as discussed in the introduction to the French drapeaux, this could be easily explained by the square flags being nailed to the pole in different orientations at different periods. The sources of 1771, 1772, and 1773, all show isabelle along the pole in the first canton. The drapeau colonel at that period also had the cantons marked with white on white in imitation of the diagonals on the drapeaux d'ordonnance. At some point after the American war, the drapeaux of Regiment Foix were lettered *FIDELIS FELIX FORTIS* (faithful, cheerful, strong) across the horizontal arm of the central cross.

Regiment Foix contributed four line companies and its grenadier company to the siege of Savannah in 1779. Although no source states specifically which line companies were sent, the presence of the grenadier company suggests that it was the first battalion of the regiment, which contained the colonel's company and the drapeau colonel.

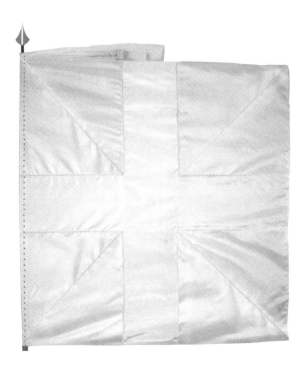

Drapeau colonel, Regiment Foix.

Drapeau d'ordonnance, Regiment Foix.

Regiment Gatinois

Regiment Gatinois was created in 1776 from the Second and Fourth Battalions of the ancient Regiment Auvergne, originally raised in 1606. The balance of the regiment, reorganized on the two-battalion model, remained on the French establishment under the original name. The new regiment was given the name Gatinois, which had previously belonged to a much younger regiment which had been disestablished in 1749.

The drapeaux of Regiment Auvergne were violet and black; the drapeau d'ordonnance of the new Regiment Gatinois was also violet and black, but with each canton being cut on the diagonal from the outer ends of the white cross, with half violet and half black. Possibly one of the original drapeaux was simply altered, with each corner being cut off and then resewn onto the opposite color. Van Blarenberghe clearly shows this drapeau at Yorktown, the arrangement of the colors being black in the outer corners in cantons one and four, and in the inner corners next to the cross in cantons two and three.

Regiment Gatinois participated in both the siege of Savannah in 1779 (one company only) and the siege of Yorktown in 1781. Due to its gallant performance in the capture of British Redoubt Number Nine at Yorktown on the night of October 16, 1781, the regiment was rewarded with return of its traditional name of Auvergne, now Royal Auvergne to distinguish it from the parent organization. Due to the relatively short period the regiment existed under the name Gatinois, it is not included in most documents on French regimental flags.

The purple cantons shown for Auvergne in documents up to 1773 are a fairly clear bright violet. Mouillard and Susane in the nineteenth century show them as deep indigo closer to blue. Richardson, citing a series of flags presented by France for the 1981 bicentennial of Yorktown, describes the colors for Gatinois as black and "Marine blue," thus completely discounting the connection between the parent regiment, as well as the regiment's much-prized redesignation as Royal Auvergne.

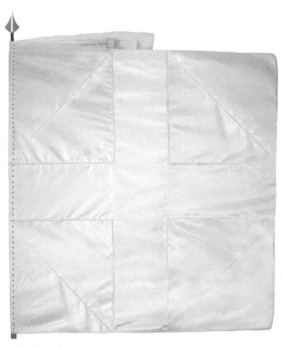

Drapeau Colonel, Regiment Gatinois (Royal Auvergne).

Drapeau d'ordonnance, Regiment Gatinois (Royal Auvergne).

Regiment Hainault

The Regiment Hainault that participated in the American War of Independence had been redesignated from the venerable Regiment Vendome in 1762 and maintained that regiment's seniority and drapeaux. Another Regiment Hainault, with completely different drapeaux, had existed from 1684 to 1762.

No two sources have exactly the same description or depiction of the drapeaux of the Regiment Hainault associated with the American war, although all are close enough that the flag would be easily identifiable on the field, as the quarters are four different colors, always including violet, green, and blue. The color of the first canton (upper corner next to the staff) is variously identified/illustrated as aurora, feulle morte, brown, olive drab, light green, and in the 1771 tableau, an indeterminate silverish gray. All sources agree on the other three colors in cantons two, three, and four, but show them in every possible position. This cannot be explained by the wrong side of the flag being attached to the pole, since the sources do not even agree on which colors are diagonally opposite. The two sources closest to the American war, the Tableau of 1771 and Montigny's plate of 1772, both show violet, green, blue, in cantons two, three, and four, respectively.

Hainault was stationed on the French island of St. Dominique in 1779. A detachment of several companies, including the single grenadier company and the balance fusiliers, participated in the siege of Savannah in 1779. If the unit sent was a single battalion rather than picked companies, the presence of the grenadier company would suggest the regiment's first battalion, which included the colonel's company and the drapeau colonel.

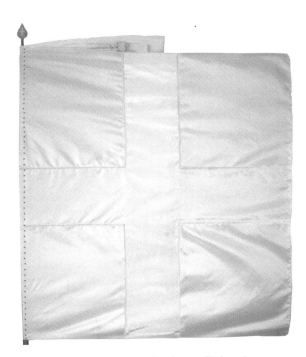

Drapeau colonel, Regiment Hainault.

Drapeau d'ordonnance, Regiment Hainault.

Legion Lauzun

Lauzun's Legion, the Volontaires Étrangers de Lauzun, was created in 1780 in part from Lauzun's earlier command in the Volontaires Étrangers de la Marine raised in 1778 specifically for the impending war with Britain. The only contemporary source which refers to flags of Lauzun's Legion in America is the initial table of organization which specified two flag-bearers, one on foot (*porte-drapeau*) and one mounted (*porte-etendard*). The records contain the names of the men who held these positions, but nothing about the flags themselves.

A legion was a composite force of infantry, cavalry, and artillery—basically a tiny self-contained army—about the size of a standard regiment. All legions in French service were proprietary units raised by *gentilhomme* colonels and traditionally did not carry flags. In the Tableau of 1771 both legions and hussar regiments are specifically noted as "corps sans drapeaux," and Montigny's plates of 1772 show the uniforms of all legions and hussars then in service, but no flags.

Nonetheless, per the original establishing order, the infantry contingent of Lauzun's Legion carried a drapeaux like other infantry on the French establishment. This was probably the same drapeau that Lauzun had procured for his earlier legion and is generally believed to have been modeled on the drapeaux of the Royal Volunteers (*Volontaires royeaux*) first created in the Seven Years' War: white cross, all four quarters blue with three gold fleur-de-lis in each.

The Legion cavalry, styled hussars, was uniformed and equipped as light cavalry. It carried a small *étendard* (standard). In the French establishment, only dragoons carried guidons, and these were of a very specific design: long and tapered, swallow-tailed with rounded points, and the devices and mottoes parallel to the lance, so they appeared right side up when the lance was held parallel to the ground with the flag hanging down. They were also generally much larger than étendards. Early in the eighteenth century some hussar regiments carried swallow-tailed étendards or guidons, but of a very different shape from those of the dragoons—shorter, and more rounded toward the fly, with their emblems right-side-up like other standards. In the general reorganization of the French Army in 1762, flags of either type were abolished for hussars; as mentioned above, both the Tableau of 1771 and Montigny's plates of 1772 reflect this. In June of 1772, however, after ten years of complaints, hussars were re-authorized étendards. According to Charrie, these were to be made with the royal sun and motto on the obverse and arms of the proprietary colonel on the reverse. No specifications are given as to their basic size or shape. An existing étendard/guidon of hussars circa 1758, just before their use was discontinued, shows a smallish swallow-tailed flag with rounded points and embroidered design displayed horizontally. In the Tableau of 1773, the re-authorized étendards/guidons for legions or hussars are shown as swallow-tailed flags indistinguishable in the tiny drawings from the guidons of the dragoons, except for their designs being horizontal rather than parallel to the staff. Only the reverse sides of these étendards are shown, each bearing the arms of its proprietary colonel.

The étendard of Lauzun's hussars would have been made of two layers of silk with the designs embroidered in metallic and colored silk threads, bound on all sides, including the pole edge, by a heavy bullion fringe of gold and/or silver, and accompanied by cord and tassels matching the fringe. The étendard was nailed to the pole through a separate silk sleeve sewn along the outside of the fringe on the leading edge. Judging from the étendards of hussars before 1762, and the new model guidons post-1783, it would have been about thirty-three to thirty-four inches on the pole by forty inches fly, which would require it be pieced together, as available silks were generally twenty-eight inches wide. On one side were embroidered the arms of the duc de Lauzun: a shield quartered gold and red, supported by two griffins in gold, a ducal coronet above, and below a scroll with motto *PERIT SED IN ARMIS* (They perish only in arms), all on a slate gray background.[4] The opposite side was white with the golden sun and Royal motto *NEC PLURIBUS IMPAR*. Assuming the shape to be a shortened guidon, there was probably a gold fleur-de-lis in each corner. There is no compelling reason to believe that the étendard of this Legion, which had been created in 1780 and not returned to France until late in 1783, would have had the dragon and motto *VIGILENTIA* which was ordered for French guidons in 1783, though this pattern is described in later lists for Lauzun's post-war regiment in France. It is also unclear which side of the flag was which. After citing the Tableau of 1773, which shows the colonel's arms on the reverse of all hussar étendards, Charrie then describes each of those flags individually with their colonel's arms on the obverse. It appears that like the which-side-is-up orientation of the French infantry drapeaux when nailed to their poles, it was totally immaterial which side was front and which was reverse on French étendards.

The lance for both guidons and standards was traditionally shaped somewhat like an ancient knight's lance, narrow at the top, widening considerably in diameter at a point about one-third from the bottom, and an extreme narrowing in the middle of that portion for a handhold. By this period, however, it was becoming fashionable among hussars and other light horse, to carry light lances of a more uniform taper with a less prominent narrowing for the handhold. A long iron rod usually ran along the midsection of the lance, with a ring to slide along it, to be clipped to the bearer's bandolier, similar to a carbine sling. The newer light lances coming into fashion at the time had a simple ring to attach to the bandolier. There was a small leather boot or socket attached to the stirrup for the butt end of the lance to sit in while mounted. There was no standard pattern for the lance points, though in general they were smaller and more compact than piques of the infantry drapeaux. The overall height including the spear and butt ferrule was approximately nine feet.

Étendard, Lauzun's Legion, Hussars (obverse).

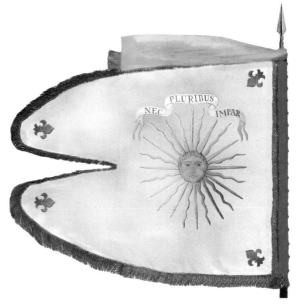

Étendard, Lauzun's Legion, Hussars (reverse).

Drapeau d'ordonnance, Lauzun's Legion, Light Infantry.

Regiment Rouergue

While virtually every listing of French regiments involved in the American War of Independence includes the Regiment Rouergue, it is also universally agreed that the regiment reached America too late to take any part in the war. The drapeau d'ordonnance of the regiment had four green cantons with a red diamond centered in each. The Tableau of 1771 and Montigny's plate of 1772 both show the diamonds replicated in white on white in each quarter of the drapeau colonel.

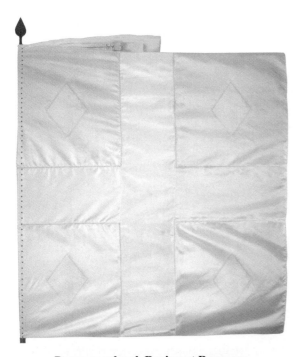

Drapeau colonel, Regiment Rouergue.

Drapeau d'ordonnance, Regiment Rouergue.

Regiment Royal Deux Ponts

Regiment Royal Deux Ponts was the youngest of the French regiments involved in the American war. As such it had the lowest seniority in 1781, putting it at the very end of the French line at the surrender ceremonies at Yorktown, and consequently its drapeaux show up as closest to the viewer and are quite prominently displayed in van Blarenberghe's painting of the event. Also known by its German name of Zweibrucken, it was a German regiment created and accepted into the French Army in 1757. The Library of the Minister of War in Paris has (or had) a very detailed drawing of both drapeaux of the new regiment, dated 1757 in the margins. Montigny's print of 1772 inexplicably shows a flag of standard French pattern, with the cantons red and violet, but the Tableaus of 1771 and 1773 show the drapeaux as authorized and drawn in 1757. Taken along with van Blarenberghe's painting, it is quite certain what the regiment carried in North America, any quibbling being only in the details.

The size of these drapeaux is not known. If made in Germany, they were probably about fifty-six inches square, made of three eighteen-to-nineteen-inch widths of silk, as other German flags. French sources, however, routinely draw them the same size as other French drapeaux, approximately sixty-eight to seventy inches per side. Perhaps most importantly, they are portrayed in van Blarenburghe's painting as the same size as all other flags dotting the line of French troops. While the drapeau d'ordonnance was clearly made up of many small pieces, the drapeau colonel is shown here as being made of the same pieces as other French flags—two standard widths of twenty-eight inches plus one half-width of fourteen inches.

The drapeaux colonel of the Royal Deux Ponts had a white field with gold fleur-de-lis semé, the overall pattern being interrupted by a golden sun in splendor (sun with a classical human face) and the coat of arms of the Duke of Deux Ponts/Zweibrucken, including the collar of the *Ordre du Saint-Esprit* (Order of the Holy Spirit), displayed with full mantling, and surmounted with a ducal crown with red interior. Above the sun, on a blue scroll, was the French monarch's Royal motto *NEC PLURIBUS IMPAR*. As the scroll was painted on the silk and overpainted on the reverse, the motto would read correctly on both sides of the flag. All depictions of this drapeau show three fleur-de-lis in the upper corners above the motto scroll, and it is probably this that Johann Dohla of the Anspach-Bayreuth regiment saw at Yorktown and recorded in his diary, "on the right wing of each regiment the French paraded white silks adorned with three silver lilies."

The drapeau d'ordonnance featured a white St. Andrew's cross with two fleur-de-lis on each arm, pointing toward the corners of the flag, and the Royal crown of France in the center, with fleur-de-lis on its rim and a red velvet cap inside. The triangles defined by the cross were also of white silk, the upper and lower with five wavy red stripes, the left and right with five wavy blue stripes. The stripes do not appear to be perfectly aligned. While this might be attributed to the relative skill of the draftsmen making the various drawings over many years, it is also likely that any originally intended pattern—the stripes appear somewhat narrower nearer the outer corners of each triangle—simply could not be perfectly accomplished in sewing thirteen wavy stripes per canton and then fitting the resulting triangles into a reasonably accurate diagonal cross. Besides all the pieces having to be cut and joined along their wavy edges, each completed triangle would have to be cut on the bias—across the natural grain of the silk—to be sewn into the complete flag. It is highly unlikely that the wavy lines were painted onto the silk—any painted parts of the cloth tended to become somewhat stiff and brittle, and paint was therefore rarely, if ever, used where the painted design ran off the edge of a flag.

In each triangle was painted a coat of arms in full color, crowned and mantled. The coats of arms in the triangles are a breakdown of those of the families/territories represented in the combined coat of arms on the drapeau colonel. As portrayed in the original drawing of 1757, all are positioned with their natural base toward the center of the cross, thus the one in the bottom triangle is upside down and those on the right and left lie sideways. The plate from *Troupes du Roi, 1757* shows the four coats of arms all "right side up," which perhaps is how the flag was first made and recorded, but newer flags made for the regiment by early 1770s and recorded in the Tableaus of 1771 and 1773 agree with the original approved design. Van Blarenberghe shows them in this orientation as well; though admittedly very tiny, and without great detail, the vertically divided coats of arms appear horizontal in the right and left triangles.

The arms in the blue-striped triangles on the left and right display the combined arms of Bavaria (blue and white lozenges in a checkerboard pattern) and Palatine (a golden lion with red claws and red crown on black). These two provinces had long been joined, their combined coat of arms showing two lions and two sections of blue and white lozenges quartered, thus the two devices on the right and left triangles of this flag are not repetitions, but the separated portions of the traditional arms. In the upper red-striped triangle are the combined arms of Veldenz (a blue lion with red claws and a gold crown on white), and Hohnstein (checkerboard of red and white). In the lower triangle are the combined arms of Ribeaupierre (three red shields on white) and Hohenack, which were traditionally allied under a single prince (three black eagles' heads with gold crowns, on white).[5] Each shield with its various devices is surrounded by the collar of the Order of the Holy Spirit. The ducal crown and decorative mantling are the same on each coat of arms, on both drapeaux, showing an ermine interior and where the mantle turns toward the viewer, the arms of Hohnstein and Hohenack on one side and the arms of Bavaria and Palatine on the other. Because the mantle was imagined to have the full coat of arms on the reverse, a little bit of the blue lion of Veldenz and the golden lion of Palatine show where the mantle is rolled forward just below the crown. Due to their central position in the complete coat of arms, the three red shields of Ribeaupierre do not show up in any of the parts of the mantle facing the viewer.

Drawing for drapeau colonel, Regiment Royal Deux Ponts, dated 1757. Bibliothèque Nationale Française.

Drawing for drapeau d'ordonnance, Regiment Royal Deux Ponts, dated 1757. Bibliothèque Nationale Française.

Detail of the coat of arms of the Duc de Deux Ponts (Zweibrucken) as shown complete on the regiment's drapeau colonel and divided into quarters on the drapeau d'ordonnance.

Drapeau colonel, Regiment Royal Deux Ponts.

Drapeau d'ordonnance, Regiment Royal Deux Ponts.

Regiment Saintonge

Regiment Saintonge had been created in 1684 and was number eighty-five in seniority in the French Army in 1781. Its white drapeau colonel, and colored drapeau d'ordonnance, can be seen in van Blarenberghe's painting *Surrender at Yorktown.*

The drapeau d'ordonnance of Regiment Saintonge has the white cross with each of the four quarters divided into four triangles colored red, blue, green, yellow. The drapeaux colonel at this period probably had each quarter mimicking the drapeaux d'ordonnance with each canton divided into four triangles by white stitching on white. The positions of the colors within each quarter of the drapeaux d'ordonnance are usually shown with red opposite yellow, and blue opposite green, but as Gherardi Davis stated in 1907, "The sequence of these colors does not seem to be determined, and the flag is, therefore, differently colored in different books."

As implied by Davis, and noted in the general introduction, this need not suggest that different illustrations done at different times are incorrect, rather that the exact sequence of the colors was not important to identification of the regiment in line of battle. As noted in the introduction to the French drapeaux, it was not unknown for the square flags to be attached to their poles by the "wrong" edge. Considering the complexity of the construction of the Saintonge colors, all done by hand, it should not be surprising that many iterations made over many years might come out differently. With the four quarters all made alike (red opposite yellow and blue opposite green), there are four possible orientations, but since the silk can be flipped over, so instead of red being on the left and yellow on the right, yellow is on the left and red on the right, there are actually eight possibilities. With eight possible arrangements for each quarter, which theoretically could be repeated (some drawings show two of the four-color quarters in identical orientations), there are

Montigny's drawing of the uniform and drapeaux of Regiment Saintonge in 1772. Note that canton four, lower right, has the colors in a different arrangement from the other three, with green opposite yellow instead of the usual green opposite red. Note also the drapeau colonel with the cantons divided by stitching to mimic the colored drapeau d'ordonnance. Bibliothèque Nationale Française.

over four thousand possible arrangements of four four-color quarters to make one flag. If the sequence of colors is not always the same—if red can be opposite green and yellow opposite blue, or red opposite blue and yellow opposite green–the number of possible arrangements is astronomical.

The reconstruction here presented is based on van Blarenberghe's painting of the regiment at Yorktown, which is, perhaps not coincidentally, the same as the original drawing of 1721.

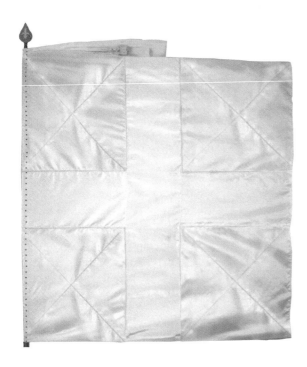

Drapeau colonel, Regiment Saintonge.

Drapeau d'ordonnance, Regiment Saintonge. Flag reproduction by author.

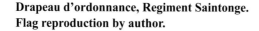

Regiment Soissonnais

Regiment Soissonnais was created in 1684 but amalgamated with Regiment Briqueville in 1762. While maintaining its original seniority, the regiment lost its original drapeaux, adopting those of the younger regiment. All original sources agree that the drapeau d'ordonnance of Soissonnais had cantons cut into triangles of red and black, displayed pinwheel fashion, with the red being along the staff in the first canton, and this is how it is portrayed in van Blarenberghe's painting of Yorktown. Richardson states that "The red had faded to a rose color by the time the regiment marched to Yorktown according to eyewitnesses," but does not site his source for this. Gherardi Davis, in his painting of this flag done in 1907 and published in *The American Heritage Book of the Revolution* in 1958, also shows a light rose color. According to the Tableau of 1771 and Montigny's plate of 1772, the drapeau colonel had the diagonals in each canton marked out by seams.

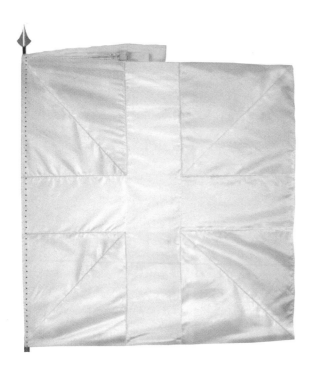

Drapeau colonel, Regiment Soissonnais.

Drapeau d'ordonnance, Regiment Soissonnais.

Regiment Touraine

Regiment Touraine served with Rochambeau's army and was present at the siege and surrender of Yorktown. Most original sources agree that the colors of the drapeaux d'ordonnance were aurora, blue, green, and red, in cantons one, two, three, and four, and this is how the flag was portrayed in van Blarenberghe's painting of the surrender ceremonies. Only two earlier sources disagree: the Tableau of 1771, and Montigny's plate of 1772. The drawing on the tableau is very badly colored, but seems to agree with the 1772 plate, which shows cantons as yellow, feuille morte, blue, red. The Tableau of 1773, however, again shows the earlier documented colors, and van Blarenberghe's painting confirms it.

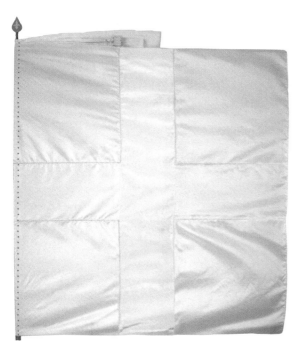

Drapeau colonel, Regiment Touraine.

Drapeau d'ordonnance, Regiment Touraine. Flag reproduction by author, currently on display at US National Guard Memorial Museum, Washington, DC.

Regiment Walsh

Regiment Walsh had originally been the Royal Irish Regiment of Foot Guards, but in 1688 had sided with the defeated King James and marched into exile in France. Accepted into the French Army in 1697, it was known by the name of each subsequent colonel, thus its drapeaux show up in different sources under different names. In 1721 it was known as Dorington, in 1748 and 1757 as Roth or Rooth, in 1766 as Roscommon, in 1770 as Walsh. It was probably at the time of the reorganization of all regiments to the two-battalion model in the 1760s that the drapeaux of the regiment were changed from their traditional Irish Guards pattern to a more standard French style with cantons of violet and feuille morte as shown in the Tableaus of 1771 and 1773, and Montigny's plate of 1772. (Montigny also says the reverse of the flag was blue.) In addition, there had been great difficulty in maintaining the regiment at full strength with Irish recruits, which may have influenced a withdrawal of the traditional Irish drapeaux. The regiment was even discontinued for a time in 1775.

Upon strenuous protest of the displaced Irish officers, however, the regiment was reconstituted in 1776. It seems likely that it was at this point the regiment was restored its traditional drapeaux. The drapeau colonel, white with a white cross, had in its center an English crown—distinguished by having crosses as well as fleur-de-lis on its rim—above the letters JR, for Jacobus Rex (King James), in large gold script. The drapeau d'ordonnance was white with a red cross of St. George, in the center an English crown surmounted by a crowned lion. The red cross on this drapeaux is sometimes shown with a white outline, like that on the drapeau d'ordonnance of Regiment Dillon. Early drawings and descriptions do not show such a detail however, and the word description in 1748 simply says white with a red cross, whereas the same source specifically states a red cross bordered in white for Regiment Dillon and the other Irish regiments.

Several fusilier companies of Regiment Walsh were part of the French combined assault column at Savannah in 1779. If these companies were landed as an intact battalion before being parceled out to the combined column, one of the drapeaux may have accompanied, but which one would depend on which companies were committed.

Drapeau colonel, Regiment Walsh.

Drapeau d'ordonnance, Regiment Walsh.

German Regimental Fahnen in North America

INTRODUCTION: GERMAN FAHNEN IN NORTH AMERICA, 1776–1783

Germany in the second half of the eighteenth century was not a unified nation, being made up of dozens of small principalities, each with its own military traditions, and several with sizable military establishments ready to be contracted out as needed. In general, these establishments followed one of two models: the Prussian system instituted under Frederick II of Prussia, or the older model of the Holy Roman Empire under the Austrian emperors in Vienna. German military colors, singular *Fahne*, plural *Fahnen*, but sometimes referred to collectively as *Feldzeichen*—literally "field signs," generally fell into one of these two styles as well, with Fahnen of Brunswick, Hesse-Cassel, and Hesse-Hanau closely following Prussian models, while those of Waldeck and Anhalt-Zerbst were apparently (no originals have survived) on the Austrian model. Anspach-Bayreuth was an outlier; its Fahnen were embroidered rather than painted and had a different design on each side.

A common denominator among all the German regiments was that each regiment had one Leibfahne (literally body flag, as in the English "bodyguard") carried by the Colonel's company, the first company of the first battalion, and three to four other flags, all the same, depending on the number of companies and battalions in the regiment. These were variously called Regimentsfahnen, sometimes Kompaniefahnen, and sometimes Ordinairefahnen, using one of the Frenchified military terms of the day. In most German/ Austrian regiments the Leibfahne was predominantly white, though in the Hesse-Cassel regiments in North America the single Leibfahne may have been simply a different color combination from the company flags (discussed in detail in the Hesse-Cassel section), which were all the same within each individual regiment, and generally—but not always—had some color relationship to the secondary color of the Leibfahne, or to the uniforms. In single-battalion regiments each line company had one Fahne. Grenadier companies or independently fielded companies of jaegers or light troops did not carry flags. In two-battalion regiments, such as the Anhalt-Zerbst regiment, there was a single Leibfahne and one Regimentsfahne in the first battalion and two Regimentsfahnen in the second battalion.

A Note on German Colors

In general, the colors used in German Fahnen were more or less bright primary colors and I have used the standard translations for red, green, blue, black, yellow, orange, and white. Of the colors mentioned in German sources that are unfamiliar or subject to interpretation are the following:

Pfirsichblüt: Literally "peach blossom," a deep, intense pink, rose, or fuchsia, often associated with the Erbprinz, or Crown Prince, of the Hessian territories. Sometimes translated as purple; but purple in modern English generally means violet—which pfirsichblüt is not.

Detail, *Battle of Trenton, December 26, 1776*, by Don Troiani, 2008, oil on canvas. Photo courtesy of the artist.

Paille: Literally "straw." A very light yellow.

Cramoisin/Karmesin: Crimson. A deep dark red, more intense and somewhat cooler or bluer than true red (*rot*).

Moosgrün: Moss green, a dark slightly grayish or olive green, used for Hessian Regiment Prinz Carl.

A Note on German Regimental Titles

German regiments throughout this period were known by the names of their colonels-in-chief, *Chef* in German, often a titled aristocrat or member of the reigning family. This officer was generally not the commander of the regiment in the field, although he might be in some other command position at brigade level or above, which included the regiment with his name. A few regiments were numbered by the jurisdictions which had raised them—the Waldeck Regiment, for example, was technically the Third Regiment of that principality—but these numerical designations were not used in British orders or correspondence. In general, the regimental names did not change during the course of the war, except in the Hessian service, where a number of regiments went through several name changes as their colonels-in-chief took responsibility for different regiments, were promoted above regimental level, or in the case of Regiment Rall, killed in action.

It should also be pointed out that the term "Hessian" was very loosely applied by American sources both during and after the war to apply to any German unit. Thus, one will often see references to Hessian troops and flags captured at Saratoga, where they were actually Brunswick/Braunschweig regiments, or Hessian colors taken at Yorktown, where eight of the eighteen Fahnen captured were actually from Anspach-Bayreuth.

A Note on Sources

In all, at least 114 German Fahnen were carried in North America during the American War of Independence— possibly a few more—but at least four from Anhalt-Zerbst, two from Waldeck, five from Hesse-Hanau, twenty from Braunschweig, seventy-five from Hesse-Cassel, and eight from Anspach-Bayreuth. Of these, thirty-five were captured, and of those, only six more or less complete flags remain, and scraps of five more. Of the seventy-nine returned to Germany, either by stealth, or through regular redeployment at the war's end, not a single German flag associated with the American War has survived.

Contemporary illustrations, documents, and other archival sources are discussed under the separate German headings.

Anhalt-Zerbst

Nothing at all has been recorded or found on this unit's Fahnen, except what might be concluded from its organization and traditions. The Anhalt-Zerbst Regiment was the most completely Austrian of any of the Auxiliary troops sent to America. It numbered only about 475 officers and men but was divided into two battalions as per the Austrian model and uniformed in white Austrian style uniforms. Presumably it carried four Fahnen, as other Austrian regiments in service to the Empire: one white Leibfahne and one colored

Regimentsfahne in the First Battalion, two colored Regimentsfahnen in the Second Battalion. This regiment was the last of the German Hilstruppen to come to America, arriving in Canada in 1778, and was not engaged in any active campaigns or battles.

Ansbach-Bayreuth

Ansbach-Bayreuth was several geographically separated small German states under one prince. The two largest, Ansbach and Bayreuth, were only joined under the Markgraf Christian Friedrich Carl Alexander of Brandenburg-Ansbach in 1769. Two regiments, each organized on the Prussian model of a single battalion, but with only four line companies each carrying one Fahne, were sent to America. The two regiments sent were nominally identified as one from each of the two domains, and sometimes called the First and Second Ansbach-Bayreuth, but as with other German regiments, they were more generally referred to by the names of their colonels, Voit and Seybothen. They were second-to-last of the Hilfstruppen to arrive in America, landing in New York in June 1777.

The two regiments served together, and both were present at the Battle of Newport, Rhode Island, where they may have advanced against the First Rhode Island Regiment, which had several companies of Black soldiers. There is no evidence whatsoever that there was a hand-to-hand scuffle over a flag of either of the Ansbach-Bayreuth regiments, however, nor was one captured, as suggested in a rather fanciful rendering readily found on the internet.

The traditional view, based on four remaining Fahnen of the eight originally captured at Yorktown, is that both regiments carried Fahnen of the same pattern and design. However, recent research suggests that the four nearly identical captured Fahnen may all have belonged to the Bayreuth Regiment, and that the Ansbach Regiment may have carried four Fahnen of an entirely different design, none of which have survived.

A nearly contemporary post-war painting of Hessian Major August Christian Noltenius at the Battle of Rhode Island includes small background depictions of German troops advancing under blue and red horizontally striped flags. The uniform Noltenius wears in the painting appears to be a somewhat later style than that worn in the American war, and nothing is known of the artist, though almost certainly he was not an eyewitness to the battle. Similar flags, some red and blue striped with a large cypher surrounded by a wreath, some red and blue striped with a red eagle at center, were illustrated in the German modeling magazine *Heer und Tradition* (date unknown, circa 1970?) under the title "*Infanteriefahnen—Muster in der Markgrafshaft Ansbach im 18. Jahrhundert*" (*Infantry Flags—Pattern of the Markgrafshaft of Ansbach in the Eighteenth Century*). The flags are of the style generally associated with German Fahnen of the Seven Years' War, and the cypher appears to be that of Markgraf Charles Wilhelm Friedrich, who died in 1757. An existing Ansbach-Bayreuth Fahne dating to after the American war is striped diagonally black and white. It is embroidered with the Prussian Order of the Red Eagle similar in style to the reverse of the Fahnen captured at Yorktown, and has Alexander's four initials C, F, C, A, in the corners. An undated military print labeled only "Preussinf-Regt-Nr-56-Ansbach" (Prussian Infantry Regiment No. 56-Ansbach) shows a contemporary soldier carrying the same Fahne, though the corner initials are not clear in the drawing. Alexander sold his lands to the king of Prussia in 1791 and the Ansbach Regiment became the Fifty-Sixth Regiment in the Prussian Army, at which point it received new Fahnen of the standard Prussian pattern, as verified in many references on Prussian flags of the period. Two more post-war Fahnen exist, identified to the Anspach-Bayreuth Regiment of 1785. The Kompaniefahne is similar to the reverse side of the Yorktown flags, with the red eagle and motto *PRO PRINCIPE ET PATRIA* (For Prince and Fatherland). It also has Alexander's initials in the corners. The Leibfahne of the regiment has a panoply of arms and flags painted at its center, including four—possibly five—striped flags: one black and white, one white and red, one white and blue, one red and blue, and one, almost hidden, of red and white. The motto is *PRINCEPS ET PATRIA*, meaning "Prince and Fatherland." Striped fields are so unusual among German flags, that the inclusion of them on this Fahne of the combined regiment might be a deliberate harking back to a tradition of striped Fahnen of different color combinations carried by Ansbach regiments in the past. Unfortunately, none of this gives enough information for a reasonable reconstruction of what Fahnen the Ansbach regiment may have carried in America—assuming they were not one or more of the surviving Fahnen captured at Yorktown—and there are no contemporary accounts describing them in any way.

Of the four Ansbach-Bayreuth Fahnen that were captured and still exist, they are unusual among German Fahnen in being embroidered rather than painted and being two-sided with a different design front and back. In overall appearance they hark back to the German patterns in vogue during the Seven Years' War rather than the more progressive Prussian-inspired Fahnen of Braunschweig and Hesse. Among the four that still exist, the only important distinction is that one is embroidered 1770, two are embroidered 1775, and on one the date is missing. The 1770 flag is made of figured silk of a different pattern, but the embroidery is virtually identical on all four. There is no way to tell whether any of these was considered a Leibfahne—maybe the one with the earlier date? A total of eight flags was captured from the two Ansbach-Bayreuth regiments, so it is also possible that there were two that would have stood out in some distinctive way as Leibfahnen but are not among those that have survived.

Each flag is two-sided, with a different embroidery on each side—in a sense they are two flags sewn back-to-back. Each is made of three panels of approximately eighteen and a half inches—the width of silks used in Prussian, Hessian, and presumably Braunschweig Fahnen—but sewn vertically rather than horizontally as one would expect. The innermost panel is cut about five inches narrower and the silk then used for the pole sleeve, so the flag flying is almost exactly square at fifty inches each direction. The 1770 flag *is* exactly square, the other three flags seem to be about two inches less on the staff.

The three intact Fahnen are nailed to their staffs, but not all the same—one of the 1775 flags has the nails in three rows, one row staggered, to give a checkerboard pattern all around the staff rather than a straight line up one or both sides. As with most German military flags, the tassels are suspended on a broad tape, in this case plaited or braided rather than woven, in silver, gold, and red. The tassels are typically German in shape, and in the same colors. The finials are fairly large, approximately nine inches tall, cast with Alexander's cypher.

The obverse of each flag has besides the crown, wreath, and date, the initials "M. Z. B." for *Markgraf Zu Brandenburg* and the large dramatic cypher "SETCA" for *SINCERE ET CONSTANTER ALEXANDER* from the motto of the Prussian Order of the Red Eagle, "Truthfully and Steadfastly," plus the name of the current Markgraf, Alexander. The reverse side of the flag shows the Red Eagle itself under the motto *PRO PRINCIPE ET PATRIA* (For Prince and Fatherland).

As Charles Willson Peale had done for Washington and the flags captured at Trenton in 1776, his brother James Peale did for Washington and the colors captured at Yorktown in 1781. Again, so far as is known, Peale had the original flags to work with. Sometime after the surrender, Congress gave at least one of the Ansbach-Bayreuth Fahnen, as well as one British colour, to General Washington and it remained in his family for many years. In the 1850s it was housed in the Grand Masonic Temple in Alexandria, Virginia. Then suddenly in about 1858 two more flags of identical design surfaced at West Point and the one in Alexandria was sent there as well. In 1900 the fourth flag was found in a box marked "unidentified" at West Point. Currently one of the 1775 Fahnen can be seen at West Point, one at the Smithsonian, and the 1770 Fahne at the Visitors Center at Yorktown. A very complete survey of the four Ansbach-Bayreuth Fahnen belonging to the federal government is James W. Lowry, *A Yorktown Surrender Flag—Symbolic Object*, published by National Park Service, Harpers Ferry, in 1989.

Ansbach-Bayreuth, obverse. This Fahne is shown in James Peale's portrait of Washington at Yorktown. (See entry for British 76th Regiment) Digital reconstruction from author's photos of original Fahnen on display at Smithsonian Institution, West Point, and Yorktown NBP.

Ansbach-Bayreuth, reverse. This Fahne is shown in James Peale's portrait of Washington at Yorktown. (See entry for British 76th Regiment) Digital reconstruction from author's photos of original Fahnen on display at Smithsonian Institution, West Point, and Yorktown NBP.

Detail of original on display at National Museum of American History, Smithsonian Institution, Washington, DC. The heavy metallic threads in the embroidery are greatly tarnished and the reds and greens faded. Note the floral pattern of the silk damask. These flags were seamed top-to-bottom, probably to line up the patterns, like hanging wallpaper. Photo by author.

Detail display at Yorktown NBP. It is impossible to tell how deep the reds were originally, though similar flags with painted eagles are a fairly deep scarlet or madder red. Here the eagle was done with several different colors of thread; the breast and tops of the wings are considerably lighter than the body and flight feathers. The greens, blues, and black, are close to their original colors. Note the floral pattern of the silk damask. Photo by author.

Ansbach/Bayreuth finial, watercolor by Gherardi Davis. Gherardi Davis papers, Manuscripts and Archives Division, The New York Public Library.

Ansbach/Bayreuth finial, pencil rubbing of original, from Gherardi Davis papers, Manuscripts and Archives Division, The New York Public Library. From tip to bottom center where it originally was attached to ferrule, spearpoint is five inches. Overall height of finial approximately eleven inches.

Braunschweig (Brunswick)

The Fahnen of Braunschweig are fairly well authenticated, even though no originals have survived. Braunschweig-Wolfenbüttel was a middling-sized principality in northwest Germany, bordering on Hanover, the ancestral home of the English Kings George. Braunschweig was the first of the German states to conclude a treaty with Britain for Hilfstruppen. It had a strong military tradition and had been allied with Britain in the Seven Years' War. During the American War of Independence, Braunschweig contributed four infantry regiments and one dismounted regiment of dragoons.

Braunschweig regimental Fahne, Model 1754. This example is one of the four Regimentsfahnen of the Regiment Prinz Friedrich. Flag reproduction by author.

In 1754 the Braunschweig forces were reorganized and re-equipped on the Prussian model. This included regiments of a single battalion of five line companies, each carrying one Fahne, and one of grenadiers—for a total of approximately six hundred fifty officers and men. The grenadier companies were separated from their parent regiments and formed into a combined battalion of grenadiers, which did not carry Fahnen. The new Fahnen of the Braunschweig infantry were modeled very exactly on the Prussian. Like the Prussian, and unlike almost all modern representations which show them as square, the new flags were slightly taller on the staff than wide, the proportion being approximately seven to six. Each was made of three silk panels approximately eighteen and a half inches wide, for a total height of fifty-five to fifty-six inches when finished, and a width of about forty-six to forty-eight inches. In the center was a large red oval—almost universally portrayed too small in later paintings and prints—featuring the white horse of Hanover (also known as Welfenross, from the ancient Guelph or Welf family of Saxony, Hanover, Lunebourg, and Braunschweig). The horse is displayed "courrant," that is, running or leaping, with the hind legs on a green mound and the front legs roughly together and extended. According to the normal rules of heraldry, the horse should be running to dexter, its own right or the viewer's left, but the earliest depictions of the Prussian-style flags introduced in 1754 show the horse running toward the fly end of the flag. Perhaps this too was in imitation of the Prussian Fahnen in which the Royal eagle is always shown racing toward the fly. Above the horse on the Braunschweig Fahnen was the motto in a scroll, *NUNQUAM RETRORSUM* (Never Backward), the whole surmounted by a crown and surrounded by a Prussian-style wreath in gold or silver, depending on the buttons and cap-fronts of the regiment. The Brunswick crown in this period is always portrayed with white ermine below the traditional red velvet interior. The wreath was painted over the seam that joined the central red panel to the field of the flag. Four undulating blazes or flames of a contrasting color, their points just touching the seam holding the central oval, radiated out to right and left, top and bottom, forming a cross. Each of these blazes had a stylized flaming grenade, all with the flames pointing inwards. In later and modern drawings these are often made to look like a ball with flames shooting out, but originals both Prussian and Hessian depict them looking more like comets, or even jellyfish. In each corner of the flag was the cypher of the hereditary prince, Carl 1, also crowned and surrounded by a wreath. In line with the Prussian models, these would have been much closer to the corners than in most illustrations. As the cypher was two capitals "C" entwined and reversed, it was identical in each corner and appeared the same as seen from either the front or the back of the flag. Like the Prussian and Hessian Fahnen, all the gold or silver elements on the flags—crowns, wreaths, grenades—were outlined in black and had black or brown shading.

As in other German regiments, the Braunschweig Leibfahne and Regimentsfahnen were different colors. Unlike the Hessian Fahnen, there is mostly agreement on the colors of flags of the Braunschweig regiments. Gherardi Davis received a listing from the Vaterländisches Museum zu Braunschweig (Braunschweig Archives) in 1907 of the colors of the Regimentsfahnen but not the Leibfahnen. It was probably understood that the Leibfahnen in every case was white, so from the descriptions of the regimental Fahnen, it would be relatively clear what the accompanying Leibfahne would be. In the case of the Regimentsfahnen having black ground and yellow cross for example (Regiment Prinz Friedrich), the Leibfahne would be white with the same yellow cross. In the case of the two regiments that had a white cross, their Leibfahnen could not have white crosses on a white ground, so the cross was instead the same color as the ground color. According to Georg Ortenburg's in-depth study of Braunschweig troops from the seventeenth through the nineteenth centuries, all the Leibfahnen were white with the cross of a secondary identifying color.[1] His listing of the Regimentsfahnen is identical to Braunschweig Archives list as received and published by Davis in 1907. Herbert Knötel, better known to American military historians from his work done mostly in the first half of the twentieth century, believed that the Leibfahnen followed the Prussian model in simply reversing the two primary colors—ignoring the fact that Prussian Fahnen also

Braunschweig corner cypher. All such ornamental elements in either gold or silver were outlined in black—which of course does not show well on the black flag.

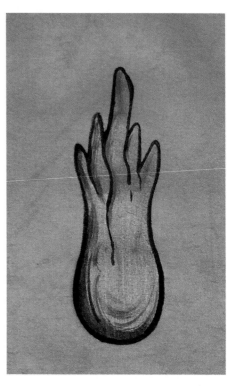

German-style flaming grenade as portrayed on Prussian, Hessian, Braunschweig Fahnen from 1750s through end of the First World War. As each was individually hand-painted, they all vary a bit in the wavy flames and the shading.

reversed the color of the central panel on which the Prussian eagle was displayed, while the Braunschweig Fahnen always had a red central panel for the white horse of Hanover. He suggested that Leibfahne of the Regiment Prinz Friedrich, for example, would have been yellow with a black cross, whereas Ortenburg says it was white with the same yellow cross as the four Regimentsfahnen.

Each flag was sleeved with a single color matching the field of the flag and mounted on a staff with brass (or silvered?) nails about one inch apart. Whether nails were on one side or both sides of the staff is unknown. Since the flags were sleeved, it would only take one or two nails at the top to keep them on the pole; the long row (or rows) of nails was traditional and decorative rather than necessary. The staff was approximately ten feet tall including the cast brass spear. This was leaf-shaped, with an open-work representation of the crowned cypher, apparently closely copied from Prussian models but with the "FR" for Friedrich Rex replaced with the double "C" for Carl. Whether these were gilded or silvered to follow the metal of each regiment is unknown. The smaller and more complex finial shown in many secondary illustrations of Braunschweig infantry Fahnen actually belongs only to the standards of the dragoons. (Contrarywise, some reconstructions of the dragoon standards imagine them with an infantry-style leaf-shaped spear.) Each Fahne was accompanied by tassels on a bullion ribbon approximately one inch wide, and about half the height of the flag. This is sometimes shown tied in a bow, sometimes merely hanging down. Although there are no contemporary records to verify their color, they are generally shown as silver with gold highlights.

Re-created Braunschweig finial, based on original drawings and existing Prussian models. Approximately nine and a half inches. Silver and gold tape at base of finial is for the tassels. German tassels were traditionally suspended on a broad tape or ribbon rather than cord.

German-style tassels, traditionally portrayed in silver and gold for Braunschweig regiments. Approximately eight and a half inches from top of bead to bottom of fringe. Reproduction by author. Ansbach tassels are very similar except in black and gold.

Three Braunschweig regiments—von Riedesel, von Rhetz, and Specht—along with the Hesse-Hanau regiment, were captured at Saratoga. The commander of the German forces, General Riedesel, was accompanied by his wife, who left a very complete diary of the entire adventure. With the terms of the capitulation somewhat in dispute, the flags of all the German regiments were reported as burnt and not given up to the Americans. In fact, the staffs only were burned, the silk Fahnen and their accompanying tassels hidden away in a mattress in Madame Riedesel's baggage, which was not searched as she accompanied the army into captivity. These made their way with Madame Riedesel back to Braunschweig in 1783 and were deposited in the state arsenal. What became of them thereafter is not known, though it is suspected they were burned with "der anderen Fahnenbeute," the other flag-booty, in Paris in 1814.

The Prinz Friedrich regiment had been left behind to garrison Ticonderoga and was not part of the Saratoga convention; presumably their Fahnen were also returned to Braunschweig at the end of the war and lost or burnt with the others during the Napoleonic period.

Braunschweig also sent a regiment of dragoons, which was deployed dismounted as a light battalion. It is generally agreed that this unit took four swallow-tailed standards (Standarten—there was no German word for guidon at the time), one per squadron, but that these were not used in the field. The Braunschweig Archives sent Davis black-and-white drawings and detailed descriptions including the colors of the various parts of the design. All four standards were blue silk and were painted, not embroidered. They were two-sided, with the coat of arms of Braunschweig on the obverse, crowned and in a gold laurel wreath, and the white horse of Hannover in the same wreath on the reverse. The horse was painted directly on the blue silk—no red background. In each corner was a gold heraldic rose. The exact size is uncertain. If each was made of one and a half widths of the standard silks used throughout Germany for infantry Fahnen, like two existing Hessian standards of roughly the same period, they would be approximately twenty-six inches on the lance. This seems reasonable and would put them entirely in line with standards and guidons of most other European nations at the time. Each standard had a pole sleeve and a row of nails like the infantry Fahnen. They had neither fringe nor cord and tassels. Judging from the size of the standards in the drawings, the lances were probably about eight feet long, and topped with a tall spear of a more compact but intricate design than the infantry. The spear was gilded. The pole was not a smooth shaft from top to bottom but had handhold portions turned into the wood. It is not known whether there was a bar for a slide-ring to attach to a guidon-bearer's bandolier; these were gradually going out of style as the century neared its end. What became of these standards after the war is unknown.

Regiment Prinz Friedrich

The Fahnen of the Regiment Prinz Friedrich were a Leibfahne white with yellow cross, and four Regimentsfahnen of black with yellow cross. Both Ortenburg and the Braunschweig Archives correspondence with Davis in 1907 agree on this. The wreath, crowns, and grenades were all painted in gold. Some

Leibfahne, Regiment Prinz Friedrich.
Regimentsfahnen, Regiment Prinz Friedrich.

sources mistakenly follow Herbert Knötel's belief that the Braunschweig Fahnen followed the Prussian system of reversing the colors for Leib- and Regimentsfahnen, showing the Leibfahne yellow with black cross, while others seem to agree that the Leibfahne was indeed white, but depict it with a black cross.

Ensign Julius Friedrich von Hille mentioned in his journal of his having raised the Leibfahne of the Prinz Friedrich Regiment over the ramparts of Fort Ticonderoga when it was evacuated by American troops and occupied by the British and Braunschweig Army on July 6, 1777. Prinz Friedrich remained at Ticonderoga during the subsequent campaign that ended with the surrender at Saratoga, thus its Fahnen were neither surrendered nor burned nor hidden, and presumably were returned to Braunschweig at the end of the war, but subsequently lost.

Regiment von Rhetz

The Leibfahne of Regiment von Rhetz was white with a green cross, the Regimentsfahnen green with white cross. Ortenburg and the Braunschweig Archives' response to Gherardi Davis in 1907 both agree on this. The wreath, crowns, and grenades were painted in silver. Somewhere along the line Herbert Knötel suggested that the Fahnen of this regiment were white with blue cross and blue with white cross, and this combination has been copied in many secondary sources. These are sometimes shown with the traditional Braunschweig light blue (hellblau), sometimes with dark. Ortenburg's complete list of Braunschweig regiments of the period includes the Leibregiment, which did not serve in America, as having a Leibfahne of white with blue (blau) cross and Regimentsfahnen of blue with white cross. Ortenburg also states

Leibfahne, Regiment von Rhetz.

Regimentsfahnen, Regiment von Rhetz.

categorically that all the Leibfahnen were white with different colored crosses and identifies a white with light blue (hellblau) cross as belonging to Regiment von Riedesel. Knötel believed that the colors of the Leib- and Regimentsfahnen were simply reversed, as in the Prussian system. A yellow and light blue combination for the Regiment von Riedesel was fairly well established, as was black and yellow for Prinz Friedrich and red for Specht. So presumably with the Prussian model in mind, Knötel identified a white Leibfahne with blue cross as belonging to the fourth regiment to serve in America, von Rhetz, and then further surmised that Regimentsfahnen of blue flags with white cross must accompany. However, the blue/white combination actually belonged to the Leibregiment, which was never in America. Apparently Knötel was completely unaware of any green Fahnen. Regiment von Rhetz was captured at Saratoga, and its Fahnen were among those hidden in Madame Riedesel's baggage and returned to Braunschweig in 1783, but these had disappeared long before Knötel was doing his research.

Regiment von Riedesel

The Fahnen of Regiment von Riedesel were white Leibfahne with light blue (hellblau) cross, and four Regimentsfahnen of yellow, also with the light blue cross. The wreath, crowns, and grenades were painted in silver. When Davis corresponded with the Braunschweig Archives in 1907, he received an illustration of one of the von Riedesel yellow and blue Fahnen as an example of the pattern which all the Braunschweig infantry Fahnen followed. The von Riedesel Fahnen were among those spirited away by Madame von Riedesel after the surrender at Saratoga.

Leibfahne, Regiment Riedesel.

Regimentsfahnen, Regiment Riedesel.

Regiment von Specht

The Fahnen of Regiment von Specht were a white Leibfahne with red cross, and four red Regimentsfahnen with white cross. There seems to be no controversy among sources for this regiment. The wreath, crowns, and grenades were painted in gold. The Fahnen of Regiment von Specht were among those spirited away in the baggage of Madame Riedesel after the surrender at Saratoga in 1777.

Leibfahne, Regiment von Specht.

Regimentsfahnen, Regiment von Specht.

Braunschweig Dragoons

The Braunschweig Regiment of Dragoons brought four Standarten (standards or guidons) to America, one per squadron, but as the regiment fought dismounted as light infantry there was no tactical use for them, and they were thus left in garrison in Canada or possibly Ticonderoga. Presumably these standards were returned to Braunschweig in 1783 and lost with all other Braunschweig Fahnen during the Napoleonic wars.

These standards are often portrayed in secondary works in the style of those used by Prussian cavalry of the period—swallow-tailed, embroidered, and heavily fringed—with the white horse on a red field at center and the reigning prince's cypher in the four corners. However, the Braunschweig Archives sent Gherardi Davis in 1907 a very detailed drawing of both sides of these standards as well as description of all the colors of the component design. Apart from being traditional Braunschweig light blue, these differ in almost every detail from the imagined Prussian-style guidons. The letter to Davis specifically notes that they were painted, not embroidered. They were two-sided, with the coat of arms of Braunschweig on the obverse, crowned and in a gold laurel wreath, and the white horse of Hanover in the same wreath on the reverse. The wreath is tied with a red ribbon below the Braunschweig arms on the obverse, with a white ribbon below the horse on the reverse. The horse was painted directly on the blue silk rather than on a red background like the infantry Fahnen. In each corner was a gold heraldic rose. (Details on size, construction, and lance are in the introduction to the Braunschweig section.)

The guidons shown here are colorized versions of the drawing sent to Gherardi Davis in 1907.

Standarten, Prinz Ludwig Dragoons (obverse). Gherardi Davis papers, Manuscripts and Archives Division, The New York Public Library. Photo by author.

Standarten, Prinz Ludwig Dragoons (reverse). Gherardi Davis papers, Manuscripts and Archives Division, The New York Public Library. Photo by author.

Hesse-Cassel

Hesse-Cassel was a smallish German principality, entire population a little over 350,000, of which approximately 7 percent were in the Hessian military, either active regiments or garrison. Of all the German states, Hesse-Cassel sent by far the greatest number of soldiers to America, some fifteen regiments of infantry, four battalions of grenadiers, a small corps of jägers, and a contingent of artillery. Each of the fifteen infantry regiments carried five Fahnen, one per line company. The companies were administrative units only; in line of battle the battalion was deployed as eight platoons, with the five flags massed at the center. Hessian records make clear that the five garrison regiments sent to America, including Grenadier Regiment Rall, which despite its uniforms and title was equipped and treated as any other infantry battalion, were brought to the same standards as the field regiments in all arms, accoutrements, and flags. Of this total of seventy-five Hessian flags in America, twenty-five were captured—fifteen with three regiments at Trenton, and ten belonging to two regiments at Yorktown. Of these, two fairly complete flags and scraps of at least five others still exist in Philadelphia. Due to this, most of the common physical characteristics of the Fahnen can be very accurately known or reconstructed. There is considerable dispute and discontent, however, over just which regiments had flags of which colors, as well as whether the Leibfahnen were all white, or were different colors for the different regiments.

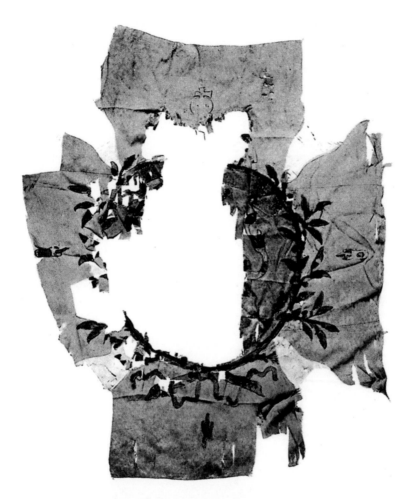

Remnant of Hessian Fahne captured at Trenton. Photograph by Gherardi Davis, 1907. When background was removed for original publication, the interior of the large crown was mistakenly cut away also. In reality, the faded green silk is still intact above the motto scroll, but all traces of paint have been lost.

The Hessian Fahnen, like those of Braunschweig, were based very closely on the Prussian. They were constructed in exactly the same way as Prussian Fahnen—three panels of eighteen-and-a-half-inch silk sewn selvage to selvage, and a large oval cartouche in the center, surrounded by a painted wreath that covered the seams. The overall size is fifty-five inches on the pike by forty-six-plus-inches wide. The eckflamen (corner blazes), on those that had them, come to a point just where they meet the central panel. Each Fahne had a pole sleeve of the same color as the field of the flag. This was a separate piece, the flag with (or without) eckflammen was not simply rolled around the pole and sewn down. In the quarters of the flag to the right, left, and below the central wreath was a flaming grenade. These are sometimes portrayed in secondary sources as a ball with flames shooting out, and in the Thalmann plates (addressed below) they look like tulips. They are probably meant to look like a round grenade flying through the air completely enveloped in flame.

Hessian regimental Fahne, first in use circa 1770. This example is one of the four Kompaniefahnen of the Regiment Rall. Note that flaming grenades are even more simplified than the Prussian Fahnen they were modeled on, as seen on Braunschweig Fahnen. Flag reproduction by author, currently on display at George Washington Museum, Mount Vernon, Virginia.

The eckflamen are all cut to identical shape, but, like Prussian models, two are reversed, and the corner cyphers—FL for Friedrich Landgraf—are also reversed, so that two read correctly as seen from either side of the flag. Unlike many contemporary and later drawings, the wreaths surrounding the corner cyphers overlap the edges of the eckflammen and extend a little into the differently colored field of the flag. The small crowns on the corner cyphers ought to have been filled with red, but there seems to be no trace of red paint on the white silk of the remaining captured flags in Philadelphia. The interior of the large crown above the wreath ought to be red as well, and perhaps it was on most Hessian Fahnen, but Charles Willson Peale had the original captured flags to work with on his monumental paintings of *Washington at Princeton*, and he portrays them as being gold inside. Gherardi Davis inspected both the original Fahnen in Philadelphia as well as Peale's paintings in 1907 and also concluded that the interior of the crown was gold. Perhaps this varied depending on the whim of the painter—the lions on the two remaining flags, while having identical outlines, are painted with the red and white stripes in very different positions. While the small crowned wreaths in the corners are virtually identical in size and arrangement of all details to the Prussian models, the central wreath and cartouche on the Hessian Fahnen is considerably bigger, twenty-six by twenty-two inches on the Hessian versus only twenty-two by nineteen on the Prussian. The crown is also bigger—and with the larger center panel and larger crown, there is simply no room for a flaming grenade in the top quarter of the Hessian flags. Letters from the Hessian Archives sent to Davis in 1907 list the silver or gold metal associated with the uniforms of each regiment—their buttons and cap-fronts. Like the Braunschweig and Prussian flags, the wreaths, cyphers, and grenades on the Hessian Fahnen followed the color of the metal of each regiment's uniforms. Contemporary illustrations suggest that on the Hessian flags, however, the crowns were always gold, even where the wreaths and other details were silver. On the Thalmann plates (described below) the wreaths and grenades are always silver, the crowns and cyphers always gold. We know this is incorrect however as the remnants of three original Fahnen in Philadelphia all have central and corner wreaths, plus grenades, in gold, agreeing with the metal uniform details of the regiments to which they belonged. A series of plates made in 1785 shows the large and small wreaths, whether gold or silver, as having green leaves intermixed, but no portion of any fragment of the original Fahnen in Philadelphia shows any trace of green, either whole leaves or any secondary highlights or shading. Like their Prussian models, the leaves are painted solid in either gold or silver (all the captured flags had gold), outlined in black, with details and shadows added in deep brown or black.

Hessian corner cypher. All such ornamental elements in either gold or silver were outlined in black. Note that wreath extends into the colored field of flag. Only one crown still exists from the flags taken at Trenton. There is no evidence, not even reddish stain on the white silk, of the interior of the crown being red.

The reproductions shown in this book are made from tracings of the two originals in Philadelphia. For some unknown reason, the head of the Hessian Lion is turned to the rear. In heraldic terms he is rampant regardant. This was not the case in earlier—nor again in later—versions of Hessian flags, but it is shown in the earliest contemporary illustrations from this period, and in Peale's paintings of the captured flags. It is currently impossible to tell from the remains of the two originals in Philadelphia; it was suggested by a conservator in the 1990s that they had been "mechanically laundered," which caused additional paint loss since the photographs by Davis in 1907. Purists may note that a heraldically "correct" version of the lion ought to start with white at the top, and that is how it is shown in contemporary illustrations of the Fahnen, but three existing Hessian cavalry standards, contemporary portraits of Landgraf Friedrich with a standard and Fahne in the background, and Peale's paintings taken from the original flags captured at Trenton, all show the stripes starting with red at the top of the lion's head. It should also be noted that the Hessian Lion in heraldry is described as striped in silver and red, but on flags it was virtually always portrayed as white and red.

Washington at Princeton, **by Charles Willson Peale, original painted 1779. As many as nine full-sized copies were painted by Peale within a few years, as well as several of just the upper three-quarters of the composition, which do not show the flags at Washington's feet. It is difficult to sort out just how many individual flags are portrayed. But at least one white Leibfahne, and—depending on the count—either one or two green Kompaniefahnen of Regiment Rall, plus either two or three black Fahnen of von Knyphausen, are visible. Note that in this painting, possibly the first copy done by Peale, the motto on the black Fahne on the ground is lettered "PERCULA" while the other visible flag has the correctly spelled "PERICULA."**
Public domain, US Senate Chamber, United States Capitol, Washington DC.

The lion wears not a full crown, but a ducal coronet, as in heraldic portrayals of the Hessian Lion going back to the fifteenth century. Another interesting detail corroborated by Peale's paintings is that the motto *NESCIT PERICULA* traditionally translated as "ignorant of fear" or "knows no fear" is misspelled *NESCIT PERCULA* on some of the flags. Peale's first paintings of the Trenton flags show this misspelling, and it is misspelled the same way on one of the illustrations done of the flags returned to Germany after the war. Someone with a better knowledge of Latin than Peale apparently pointed this out, and it was corrected in later copies of Washington with the captured flags. But Peale had seen the original Fahnen, not the German illustrations. Apparently at least some of the flags actually did have the Latin motto misspelled, a not entirely uncommon mistake among flags individually hand-painted in great numbers.

The Hessian Fahnen were nailed to their staffs with a row of forty to fifty nails down each side of the pole sleeve, through a reinforcing ribbon or tape that matched the color of the sleeve. The staffs were untampered, about an inch and a quarter in diameter. Some illustrations suggest that they were painted white for some regiments; surviving staffs of Hessian guidons and most other German infantry Fahnen are simply stained or varnished a deep brown. The staff was topped with a brass finial with Friedrich's cypher and crown. As with so much else, most of the originals have been lost—some were among French war trophies burned and thrown into the Seine in 1814, later fished out and put on display at the Invalides where they were drawn in 1904, but then lost again in World War II. At least one crude finial made by cutting or stamping through sheet metal exists and has been published online. The finial shown here, from a private collection in Germany, is virtually identical to the contemporary Prussian models, with only the crown slightly modified and the FR of Friedrich Rex replaced with FL for Friedrich Landgraf.

But again, we have a mystery embodied in Peale's paintings, for Peale portrays very odd finials on the flags. And again, we must remember that he had the originals. In 2008 an amateur historian

Original Hessian finial, private collection, Germany. Courtesy German PC Hans Eichel. Two identical finials of this pattern were at one time in the collections of *Les Invalides*, drawings published in *Les Trophees de la France*, 1907. Overall height nine and a half inches.

digging around a British Revolutionary War campsite at Monck's Corner, South Carolina, found the very spear—identical to Peale's painting. What it was doing in South Carolina is not known, there were very few Hessians ever in the vicinity, but there is little doubt that this is what Peale painted. And it appears on the flags of two regiments, both old and new—Knyphausen's had been on the Hessian establishment for years, and Rall's had been "promoted" from a garrison regiment to a regular field regiment at the time of the subsidy treaty with Britain and equipped like all other field units.

All Fahnen were accompanied by red tassels with silver or gold details, probably suspended on a broad ribbon or tape like other German Fahnen. Based on studies of Hessian uniforms, and as shown in contemporary illustrations, it has been suggested that all regiments should have tassels of red and silver, as it is known that all Hessian officers' sashes had tassels of red and silver regardless of the metal associated with their individual regiments. An original tassel in the First Troop Philadelphia City Cavalry Museum appears to be red and gold, though due to its age and the propensity for silver to tarnish and vary in color, it is difficult to tell whether it may have originally been red and silver.

As mentioned above, there is considerable disagreement as to the colors of the Fahnen carried by the individual Hessian regiments in North America. Gherardi Davis corresponded with Hessian archivists in Cassel and Marburg in 1907 and came up with a list in which the Leibfahne carried by each regiment is a different color from the Kompaniefahnen, but not white—just different, the colors reversed, or a new color added. Recent scholarship and reconsideration of the known sources by Frédéric Aubert in France, assisted

Hessian tassel from one of the Fahnen taken at Trenton. It is not certain whether this is red and gold or red and silver. The fringe is somewhat shorter than extant Ansbach and Prussian tassels; the overall length of the Hessian tassel is about eight inches. Photo courtesy of J. Craig Nannos, Curator, First Troop Philadelphia City Cavalry Museum, Philadelphia.

by Michael Zahn in Germany, however, make a good case that the Leibfahne was white in every regiment and only the Kompaniefahnen were various colors.

There are four basic contemporary or near-contemporary sources for Hessian Fahnen, and one mid-twentieth century source that must be taken into account as its author and artist are better-known in European military history circles. First, the so-called *Fahnenbuch*, dated 1783, was consulted by the Ducal Archives in Cassel and cited by Gherardi Davis. This book in Cassel comprised a number of unbound plates, and according to the archivists who corresponded with Davis, did not include flags of the five regiments captured in America. In some cases, the pictures had been "updated" sometime after 1785 by overpainting the "FL" in each corner with "WL" for Wilhelm Landgraf, Friedrich's successor. The paints appear to be opaque watercolors, much chipped and probably discolored a century and a quarter after they had been made. Only one picture from the Fahnenbuch survives, as a plate in Davis's book, and that one is not in color—the Fahnenbuch itself apparently did not survive World War II. It is not known whether the original plates were labeled with regimental names, and it is not clear how the archivists in Cassel ascertained which flags belonged to which regiment. Nonetheless, a letter sent to Davis in 1907 described twelve Fahnen belonging to six regiments. No declaration was made as to which was the Leib- and which

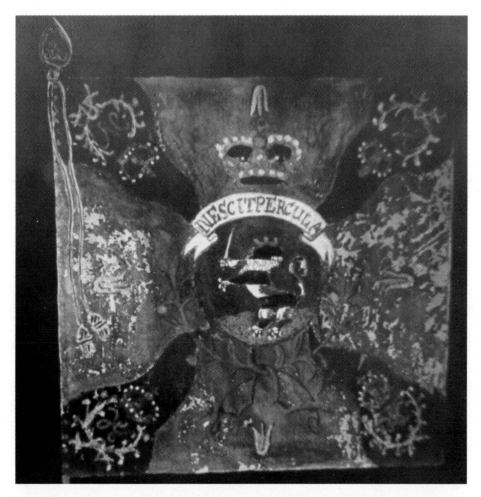

Only known plate to survive in any form from "Fahnenbuch," in Hessian Archives before World War II. Notice Latin motto *PERICULA* is misspelled *PERCULA*, also that cyphers "FL" in corners have been overpainted with "WL." Photo Gherardi Davis, from *Regimental Colors in the War of the Revolution*.

the Kompaniefahnen in each case. Included on the list were three that do not show up in any other compilation—moss green with red corner blazes, light yellow with blue corner blazes, and dark yellow with blue corner blazes. Two of these might reasonably be assigned to other regiments, however, as will be discussed in the individual unit entries. It is unfortunate that the Fahnenbuch has been lost. There is reason to believe that some of the flags described by the Cassel archivists and Davis did in fact represent Fahnen of regiments captured in America, that some may have belonged to garrison regiments, and that others may have been so faded or discolored that they were simply not recognized for what they originally were. The original correspondence between Davis and the Hessian archivists is in the manuscript collections of the New York Public Library.

The second source is a series of plates by G. F. Thalmann, in the library of the Hessischen Staatsarchiv Marburg. Titled *Abbildung und Beschreibung des Fürstlich Hessen-Casselischen Militair-Staates unter der Regierung Landgraf Friedrich des zweiten, bis zum Jahre 1786, gezeichnet von G. F. Thalmann* (*Illustration and Description of the Princely Hesse-Cassel Military State under the Reign of Landgrave Friedrich II up to 1786, drawn by G. F. Thalmann*), the folio includes some 534 pages comprising four components: historical text, uniform plates, Fahnen plates, and what might be called "allegorie" or "monument" illustrations, each of which shows what appears to be a tombstone or monument with the date of the founding of the regiment and two flags belonging to that regiment crossed over the stone. Not all regiments of the Hessian establishment are shown in all three illustration categories—full-page flag pictures are included for only nine of the fifteen regiments that served in America—no Fahnen are shown for the five garrison regiments or for Infantry Regiment von Donop. The nine full-page flag drawings have been re-colored and individually reprinted many times in many versions, in books and online. The nine Fahnen plates, and uniform plates of all fifteen regiments that served in America, were collected and published in a limited series in 1976/1977 for the bicentennial of the Hessian entry into the American War by Hans-Enno Korn, under the title *Fahnen und Uniformen der Landgräflich Hessen-Kassel'schen Truppen im Amerikanischen Unabhängigkeitskrieg 1776–1783* (*Flags and Uniforms of the Landgraf Hesse-Cassel Troops in the American War of Independence, 1776–1783*). The Thalmann plates show only one Fahne for each of the included regiments. Korn suggested that these represented the Leibfahne of each regiment, but most other researchers assume they are the Kompaniefahnen. The 1786 date in the title of the Thalmann collection seems to be accurate as reflected in the names of the regiments, several of which changed in the years after the war. However, many of the uniforms shown are those worn before 1783, and the title clearly states that it is intended as a history *up to* 1786, not a snapshot of what was currently to be seen in the Hessian military, so the plates may be reasonably supposed to show the flags as they appeared sometime shortly after the regiments' return. These two lists, the Fahnenbuch and the Thalmann Fahnen pictures, along with Gherardi Davis's book and supplement of 1908–1910, were used throughout most of the twentieth century as primary sources for information and illustration. The monument plates in Thalmann were generally overlooked, as in most cases they showed only a plain white flag and a plain single-color flag, loosely furled on the staff, without any details.

Taken as a separate source (the third of our four), however, the monument plates in the Thalmann collection lend support to the idea that all Hessian regiments—like those of Braunschweig and Hannover, and most, but certainly not all, Prussian regiments—carried a white Leibfahne and variously colored Kompaniefahnen. (An important caveat is that the white Leibfahnen of Braunschweig and most of those of Prussia were white with an additional color related to the company flags of the regiment. Of Hessian Fahnen in contemporary illustrations there are indeed all-white Leibfahnen, but not a single one showing white with another color in the eckflammen, or corner blazes.)

While the monument Fahnen are depicted only as furled flags with little or no detail, each clearly shows a predominant color, and with few exceptions that color is identical to the fourth commonly encountered

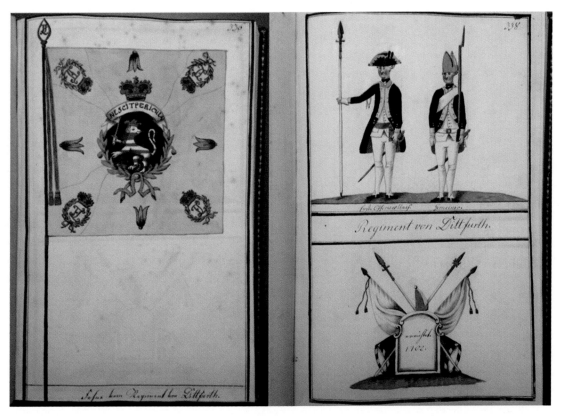

Pages from Thalmann's *Abbildung und Beschreibung des Fürstlich Hessen-Casselischen Militair-Staates* **unter der Regierung Landgraf Friedrich des zweiten, bis zum Jahre 1786,** **showing Fahnen plate and accompanying uniform and "monument" plates. Hessischen Staatsarchiv Marburg.**

source, *Abbildüng derer Uniformen von dem Hochfürstl: Hess: Casselischen* (*Illustrations of the Uniforms of the High-Princely Hesse-Cassel Military*). This series of fifty-two plates was made circa 1785–1786, based on the regimental titles. It shows each Hessian regiment of infantry and cavalry, plus general staff and engineers, each on a separate plate. The originals were held by the Grand Ducal Cabinet Library of Darmstadt until destroyed in an air raid in 1945. For this reason, the collection is generally called the "Darmstädter Handschrift" (manuscript). Some of the original plates had been copied circa 1921 by Ferdinand Rasher, a German uniform researcher. Some plates were known only as black-and-white photos. At least six of the Rasher plates are in the Anne S. K. Brown Military Collections, Brown University Library, and some were in the estate of Herbert Knötel in Germany. Several of these can be found online. A more complete copy had been made, however, in 1912–1913, by a German soldier/artist known only as "Mick." This too, had been lost, but then rediscovered in 1998. In 1999 it was published in Potsdam, in full color, by Georg Ortenburg as *Das Militär der Landgrafschaft Hessen-Kassel zwischen 1783 und 1789* (*The Military of the Landgraviate Hessen-Kassel between 1783 and 1789*). Each regimental plate of the series shows officers and soldiers in variations of the regimental uniforms and one Leibfahne and one Kompaniefahne, all on a single page. Unlike Thalmann, the series does not intend to be a historical narrative, rather a snapshot of the appearance of the Landgraf's troops at that moment—1785–1786. As depicted in all of these plates, the Fahnen so poorly reflect the actual flags—they are the wrong shape, do not have wavy corner blazes, have the lion walking toward the fly, have wreaths not remotely like the real ones, have all the "FL" cyphers reading correctly regardless of whether on front or reverse of flag, and do not include the flaming grenades—that they might be taken for a completely new series issued to the returned regiments after the war. Nevertheless, they line up with the colors shown in the Thalmann monument plates, so regardless of the inaccuracies of detail, they seem to confirm which regiments had which colors for their Fahnen. The prints also make a distinction between gold and silver wreaths and cyphers, but with all the crowns both large and small always being gold. All the flags in these drawings but two—those belonging to Hesse-Hanau—have the cypher FL for Friedrich Landgraf, even though Wilhelm was probably the reigning prince at the time the series was completed, Friedrich having died in October 1785. Since they still have Friedrich's cypher, they cannot represent an entirely new issue or a new design on the accession of Wilhelm. The two Hesse-Hanau Fahnen included in the series both have Wilhelm's WL cypher.

The two earlier lists—Fahnenbuch and Thalmann—do not have any white flags except those of the Guards Regiment, which did not go to America, and the illustrated flags of different colors have been associated as either Leibfahne or Kompaniefahnen by different chroniclers. Dr. Fritz Dietrich and Friedrich Schirmer published an article on the Hessian Fahnen in the American War of Independence as *Uniformheft 6* in the German military modeling magazine *Die Zinnfigur* in the early 1960s (exact date unknown). An unbound copy is at Brown University. The article cites the Staatsarchive Marburg as its source, and lists Fahnen for the eleven field regiments in America 1776–1783. It does not list the four garrison regiments, and suggests that Regiment Rall, also technically a garrison regiment before the war, "probably" did not have Fahnen in America, but if it had, they were probably dark blue with red eckflammen. This would have come from the Thalmann monument plate for the Land Grenadier Regiment circa 1786. The other ten regiments are described as having both Leibfahne and Kompaniefahnen of various colors, apparently derived by combining both the Thalmann and the 1785 Darmstädter plates, in most cases taking the Thalmann picture to be the Kompaniefahnen and the Darmstädter plate to be the Leibfahne, but also incorporating

Page from the Darmstädter Handschrift. While most of the internal details of the Fahnen in these drawings are inaccurate, they help to establish which regiments carried which color Fahnen in America.

the idea that the colors of the Leib- and Kompaniefahnen were in some cases simply reversed, Prussian style. Why they ignored the white Leibfahne in every Darmstädter plate is not known, but they were clearly of the opinion that Hessian regiments during the war in America did not carry white Leibfahnen. They were not the only German military historians to hold this view. Even after the publication of Ortenburg's complete set of the Darmstädter plates in 1999, Uwe Peter Böhm, who had written extensively in the 1980s on the Hessian military of 1672–1806, could write in reference to the American war, "This leads me to the conclusion that there were *no* white Leibfahnen (as Rascher copied them from the Darmstädter Handschrift) at the time in question" (italics and parenthetical clause in original).

The Darmstädter Handschrift and the Thalmann "monument" prints, however, show two flags for each regiment, with a white Leibfahne in every case. It seems reasonable that if the Leibfahne of every regiment were indeed white, and this was well known and understood, there was no need for the chroniclers of the Fahnenbuch or the Thalmann plates to draw a white flag for every regiment, only the various colored ones specific to that regiment. Of course, this does not explain the discrepancies among the other lists as to which flags belonged to which regiments, nor why researchers in the past who were aware of the same sources drew such different conclusions. Besides Böhm, information sent to Gherardi Davis in 1907 from Hessian Archives in both Cassel and Marburg, listed two Fahnen for each regiment, but no white ones. Hans-Enno Korn in 1976 went through the entire 534-page Thalmann folio yet thought the colorful Fahnen pictured in the prints probably represented the Leibfahnen of the listed regiments. Herbert Knötel and C. C. P. Lawson, well-regarded uniform historians in the mid-twentieth century, both listed Leibfahnen as well as Kompaniefahnen as various colors, none of them white. Dietrich and Schirmer combined two source collections to come up with a list that covered at least ten regiments in America without a single white Leibfahne.

There are good reasons to accept Aubert and Zahn's idea that all Hessian Leibfahnen were white, however. First, besides the above listed sources, is the existence of the remnants of a white flag captured with at least one of the three regiments at Trenton in 1776, even though there are no white flags listed for any of those regiments in the pre-1785 sources. (Not much of this flag has survived, and its appearance in Peale's paintings of Washington show it draped in such a way that if it had corners of a contrasting color, they would not be visible, but as pointed out above, no other contemporary source shows a white Hessian flag with colored eckflammen, regardless of color.) And second, the fact that the number of different color combinations known from various sources very nearly equals the number of Hessian regiments to which they might have belonged, including the garrison regiments, whereas the theory of two flags of different colors per regiment leaves several regiments with no identified flags at all before 1785, even though other records make it clear that all regiments indeed had them for the war. But what about the two Fahnen—green with red corner blazes and yellow with red corner blazes—that were listed in the now-lost Fahnenbuch in Cassel that do not show up in any of the later compilations?

The following sections on individual regiments show the Leibfahne and Kompaniefahnen most likely carried by each regiment in America. Each entry is accompanied by discussion of the various sources and why the two flags shown are the best and most reasonable conclusion for the individual regiment addressed. Different lists and research collections are discussed and considered, hypothetical and/or post-war flags are addressed. But so as not to confuse the issue, these are not shown in photographs—only those carried in America are shown.

Leib Regiment

The Leib (literally "body" as in the English "bodyguard") Infanterie Regiment was the personal regiment of the reigning Landgraf, with Friedrich himself as its colonel-in-chief. It was also sometimes styled

Regiment du Corps in the Frenchified military terminology of the day. In 1783 the colonelship was trans-ferred to Friedrich's son and heir Wilhelm and the regiment became known as Regiment Erbprinz. Its regimental Fahnen during service in North America were a white Leibfahne and four Kompaniefahnen of yellow with deep red eckflammen.

This regiment has somewhat confused and conflicting information of what Fahnen were carried when. According to information supplied to Gherardi Davis by the Cassel Archives in 1907, taken from the water-color plates of the Fahnenbuch of 1783, the Fahnen of the Leib Regiment during its service in America did not include a white Leibfahne, rather two variations of yellow and red—one yellow with red (*rot*) corner blazes and one vice versa (*ungekehrt*) red with yellow. No distinction was made in the original Cassel letter between Leib- and Kompaniefahnen. Davis apparently saw the original plates at some later date and decided the colors were yellow with "wine red" and "wine red" with yellow. He also decided the yellow flag was the Leibfahne and the wine-red flags were the "ordinary" flags. Dietrich and Schirmer in the early 1960s reversed which flag was the Leib- and which the Kompaniefahnen and described the flags as *pfirsi-chblüt farben* (peach blossom color, a deep pink) with yellow corner blazes for the Leibfahne and yellow with *karmesin* (crimson) corner blazes for the Kompaniefahnen. Whatever sources were viewed, the reds apparently did not quite match between the two, but these descriptions readily fit the 1785 Darmstädter Handschrift plate which shows pink with yellow and Thalmann plate circa 1784 which shows a yellow flag with dark red. The small "monument" plates included in the Thalmann manuscript allow both possibilities: one plate shows a white flag paired with a yellow and red flag, another shows a white flag paired with a pink or crimson one.

Herbert Knötel, in a plate made in the mid-twentieth century, portrayed a flag-bearer with a beau-tiful deep pink and yellow Fahne unhelpfully labeled "Regimental-Colors," which could mean any of the flags that belonged to the regiment, but probably was his translation of *Regimentsfahne*, meaning not the Leibfahne.

Leibfahne, Leib Regiment.

Kompaniefahnen, Leib Regiment.

Taking all these variations, sources, and opinions into account, it seems most likely the Leibregiment carried a white Leibfahne and four yellow Kompaniefahnen with deep-red corner blazes, as portrayed in Thalmann, during its time in America.

Why these were changed to pfirsichblüt by the time they were drawn in the Darmstädter Handschrift of 1785 is not recorded, but a reasonable case can be made that the color of the Kompaniefahnen changed in 1783 when the colonelship of the Leibregiment changed from Friedrich to his son, Erbprinz Wilhelm. Pfirsichblüt seems to have been a color associated with Wilhelm—the Fahnen of Wilhelm's Hesse-Hanau regiment were pfirsichblüt and the regimental facings of the uniforms of Wilhelm's Hesse-Cassel Erbprinz Regiment between 1760 and 1783 were pfirsichblüt. It is also known that new Fahnen were presented to five regiments which had lost theirs in America, and that in at least one case—the Land-Grenadier Regiment (formerly Rall/Angelelli)—these were a different color combination from those used during the war. So new Fahnen could be obtained as needed or perhaps on demand. When Wilhelm took over the Leib Infanterie Regiment in 1783 it was re-titled Regiment Erbprinz. It is probably at this juncture that the uniform facings of its musicians were changed from their original yellow to Wilhelm's preferred pfirsichblüt—this is the only regiment on the Hessian establishment that has its musicians with different facings from the rest of the regiment's officers and soldiers. Apparently at the same time, the regiment was made fusiliers rather than musketeers and received metal-fronted caps in place of standard cocked hats. The regiment that had previously been Erbprinz became Regiment Prinz Friedrich (for Wilhelm's brother), was re-uniformed as a musketeer regiment with hats rather than fusilier caps, and had *its* uniform facings changed from pfirsichblüt to crimson. On Landgraf Friedrich's death in October 1785, Wilhelm became the Landgraf himself, and the old Leibregiment that had so recently been re-titled as Erbprinz, became the Leib-Füsilier Regiment, with its new headgear and its new Fahnen of pfirsichblüt and yellow, both duly recorded in the 1785 Darmstädter Handschrift.

Regiment Erbprinz

Fusilier Regiment Erbprinz arrived in America in the first contingent of Hessian troops in 1776 and served until captured at Yorktown in October 1781. The regiment's colonel-in-chief was Wilhelm, Landgraf Friedrich's eldest son and heir-apparent (*Erbprinz*). On the regiment's return to Hesse in 1783, the colonelship passed to Wilhelm's brother, and it became Regiment Prinz Friedrich. It was redesignated a Musketier regiment and received uniforms with a new facing color and new headgear. New Fahnen were presented and appear in the 1785 Darmstädter Handschrift plates.

The Kompaniefahnen carried by the regiment in America were crimson with blue corner blazes. The Leibfahne was probably white. The painted wreaths, cyphers, and grenades on both were silver. As the original Erbprinz Fahnen were captured at Yorktown, they were supposedly not pictured in the Fahnenbuch, although one Fahne of crimson with blue eckflammen is listed under another name. Later descriptions come from the 1785 Darmstädter Handschrift and the Thalmann Fahne plate. Dietrich and Schirmer apparently used both sources; they list the Leibfahne as crimson with blue and the Kompaniefahnen as red with medium blue, which seem to be fairly accurate descriptions of the Darmstädter Handschrift and Thalmann plates, respectively. The Thalmann book covers the entire reign of Friedrich II; the accompanying uniform plate marked "Erbprinz" shows an officer and a private soldier in the pre-1783 uniform of pfirsichblüt facings and metal-fronted fusilier cap, giving additional reason to believe the flags used in America were the same as the replacement pictured in the full-page plate. (Korn shows the post-1783 uniform with crimson facings and cocked hat of a musketeer regiment.) The Thalmann "monument" drawing also shows one white flag and one crimson, without any details.

What became of the five Erbprinz Fahnen captured at Yorktown is unknown.

Pages from Thalmann manuscript showing Fahne and accompanying uniform and "monument" plates for Regiment Erbprinz. Hessischen Staatsarchiv Marburg.

Leibfahne, Regiment Erbprinz.

Kompaniefahnen, Regiment Erbprinz.

Regiment Prinz Carl

Musketier Regiment Prinz Carl was in the first contingent of Hessian troops sent to America, arriving in August 1776, and remaining through the end of the war. Its regimental Fahnen were a white Leibfahne and four deep green (*moosgrün* or moss green) Kompaniefahnen. All painted details were gold, reflecting the metal of the regimental uniform buttons and cap plates.

Though most records agree on the deep green color of the Kompaniefahnen, there are a few contentious points to be considered. The first, of course, is that the Cassel archives, followed by Davis, and by later twentieth century researchers, maintained that the Leibfahnen were not white, but usually a variation of the colors of the other Fahnen of each regiment. Citing the now-lost Fahnenbuch of 1783, Cassel archivists wrote to Davis in 1907 that the Fahnen of Regiment Prinz Carl were moss green with red corner blazes, and moss green without corner blazes. Davis described them as green with wine red, and all green, identifying the first as the Leibfahne and the second as the Kompaniefahnen. No other sources show or describe a green flag with red corner blazes. Dietrich and Schirmer list an all-green Leibfahne, and all-green for the Kompaniefahnen, presumably taking one from the 1785 Darmstädter Handschrift, and the other from Thalmann. Interestingly, the 1921 Handschrift drawing—Prinz Carl is one of the regiments for which there are two versions—shows the flag as a medium green with corner sections of a darker green rather than a single field of a uniform color. This may have been inadvertent on the part of the artist—perhaps he had not been given complete information for the first draft and colored in the corners later. In any event, there is no evidence of any Hessian Fahne having corner blazes of the same or similar color as the field— either the flag was all one color, or it had contrasting corner blazes.

The full-page Thalmann plate for Prinz Carl shows all dark green, the accompanying "monument" plate shows a white flag and a green flag, and of course the Darmstädter Handschrift plates show white Leibfahnen for all regiments.

Leibfahne, Regiment Prinz Carl.

Kompaniefahnen, Regiment Prinz Carl.

Regiment von Ditfurth

Fusilier Regiment von Ditfurth arrived in America in August 1776 and remained through the end of the war. Its Fahnen were most likely a white Leibfahne, and four Kompaniefahnen of dark yellow, with silver wreaths and grenades. Though all sources agree on the deep yellow uniform facings and white/silver buttons and cap plates of the regiment, no two sources agree on the Fahnen. Cassel archivists in their letter to Gherardi Davis in 1907, citing the now-lost 1783 Fahnenbuch, listed two Fahnen for Ditfurth: dark yellow with red corner blazes, and dark yellow with blue corner blazes. Davis decided, and published in 1910, that these were the regiment's Leib- and Kompaniefahnen, respectively. Based on other sources, the first of these might reasonably be identified as belonging to the Leibregiment, but the same Fahnenbuch also had a different yellow and red Fahne—clearly the Cassel archivists had two yellow and reds to contend with. An additional problem raised here is that no other source specifically cites *any* Fahnen of yellow with blue corner blazes, though a case can be made for that color belonging to Garnison Regiment von Huyn (see entry for that unit).

The full-page Thalmann plate (circa 1784) shows medium to dark yellow with no corner blazes. Curiously, there are pencil lines for three blazes on the drawing, but apparently the artist was corrected before drawing in the fourth corner blaze and proceeded to paint the flag in a uniform yellow throughout. The accompanying uniform plate shows the regiment in their 1776–1780 fusilier uniforms. Perhaps the Thalmann artist began to draw the then-current (1785) flag with white corner blazes, but then left them out for his final representation of the all-yellow Fahne of the wartime regiment. The "monument" plate shows white and yellow Fahnen without any details. The 1785 Darmstädter Handschrift plate shows Ditfurth as bright yellow with white corners and the soldiers uniformed as musketeers, which they became in 1780. This is the only source showing any Fahne yellow with white, so such a combination cannot be attributed to misidentification with another regiment. Ditfurth is also one of the regiments where a duplicate

Leibfahne, Regiment von Ditfurth.

Kompaniefahnen, Regiment von Ditfurth.

Handschrift plate is known, and this second plate shows a more muted tan or orange-yellow, also with white corners, and with the motto scroll on both Fahnen red instead of gray—the only Fahnen in any of the collections with this detail. Dietrich and Schirmer again have it both ways, listing yellow with white corner blazes as the Leibfahne and all yellow as the Kompaniefahnen. All sources agree that the wreaths are silver, to be in line with the silver buttons and caps of the regimental uniform.

A primary goal of regimental flags is always ready identification in the field. Kompaniefahnen of all dark yellow might have been easily mistaken for the light yellow (paille) of Regiment von Donop or the bright yellow of Garnison Regiment von Huyn. A reasonable conclusion from the varied sources would be that the Kompaniefahnen of Regiment von Ditfurth were all dark yellow during its service in America, but that they were replaced or modified by adding white corner blazes sometime after the return to Europe and before they were drawn for the Darmstädter Handschrift of 1785.

Regiment von Donop

Musketier Regiment von Donop arrived in America in August 1776 and remained through the end of the war. Its Fahnen were the white Leibfahne common to all Hessian regiments, and Kompaniefahnen of *paille* (literally "straw," sometimes simply described as light yellow). There is less than the usual controversy—besides the standard disagreement over whether the Leibfahne was white or some color—over the Fahnen carried by this regiment. The earliest cited source for this regiment is the Cassel Fahnenbuch circa 1783. Cassel archivists wrote Davis in 1907 giving the colors of the von Donop Fahnen from the Fahnenbuch as all light yellow, and light yellow with blue. (These were identified as von Knyphausen in the letter, but Donop and Knyphausen had switched names shortly after the regiments returned to Germany, and it is known both from other records as well as the actual captured flags in Philadelphia that Knyphausen

Leibfahne, Regiment von Donop.

Kompaniefahnen, Regiment von Donop.

carried black in America, so it remains clear which regiment was meant). Davis identified the all-light-yellow as the Leibfahne and the light yellow with blue corner blazes, which he refined to "light blue," as the Kompaniefahnen. The Hessian archivists had believed that the Fahnenbuch list did not include the garrison regiments, but this yellow and blue color combination would make sense as belonging to Garnison Regiment von Wissenbach (see entry for that regiment). The Thalmann series of circa 1784 does not include a full-page plate for von Donop, but the "monument" plate shows one white flag and one of light yellow or paille. The Darmstädter Handschrift of 1785 agrees in showing the Kompaniefahnen as paille, without corner blazes, the painted details in gold, matching the metal color of the uniforms' buttons and grenadier cap plates. Dietrich and Schirmer accept the Handschrift's paille with gold details as the Leibfahne, but as the Thalmann plates do not include von Donop, they leave the Kompaniefahnen as unknown.

Regiment Alt von Lossberg

Füsilier Regiment von Lossberg was in the first contingent of Hessian troops sent to America, arriving in August 1776. In mid-1780 it became known as "Alt" (old) von Lossberg when the Regiment von Mirbach received a new colonel-in-chief, a Hessian aristocrat of the same von Lossberg family name, and to avoid confusion von Mirbach became the "Jung" (young, or new) von Lossberg. All sources agree that the Kompaniefahnen of the original Regiment von Lossberg were orange, with light or medium green eckflammen. The painted details were gold. The Leibfahne was probably all white with details in gold, though Dietrich and Schirmer, combining plates of Thalmann and the 1785 Darmstädter Handschrift, claim that the Leibfahne in this case was identical to the other four flags—orange and green. The now-lost

Leibfahne, Regiment von Lossberg (Alt).

Kompaniefahnen, Regiment von Lossberg (Alt).

Fahnenbuch identifying Fahnen of the returning regiments in 1783 did not include von Lossberg due to its flags having been lost at Trenton. Both Thalmann and the Handschrift of 1785 show orange with green corner blazes. The Thalmann "monument" drawing shows a white flag and a green flag, but as mentioned in the introductory section, the monument plates show little or no detail—a flag with green corners might appear basically green when looped up on its pole.

Regiment von Lossberg and all its Fahnen were captured at Trenton on December 26, 1776. Of the many fragments still surviving in Philadelphia of the Fahnen taken at Trenton, none is orange. It is possible that the one all-white Leibfahne at Philadelphia belonged to von Lossberg, but this seems unlikely as each regiment fought its own little battle within a battle at Trenton and the Fahnen of the different regiments would have generally been grouped within each individual regiment. American researcher Donald Holst, writing in the German magazine *Zeitschrift für Heereskunde* in 1990, suggested that Regiment von Rall had no Fahnen at Trenton and that therefore the green flags taken there must belong to von Lossberg.[2] But Holst was mistaken in believing that Rall carried no Fahnen. Johannes Reuber, a soldier in Regiment von Rall, claimed that the Fahnen captured at Trenton were recaptured at Stono Ferry in 1779. While this would not make sense for the green and black flags belonging to Regiments Rall and Knyphausen that had been taken to Philadelphia, were seen, and described there, and are still there, it would make sense for Fahnen belonging to von Lossberg if they had been separately captured and taken south by some American officer or unit at Trenton rather than being turned in at the time. It is also a confirmation by a contemporary source that Regiment von Rall did have Fahnen in America. That such captured and recaptured flags no longer exist does not much matter—*no* flags returned to Hesse after the war still survive. For further information on the Trenton flags and how they have been appraised and explained by historians, see the entry on Regiment von Rall.

Regiment von Knyphausen

Füsilier Regiment von Knyphausen was in the first contingent of Hessian troops to land in America in 1776. Its Kompaniefahnen were black with white eckflammen, the painted details all gold. The Leibfahne was probably all white, with gold details. All five Fahnen of the regiment were captured at Trenton on December 26, 1776. Sergeant Elisha Bostwick of Connecticut wrote of the Germans captured by his regiment: "their uniforms with black facings, their flag or Standard of the richest black silk & devices upon it and gold lettering in gold leaf."[3] Fragments of at least two of these flags are in Philadelphia. While some sources show the corner blazes as paille (straw), the silk on the remaining fragments appears no different from that on the green and white flags of Rall, which are documented to have been inspected by textile experts who found no traces of any dyes in the white silk portions. Charles Willson Peale shows at least two of the Knyphausen Fahnen in his paintings of *Washington at Princeton*, portraying them with the interiors of the large crowns filled in gold rather than red, and with the unusual finials shown here. He also shows the corners of the black flags as very white—not the least yellow or paille.

While all sources agree on the dominant color of the Knyphausen flags being black, some maintain that the eckflammen were paille on at least some of the flags. Dietrich and Schirmer in *Zinnfigur, Uniformheft 6* published in the early 1960s say that the regiment's Leibfahne was black with paille corners, while the Kompaniefahnen were black with white (as the original flags in Philadelphia). The authors' reasoning is unclear, as to the distinction between Leib- and Kompaniefahnen, but the Thalmann prints from which they were working, dating from 1784–1786, as well as the Darmstädter Handschrift of 1785, clearly show the Knyphausen flags as black with paille. This can be ascertained because the plates showing the uniforms make a clear distinction between white and paille breeches and vests, and the corners of the flags are the

Leibfahne, Regiment von Knyphausen.

Kompaniefahnen, Regiment von Knyphausen. All four of these Fahnen were captured at Trenton; some small pieces of one or more are still in Philadelphia. At least two of them appear in Charles Willson Peale's *Washington at Princeton*.

same color as the paille vests. The earliest records, the now-lost Fahnenbuch of 1783, made on the return of the regiments to Germany, do not show Knyphausen at all, as their captured flags obviously had not returned with the regiment. Apparently the new Fahnen presented the regiment in 1783 or 1784 were black and paille, but as stated above, the fragment in Philadelphia has white.

(The Regiments von Knyphausen and von Donop switched their names in 1784, but when this is known and taken into account, it does not really confuse the matter.)

Regiment Rall

Grenadier Regiment Rall was one of the five *garnison* (garrison, or home guard) regiments called to active service by Landgraf Friedrich for the war in America. It arrived with the first contingent of Hessian troops in America in August 1776. Rall did not have the honorific *von* attached to his own name, but as *von* simply means *of* in German, most records use the terminology "Regiment von Rall" exactly as they would with the name of any other regiment, whether the colonel was a titled individual with a "von" to his personal name or not. Though a garrison regiment, styled and uniformed as grenadiers, Hessian records make clear that the regiment was fielded and equipped exactly as any other infantry regiment, including the standard complement of Fahnen. Grenadier companies within infantry regiments, and the Hessian combined grenadier battalions made up of these detached companies, did not carry Fahnen.

All five Fahnen of Regiment Rall were captured at Trenton on December 26, 1776, along with the Fahnen of Regiments von Knyphausen and von Lossberg. Based on what remains of the captured Fahnen in Philadelphia, the color of the Kompaniefahnen of Regiment Rall was green, with white eckflammen, the painted details all in gold. The Leibfahne was white. Several are portrayed in Charles Willson Peale's *Washington at Princeton* with gold in the interior of the large crown. The paint has been entirely washed out or simply flaked away on the two fairly complete originals in Philadelphia, but Peale had the originals on hand and presumably copied them accurately. (All reconstructions of Hessian Fahnen in this book are based on careful tracings from these two originals.) Peale also depicts the captured Fahnen with the unusual finials shown here.

Although there is much confusion among sources for the colors of the Fahnen of many Hessian regiments, all sources agree on those of the other two regiments captured at Trenton: black for Knyphausen and orange for Lossberg. The green flags that still exist therefore must have belonged to Rall. The Fahnenbuch plates made in 1783 immediately after the return of the Hessian regiments did not include any of the captured Fahnen. The Thalmann "monument" plate of 1786 and the Darmstädter Handschrift 1785 show the Fahnen of the Hessian Grenadier regiment (under several different colonels' names) as either very dark (Thalmann) or very light (Handschrift) blue with red corner blazes. But both these sources were made after new Fahnen had been presented to regiments which had lost theirs during the war. Regiment Rall, by then designated d'Angelelli, had been specifically cited and returned to the Landgraf's "gracious favor" for actions at Stono Ferry and presented new Fahnen by Friedrich himself in 1783.[4] A Fahne of blue with red corner blazes depicted in the now-lost Fahnenbuch probably represented these new flags of the Grenadier regiment.

Of the fifteen Fahnen known to have been lost at Trenton, and reported to Landgraf Friedrich, fragments of only nine at most still exist, all in Philadelphia, and are green, black, or white, suggesting the Kompaniefahnen of two regiments, and the Leibfahne of one. A detailed inventory made by Donald Holst and published in a German magazine in 1990[5] averred that in contemporary records only nine Fahnen could be accurately accounted for as captured. To explain this, he posited that Regiment Rall, as a garrison and/or grenadier regiment, did not carry Fahnen. But as mentioned above, German records make it clear that it did. Fahnen of one of the regiments must have been lost in the battle, as reported to the Landgraf, but not necessarily secured by the Americans at the time, or not reported to authorities in Philadelphia. Max von Eelking mentions officers up to their necks in water trying to save the Fahnen of some regiment;[6] clearly not all the Fahnen were easily gathered up by Americans simply surrounding large groups of surrendering Hessians. Another green Fahne taken at Trenton was described in a letter by a delegate to the Continental Congress on December 31, 1776. According to Holst, this same flag was later burned "by about twenty independents . . . headed by Hancock."[7]

Men not captured with their three regiments at Trenton were reconstituted as a single battalion and served in later campaigns under various names as their colonels changed. Johannes Reuber, in his journals kept during service as a private soldier in Regiment Rall in America, recounts his reconstituted regiment's part in the Battle of Stono Ferry in South Carolina, July 20, 1779, including the burning of the American schooner *Rattlesnake*. His last sentence on the affair claims that the Hessians there recaptured the flags and cannons the Rall regiment had lost at Trenton in December 1776.[8] Many secondary sources mention this with reasonable skepticism, generally speculating as to why these flags would have been on a ship in South Carolina two years after their capture. But this does not appear to be precisely what Reuber claimed; he only says that the flags were recovered at the same time the battle was fought, not specifically that they were taken from a burning ship. He also does not claim that he personally saw these flags, only that "we" recaptured flags lost at Trenton, so the attribution to the "Rall regiment," as he still called his unit, may have been an obvious conclusion for him personally, but the flags could have belonged to any of the three

Leibfahne, Grenadier Regiment Rall. This Fahne was captured at Trenton, and small scraps of the original are still in Philadelphia. It appears in Charles Willson Peale's *Washington at Princeton*.

Kompaniefahne, Grenadier Regiment Rall. All four of these Fahnen were captured at Trenton; at least one is prominently shown in Charles Willson Peale's *Washington at Princeton*. Two of the originals and small green scraps of another are in Philadelphia.

captured regiments. If some of the Trenton booty had been taken south at some point, this might tie up loose ends both as to why there were not fifteen Fahnen turned in to authorities in Philadelphia as well as why there were no orange flags belonging to Lossberg ever found in America. What happened to these recovered Fahnen, if Reuber is to be believed that such a recapture even happened, and regardless of which regiment they may have belonged to, or whether they were returned to Hesse with another regiment, as also reported, is of little import—all Hessian Fahnen from the period have long since disappeared.

Regiment von Trümbach

Musketier Regiment von Trümbach arrived in America in August 1776. In 1778 it became Regiment von Bose. The regiment and its five Fahnen were surrendered at Yorktown. The regimental Fahnen comprised a white Leibfahne and four Kompaniefahnen of dark blue with white corner blazes, with gold wreaths and grenades, following the color of the metal of the regimental uniforms. The Leibfahne of this regiment is shown in many secondary sources both printed and on the internet as white with blue corner blazes—reversed, Prussian style, from the accepted colors of the Kompaniefahnen. There is no contemporary evidence that any Hessian flag, whether Leib- or Kompaniefahne, was white with blue or any other colored eckflammen. Friedrich Schirmer, the same artist who collaborated with Fritz Dietrich in the *Zinnfigur* listings, published in the historical uniforms periodical *Zweifarben Tücher* in the mid-twentieth century two paintings by F. Kersten which also mistakenly followed Prussian models by making the interior of the central cartouche on the dark blue Trümbach/Bose Fahnen white. There is no documentary or visual evidence for such an interpretation—the center of the Hessian Fahnen was always a medium-dark blue.

Leibfahne, Regiment von Trümbach; after 1778, von Bose.

Kompaniefahnen, Regiment von Trümbach; after 1778, von Bose.

The listing sent by the Cassel archives to Davis in 1907 did not include Trümbach/Bose, as its Fahnen had been lost at Yorktown and were not included in the Fahnenbuch, nor was there any blue or blue and white flag in that list that might be re-attributed to Trümbach/Bose. Dietrich and Schirmer described the Leib- and Kompaniefahnen, respectively, as white with blue eckflammen and blue with white eckflammen, with gold details. The full-page Thalmann plate for Regiment von Bose shows dark blue with silver wreaths and grenades, but all the Thalmann plates show silver wreaths, regardless of the uniform metals. The accompanying "monument" plate shows one white flag and one dark blue. The Darmstädter Handschrift of 1785 shows a white Leibfahne and dark blue Kompaniefahne with white corners, both with gold wreaths (grenades are omitted on all the Handschrift plates). What became of the Fahnen lost at Yorktown is unknown.

Regiment von Mirbach/Jung von Lossberg

Musketier Regiment von Mirbach arrived with the first contingent of Hessian troops in August 1776. In mid-1780 the Regiment received a new colonel-in-chief and became Regiment von Lossberg. As there was already a Regiment von Lossberg on the Hessian establishment—the two colonels-in-chief were Hessian aristocrats of the same family name—the original von Lossberg regiment became known as "Alt" (old) and the new regiment as "Jung" (young, or new) von Lossberg.

The Fahnen of the Regiment von Mirbach/Jung von Lossberg in America were a white Leibfahne and four Kompaniefahnen of orange with medium blue corner blazes, the wreaths, cyphers, and grenades silver. Cassel archivists writing to Gherardi Davis in 1907, citing the now-lost 1783 Fahnenbuch, reported for Regiment von Mirbach orange-yellow (*orangegelb*) with no corner blazes, and orange with blue corner blazes. Davis later listed the Leibfahne all orange, and Kompaniefahnen orange with light blue corner blazes. If the regiment's Leibfahne were indeed white, the orange-yellow flag could belong to Garnison Regiment von Stein (renamed von Porbeck by the time its Fahnen were recorded in 1785, see entry for Regiment von Stein).

There are two Darmstädter Handschrift plates for Regiment von Mirbach/Jung von Lossberg, one from the complete and one from the partial series, and both show the Kompaniefahne very dark orange, almost red, but not as red as the color used for the crowns and the stripes on the Hessian Lion on the flag. The color of the regimental uniform facings is sometimes listed as *ponceaurot*, or poppy red, a deep red-orange color, and it appears that the orange-almost-red flag in each plate is painted in the same color as the uniform facings on the soldiers in the plate. However, the Fahne in the full-page plate in Thalmann is clearly orange, with medium blue corner blazes, the uniforms with red facing of a different hue than the orange of the flag. The accompanying "monument" plate shows two flags, white and deep orange. Dietrich and Schirmer, combining the 1785 Handschrift and the Thalmann plates, listed the Mirbach Leibfahne as all red and the Kompaniefahnen as orange with light blue. All sources agree that the wreaths and other painted details are silver. Although the Thalmann plates were published after the original Handschrift, many of the individual plates in the series illustrate earlier uniforms and flags—indeed the full title states that it addresses the Hessian military through the entire reign of Landgraf Friedrich. The Darmstädter Handschrift, however, represents the uniforms and Fahnen as they were in 1785. In this case it seems that the orange and blue Fahnen of the Thalmann plate for Mirbach/Jung Lossberg represent the Fahnen carried throughout most of the period, including the war in America, even if at some later period they were replaced by deep red/ orange flags that matched the uniforms.

Leibfahne, Regiment von Mirbach; after 1780, von Lossberg (Jung).

Kompaniefahnen, Regiment von Mirbach; after 1780, von Lossberg (Jung).

Regiment von Wutginau/Landgraf

Musketier Regiment von Wutginau arrived in America on October 16, 1776, and remained until 1783. On October 10, as the regiment was enroute to America, General von Wutginau was replaced by Landgraf Friedrich himself as the regiment's colonel-in-chief. As there was already a regiment designated Leibregiment (of which Friedrich was also the chief), Regiment von Wutginau became Regiment Landgraf. It is not known when word of this reached America, and most early references to the regiment still address it as Wutginau, but at some point in 1777 it became more regularly known by the title Landgraf. In 1783 Regiment Landgraf (Wutginau) was renamed yet again, to Leibregiment, or Regiment du Corps, when the colonelship of the original Leibregiment was transferred to Friedrich's son Wilhelm and it became known as Regiment Erbprinz. The Darmstädter Handschrift (1785), however, identifies the old Wutginau regiment again as Landgraf, the renamed Regiment Erbprinz having reclaimed its old title of Leibregiment on the accession of Wilhelm to be Landgraf on the death of his father in 1785.

The Fahnen carried by the Regiment von Wutginau/Landgraf in America were a white Leibfahne and poppy-red (*ponceaurot*) Kompaniefahnen with wreaths, cyphers, crowns, and grenades in gold on all five.

The records on these Fahnen are as confused as the regimental title, and in some cases conflicting. The earliest known reference is from the now-lost Fahnenbuch in the Hessian Archives in Cassel. The archivist's letter to Davis in 1907 listed two flags for Regiment Landgraf: one crimson red with blue corner blazes, and one vice versa (*umgekehrt*) blue and red. When Davis presumably later saw these firsthand, he described them as dark red with light blue, and light blue with dark red, and denominated the first as the Leibfahne and the second as the "ordinary" company flags. No other sources identify either of these combinations as belonging to Wutginau/Landgraf. The crimson with blue corner blazes seems to fit both Thalmann and Darmstädter Handschrift for the Regiment Erbprinz, but as the Erbprinz Fahnen were lost at Yorktown, why would they be included in the Fahnenbuch at all?

Leibfahne, Regiment von Wutginau; after 1777, Landgraf.

Kompaniefahnen, Regiment von Wutginau; after 1777, Landgraf.

For Regiment von Wutginau/Landgraf, Thalmann shows a deep red Fahne, more scarlet than crimson, basically the same color as the insides of the crowns and the stripes on the lion, with no corner blazes. The red color appears to be the same as the collars and cuffs on the uniform plate for the regiment. The wreaths and grenades are silver, but the wreaths and grenades are silver on all the full-page Thalmann plates. The accompanying monument plate shows a white flag and a red flag without detail. The 1785 Darmstädter Handschrift shows orange with no corner blazes, but gold wreaths (all the Handschrift plates leave out the grenades). The uniform of the regiment included yellow/gold buttons and cap plates, so all painted details on the Fahnen were more likely gold than Thalmann's silver. Uniform collar and cuffs were listed in contemporary documents as *ponceaurot* or poppy red, a deep scarlet color that can appear almost as a dark orange, and although the colors of Hessian Fahne do not necessarily relate directly to uniform details, it appears that the orange color of the Landgraf Fahne in the Darmstädter Handschrift is the same as the color used on the collars and cuffs in the same picture, so presumably was meant to signify ponceaurot. Dietrich and Schirmer apparently combined these sources but decided that one represented the Leibfahne and one the Kompaniefahnen—they record the Leibfahne as all orange with gold details, the Kompaniefahnen all red with gold details.

Regiment von Wissenbach

Garnison Regiment von Wissenbach was one of the five garrison (home guard) regiments called into active service and brought up to field strength for the war in America. In 1781 the regiment became known as von Knobloch, and in 1785, at the time the original Darmstädter Handschrift plates were being made, it was identified as von Kohler. According to Hessian records, all garrison regiments were fully manned, uniformed,

Leibfahne, Regiment von Wissenbach; after 1780, von Knobloch.

Kompaniefahnen, Regiment von Wissenbach; after 1780, von Knobloch.

and equipped exactly as the regular field regiments. This included the full complement of Fahnen—one Leibfahne and four Kompaniefahnen. As with many Hessian regiments, it is not clear what colors the Wissenbach Fahnen were. There were no full-sized plates of any garrison regiment in Thalmann's compilation in 1786, and the Fahnenbuch of 1783 supposedly did not include the garrison regiments, although this probably was not correct. The "monument" plates in Thalmann generally agree with the 1785 Handschrift, but not always. The case of Wissenbach/Knobloch/Kohler is one of these discrepancies. According to the Handschrift, the regiment in 1785 had both Leibfahne and Kompaniefahnen all white with silver wreaths. If this is correct, they would be identical to the regiments of Guards, with the only difference being the yellow painted staffs of the Guard regiments, which seems unlikely. Probably the artist of the plates did not know what color the Kompaniefahnen should be. The Thalmann monument drawings—not entirely clear in some cases which drawings go with which regiment, or for which period—seem to show for von Kohler (still titled Wissenbach during its time in America) very light yellow Kompaniefahnen in one drawing, and blue in another. The monument drawings usually do not indicate the color of the corner blazes, so a reasonable case can be made that Wissenbach in America carried the misidentified Fahnen of light yellow with blue corners as described by Davis from the now-lost Fahnenbuch plates in the Hessian Archives.

Regiment von Huyn

Garnison Regiment von Huyn was one of the five garrison (home guard) regiments brought up to full strength and put on active status for the war in America. According to Hessian records, all garrison regiments were fully manned, uniformed, and equipped exactly as the regular field regiments. This included the full complement of Fahnen—one Leibfahne and four Kompaniefahnen. In 1780 von Huyn was renamed

Leibfahne, Regiment Huyn; after 1780, von Benning.

Kompaniefahnen, Regiment von Huyn; after 1780, von Benning.

von Benning, and in 1785 it become von Knobloch, under which name it appears in the Darmstädter Handschrift. The Handschrift plate for von Knobloch shows a white Leibfahne and very bright yellow Kompaniefahnen, no corner blazes, with silver wreaths. The Handschrift plates do not show the grenades at all, but like the wreaths, they would be silver to agree with the metal of the uniforms. The Thalmann monument plate shows one white Fahne and one of bright yellow. As the corner blazes often are not shown in the monument drawings, however, it seems likely that one of the Fahnen of yellow with blue corners listed in the now-lost Fahnenbuch of 1783 represented the Fahnen of von Huyn/Benning on its return from America in that year. Why the regiment under its new title of Knobloch would have had Fahnen of bright yellow without the corner blazes in 1785 is unknown.

Regiment von Bünau

Garnison Regiment von Bünau was one of the five garrison (home guard) regiments brought up to full strength and put on active status for the war in America. According to Hessian records, all garrison regiments were fully manned, uniformed, and equipped exactly as the regular field regiments. This included the full complement of Fahnen—one Leibfahne and four Kompaniefahnen. The Fahnenbuch of 1783 did not include the garrison regiments, nor were there full-sized plates of any garrison regiment in Thalmann's compilation in 1786. The Darmstädter Handschrift, 1785, shows Regiment von Bünau with white Leibfahne and crimson (*karmesin*) Kompaniefahnen without corner blazes, the wreaths in silver—the grenades, though not shown, would also be silver. The Thalmann monument plate agrees on the crimson color.

Leibfahne, Regiment von Bünau.

Kompaniefahnen, Regiment von Bünau.

Regiment von Stein

Garnison Regiment von Stein was one of the five garrison (home guard) regiments brought up to full strength and put on active status for the war in America. According to Hessian records, all garrison regiments were fully manned, uniformed, and equipped exactly as the regular field regiments. This included the full complement of Fahnen—one Leibfahne and four Kompaniefahnen. In 1780 von Stein was renamed von Seitz, and in 1783 it become von Porbeck, under which name it appears in the Darmstädter Handschrift of 1785. The Handschrift plate for von Porbeck shows a white Leibfahne and very light orange Kompaniefahnen (lighter than either of the Lossberg regiments in the same series) with no corner blazes, with silver wreaths. The Thalmann "monument" plate agrees. There were no full-sized plates of any garrison regiments in Thalmann's compilation in 1786, and the Fahnenbuch supposedly did not include the garrison regiments. It did however include a Fahne of *orangegelb*, or orange-yellow, without corner blazes, as belonging to Jung von Lossberg, but more likely representing von Stein/von Seitz on its return to Germany in 1783.

Leibfahne, Regiment von Stein; after 1778, von Seitz.

Kompaniefahnen, Regiment von Stein; after 1778 von Seitz.

Hesse-Hanau

Hesse-Hanau was an independently ruled division of Hesse-Cassel, created when Landgraf Friedrich II of Hesse-Cassel's wife, sister of George III of Great Britain, left him when he (Friedrich) converted to Catholicism, and took son Wilhelm with her. Wilhelm, as son of the current Landgrave, was Erbprinz (heir-apparent or crown-prince) of both Hesse-Cassel and Hanau and ruled his tiny fiefdom of Hesse-Hanau the same as any other German prince, treating directly with other European courts without reference to his father in Cassel. In 1776 Wilhelm signed a treaty with Britain for one regiment of a single battalion on the Prussian model with five line companies and one of grenadiers. Wilhelm also sent a contingent of artillery and another of jägers, which did not carry flags.

The Hesse-Hanau Erbprinz Regiment arrived in Quebec in 1776 with the contingent of Braunschweig troops. It was interned with the rest of Burgoyne's army at Saratoga in 1777, where it was reported to Congress that a total of twenty colors had been taken with four German regiments (three regiments from Braunschweig, and the Hesse-Hanau regiment), but that the colors had been burned rather than properly surrendered. The Fahnen of the Braunschweig regiments were famously spirited away by Madame Riedesel, wife of the German Division commander; but whether she had as motherly or collegial a relationship with the Hessian regiment as with her own countrymen is unknown. Perhaps the Fahnen of Hesse-Hanau really were burned.

Hesse-Hanau Regiment Erbprinz

There is only one relatively contemporary source for the appearance of the Fahnen of the Hesse-Hanau Regiment: *Abbildung derer Uniformen von dem Hochfuerstl: Hess: Casselischen Militair (Illustrations of the Uniforms of the High-Princely Hesse-Cassel Military)*, in the state archives in Marburg. This collection is reliably dated to late 1785 based on regimental titles—including the post-war designation of the Hesse-Hanau regiment as Grenadiers—and the fact that the Hesse-Cassel flags are portrayed with the cypher "FL" for Friedrich Landgraf, who did not die until the end of October of that year. While photos of some of the plates survive, the original collection was lost in 1945. Fortunately, a copy of the entire series was made in 1912–1913, and this was discovered and published in 1999 by Georg Ortenburg as *Das Militär der Landgrafschaft Hessen-Kassel zwischen 1783 und 1789 (The Military of the Landgraviate Hessen-Kassel between 1783 and 1789)*. This is the title generally referred to as Darmstädter Handschrift. While both titles seem to exclude Hesse-Hanau, the final two plates in the series show Hesse-Hanau units, including the regiment that had served in America, renamed Grenadier Regiment after the war, with both Leibfahne and Kompaniefahne.

The Leibfahne for this regiment is white with the full arms of Hesse, including Hanau, crowned, supported by two golden-brown lions, upon a panoply of flags and arms. The central coat of arms is not mantled (displayed on a robe or drapery background) as shown in some secondary sources. Wilhelm's "WL" cypher within a crowned wreath is in each of the upper corners. The Leibfahne portrayed for the other Hanau unit in the series shows four small wreaths with Wilhelm's cypher, one in each corner, upper and lower. This is probably correct for both units; the various elements of the flags in all the *Abbildung* drawings are far larger and take up far more space than the same designs on the actual flags they are meant to portray, and it appears that the lower two wreaths were inadvertently crowded out in the first drawing. Contemporary German Fahnen had a device in each corner, or in none—never in just the upper two.

Many secondary works portray the Leibfahne as *pfirsichblüt* rather than white. While there are conflicting sources and reasons for asserting that the Hesse-Cassel regiments carried Leibfahnen of various colors, there seems to be no supporting evidence for the Leibfahne of the Hesse-Hanau regiment not corresponding to the white flag shown in the *Abbildung* plate made after the war. Nevertheless, it is often shown as the same pink as the Kompaniefahnen. One source compounds the error by drawing the Leibfahne not only pink, but with the arms of Hesse-Darmstadt rather than Hesse-Cassel/Hesse-Hanau. Herbert Knötel portrayed the Leibfahne in his drawings circa 1940–1950 as green.

The Kompaniefahnen were pfirsichblüt, a deep magenta or fuchsia color often associated with Wilhelm. The Hessian striped lion is in a blue field surrounded by a wreath, and four corner wreaths with Wilhelm's cypher and crown, the whole being very similar to the Hesse-Cassel Fahnen in the same series. Unlike all other Hessian Fahnen, however, the central cartouche on the Hesse-Hanau Kompaniefahnen is often portrayed in secondary works with a broad flat top clearly taken from the *Abbildung*/Darmstädter manuscripts. But these drawings are very poorly done, and in fact show *all* Hessian flags with a broad flat top and wreaths shaped more like a "U" or a horseshoe than an oval. While useful for the colors of the flags, these drawings are not remotely accurate in their details when compared to existing originals or even to other contemporary drawings. There is no good reason to think the Fahnen of the Hesse-Hanau regiment did not have the same Prussian-style wreath, cartouche, and crown as other Hessian regiments.

The wreaths, grenades, and corner cyphers on both Leibfahne and Kompaniefahnen are silver, to correspond to the color of the cap plates and buttons of the regimental uniforms. The crowns are all gold. Cord and tassels would have been the same as those of other Hessian regiments, red with silver or gold details. The finials on the staffs would also have been similar to other Hessian (and most other German regiments) but with Wilhelm's "WL" cypher. All Fahnen of both Hesse-Hanau regiments are shown in the manuscripts with a long white motto scroll, but with no motto lettered onto it. Apparently, Wilhelm did not have the Fahnen of his regiment(s) painted with the same motto as those of his father, Friedrich. It seems unlikely that Fahnen were carried on parade or in the field with blank motto scrolls, but to date no research has found what motto may have been used. One secondary study—the same one that mistakenly uses the mantled arms of Hesse-Darmstadt—suggests *HASSORUM GLORIA*, or "Glory to Hesse" in Latin, without source or explanation.

The reconstructions shown here for the Kompaniefahnen follow the standard attributes of the well-documented remnants of original Hessian Fahnen in Philadelphia, very similar to the Prussian models on which they were based, with minor adjustments in the details as they differ between the Fahnen of Hesse-Cassel and those of Hesse-Hanau. The Leibfahne is based on the supposition that the 1785 *Abbildung* drawings are reasonably accurate as to what elements were included on the flag, despite how wretchedly drawn. The general style is taken from other contemporary German flags, documents, and drawings. For physical details on materials, size, and construction, see the introduction to the Hessian section.

The coat of arms displayed on the Leibfahne comprises the arms of several smaller states making up the then-current Landgrafschaft. For clarity these are described as they appear to the viewer, rather than in heraldic terms of dexter and sinister. As the arms were painted, they probably appear in the correct orientation of the reverse of the flag as well.

At center, on a blue shield, is the Hessian Lion, traditionally silver and red, but on Fahnen almost invariably done in white and red. He wears a golden crown (ducal coronet) but does not carry a sword, as on other Hessian military Fahnen. In the upper left is the red Patriarch's cross on a silver ground, representing Hersfeld. Directly below that is a red lion with blue crown, on gold, for Katzenelnbogen. At bottom left are the arms of Nidda: black above gold, with two silver stars in the black. These are sometimes described as having eight points, but drawings made in the 1750–1780s show them with six points. The lower gold section is technically an unadorned field of gold, but many contemporary prints, including the *Abbildung* drawings, show lightly rendered decorative scrolls or vines simply to add artistic flair. In the upper right, the black and gold arms of Ziegenhain are similarly rendered with light scrollwork in the gold. The silver star on black is always shown as six-pointed. At center right are two golden leopards on a red ground, representing Diez. There are no real differences between heraldic representations of leopards and lions, the leopards rarely having spots. The leopards in contemporary Hessian drawings always face forward, not toward the viewer. At bottom right are the arms of Schaumburg: on a red ground a small silver-over-red shield superimposed on a silver nettle-leaf. No two artists really seem to agree on just what a nettle-leaf ought to look like; the one portrayed here is from a print circa 1750 showing the "new" arms of Hesse-Hanau. Finally, at bottom center, the arms of Hanau: a small shield divided red-over-gold, on a field quartered with red and gold chevrons in upper left and lower right, red and gold stripes upper right and lower left. The number of stripes is not consistent, but usually three reds in each quarter.

Leibfahne, Hesse-Hanau Regiment Erbprinz (Flag reproduction by the author).

Kompaniefahnen, Hesse-Hanau Regiment Erbprinz.

Waldeck

Waldeck was a very small principality on the northwest corner of Hesse-Cassel. Its ruler was a prince of the Holy Roman Empire, and Waldeck had maintained regiments on the two-battalion Austrian model in the Emperor's service in Holland since the 1740s. In 1776 the prince offered troops to the British crown on the same general terms as other German states. To avoid stripping the regiments already committed in Holland, a new regiment was raised, and because of the wording of the subsidy treaty with Britain, it was organized on the Prussian model as a single battalion, with four line companies and one grenadier company. Again, per the language of the treaty, each line company included one Freicorporal, traditionally a promising officer cadet with a secondary duty as Fahnentraeger, or flag-bearer. This has led some sources to state that the regiment carried four Fahnen, one per company, but Spanish records of the regiment's capture at Pensacola in 1781 state that all of the flags of the British forces were taken, and specifically mention the Waldeck regiment with its two flags and two artillery pieces. Considering the strong traditional nature of most military establishments, it seems likely that this single battalion carried two flags in America just as each Waldeck battalion had always carried two flags in Holland.

There are no known extant Fahnen of the Third Waldeck Regiment. The two captured at Pensacola were taken back to Spain and at least one sent to the Cathedral at Seville in 1781. Since then, they have disappeared. The regiment was paroled by the Spanish and returned to New York where it received new Fahnen on January 21, 1783. These too have disappeared. The best clues to their appearance are drawings of four flags of Waldeck regiments captured by the French in Holland in 1746 and 1747 during the War of the Austrian Succession. These are in the manuscript books *Les Triomphes de Louis XV, Roy de France et de Navarre*, in the collections of the Bibliothèque Nationale Française. The drawings depict two pairs of Fahnen, one white and one red in each pair, with the arms of Waldeck supported by two lions rampant in gold, surrounded by draped flags in different colors.[9] An apparently contemporary painting in Spain depicts General Gálvez astride his horse and trampling three colors, two of which have a small British Union—the Sixteenth and Sixtieth Regiments were also captured by his troops—and the third all red, probably representing the Waldeck Regiment.

The Waldeck Fahnen captured in Holland and cataloged in *Les Triomphes* were two sided; the reverse of each Fahne had the arms of the Netherlands: a lion with sword in one hand and arrows in the other. The main difference between the two pairs of Waldeck Fahnen is that one pair shows three draped flags on each side of the central device, and the other shows four. All of the drawings in the manuscript are very crude; their purpose is principally to catalog the captured flags, not to give an accurate artistic representation. They do, however, attempt to accurately display the salient design features of each flag—of interest in the present case is that the relative sizes of the coats of arms or other central devices are drawn in proper proportion to the overall flag, being small in some instances and large enough to fill the entire field in others. Thus, it can be reasonably asserted that the Waldeck Fahnen did indeed have central designs that filled almost the entire field of the flags. The addition of a pole sleeve in this reconstruction is based on the fact that all other German and Austrian flags of the period had them.

The Netherlands during this period were part of the Holy Roman Empire, so the dual allegiance shown on the captured Fahnen would make sense. But there is no reason to think Fahnen made for the battalion newly raised in 1776 and committed as auxiliaries of Britain to serve in America would have incorporated Dutch elements. It is quite likely that the new Waldeck regiment would have carried Fahnen in keeping with the traditions and long service of its predecessors, however, probably a white Leibfahne and one red Regimentsfahne (as suggested in the Gálvez painting), each with the traditional display of Waldeck arms now painted on both sides. If these were generally like those of thirty years earlier, the lions on the white Leibfahne would be crowned, those on the red Regimentsfahne were not. Interestingly, the crowns on the lions appear to be imperial crowns, presumably representing the Holy Roman Emperor, rather than the princely crown as atop the Waldeck coat of arms.

The device at the center of each Fahne is the traditional coat of arms of princes of Waldeck dating to the beginning of the century. Describing the elements from left to right and top to bottom, they are: upper left, a red cross anchory (anchor cross) on silver, denoting Pyrmont; this is repeated in the lower right. Top center, three red shields on silver, for Rappoltstein; these are repeated at bottom center. In upper right are the arms of Hohenack: three eagles' heads, black with gold crowns, also on silver; these are repeated at bottom left. On all four of the captured Fahnen, the Hoheneck eagles are shown on gold. It is not known whether this was a mistake on the actual flags, or on all four drawings, which seems unlikely. Whatever the case, this slight error was probably corrected when new Fahnen were produced in 1776.[10]

In the middle row, at center, is the black eight-pointed star on a gold shield of Waldeck. To the left and right, a red lion, crowned, is displayed on silver with blue transverse billets (brick-shapes) semé, representing Geroldseck. The compartment to the left is sometimes shown with a silver lion on blue. Both versions seem to have been concurrently in use, perhaps by different members of the family, but the captured Fahnen all show the red lion of Geroldseck in both compartments. The silver lion on blue became more common in the next century and features in the current arms of the city and principality.

The original drawings of the captured Fahnen give no realistic idea of the spears or cords and tassels for these flags, although the tassels appear to be suspended on cords, not the broad tape of most German Fahnen. They also show no motto in most of the scrolls, but it is unlikely that flags were carried with blank motto scrolls. One flag has been described with the motto *PRODIT AD GLORIAM VIA* ([this] Road Leads to Glory). The traditional motto of Waldeck, *PALMA SUB PONDERE CRESCIT* (The Palm Grows/Thrives Under Stress), may have been on some of the Fahnen, but there is nothing to substantiate this conclusively one way or the other.

Regimentsfahne of a Waldeck regiment captured in Holland in 1747. From *Les Triomphes de Louis XV*, Bibliothèque Nationale Française.

Leibfahne, Third Waldeck Regiment
(Flag reproduction by the author).

Regimentsfahne, Third Waldeck Regiment.

Spanish Regimental Banderas in North America

INTRODUCTION: SPANISH BANDERAS
IN THE AMERICAN WAR OF INDEPENDENCE, 1779–1783

Of all foreign regiments participating in the War of American Independence, the Spanish units have been the least well documented in American sources. While Spanish contributions to the American cause were undeniably great, Spain entered the war in 1779 as a formal ally of France against Britain and was never formally allied to the United States. In addition, Spanish troops campaigned principally in the contested western and southern theaters of North America, in the areas now comprising Louisiana, Mississippi, Alabama, and Florida, rather than in the established colonies—states after July 1776—along the Atlantic coast. Until fairly recently, few works available in the United States even included the names of specific Spanish units, and those that did generally could not distinguish between full regiments or battalions, and detachments of companies or picked men. Only recognized regiments or battalions would have carried their unit-specific colors, ad hoc formations or detachments would not. There were no full regiments of Spanish cavalry involved in the campaigns in North America, though there is a guidon in Spain attributed to the Dragons de America, which is described in its turn. As there were no organized battalions of artillery, Spanish artillery flags are not addressed here.

As in other European armies, the Spanish infantry regiments carried two types of colors—generally termed *banderas* in Spanish—one *Coronela* (Colonel) and two or more *sencillas* (simples) also sometimes termed either *ordenanza* or *batallona* (ordonnance or battalion). King Carlos III ordered banderas of a new size and new patterns in 1762, also reducing the number of flags carried. These changes were described and made permanent in a Royal Order published in 1768. The paragraph relating to banderas was brief and to the point:

> Title I, chapter VII: In each battalion there must be two banners, whose bannerols are to be red, and the staffs of the height of eight feet and six inches including the *regatón* and *moharra* (butt ferrule and spear/finial); the first flag will be white with the shield of my Royal arms; and the other three of each regiment white with the Cross of Burgundy, and in those and these [Coronelas and sencillas] will be placed, at the extremity of the corners, the arms of the Kingdoms and Provinces from which their respective unit titles are derived, or the private devices that they have used, and are used, with my Royal approval.

Line regiments during this period had two battalions; thus the references to two flags per battalion, but the other *three* of each regiment. The first battalion of each regiment carried the Coronela and one sencilla, the second battalion two sencillas. Light regiments had only a single battalion, which carried one Coronela and one sencilla. Later Royal Orders reduced the numbers of banderas carried, but for all practical purposes, the design and details of manufacture of both Coronelas and sencillas remained virtually identical through the end of the Napoleonic period, circa 1815.

Detail, *Por España y por el Rey, Gálvez en América (For Spain and for the King, Gálvez in America)*, by Augusto Ferrer-Dalmau, 2015, oil on canvas. With permission of the artist.

Detail of the Royal Arms of Carlos III at center of each *Coronela*, or colonel's bandera, pattern of 1762, of each Spanish regiment. The Royal arms are surrounded by the Collar of the Order of the Golden Fleece. The entire design is appliquéd of different colors of silk, all the seams accentuated with black cable stitched to both sides of flag. Smaller details— eagles, fleur-de-lis, the smaller lion, the interior of the pomegranate—were embroidered. The colors of the flames between the links of the Collar, and the color within the links, varied randomly from one flag to the next. Flag reproduction by the author, based on original bandera of Regimiento Hibernia, circa 1790, and others at Museo del Ejército, Toledo.

The new Coronela introduced in 1762 had a white field with very large Royal coat of arms at center, topped by a large crown, and surrounded by the collar of the Order of the Golden Fleece. Each corner bore the coat of arms of the individual regiment to which it belonged. These were displayed in a stylized frame the same for all regiments, with a ducal crown (without arches or globe), cannons, and flags. The frames included a forked section on each side drawn to appear to pass behind the main frame. The negative spaces between these branches and the main frame are sometime portrayed in secondary sources as showing the white silk of the field of the flag, but all existing banderas show that it was the same color as the rest of the frame, a medium light yellow or gold. The new Coronela did not include the Burgundy cross or the supporting lions of older patterns. (These details remained in use for Guards regiments, but none of these deployed to America). As the regimental badges were not at the ends of a cross as on the older flags, they were portrayed right-side-up, rather than pointing toward the corners.

Sencillas had a white field with a red cross of Burgundy, an X-shaped cross with several short projections on each arm, traditionally meant to signify the rough-cut cross of St. Andrew, made of two tree trunks with their branches cut short, rather than squared wooden beams. At the ends of this cross were repeated the regimental badges, with their tops pointing toward the corners of the flag. The badges were identical to those on the Coronela of the same regiment, though usually somewhat larger on the sencillas than on the Coronelas, approximately sixteen to eighteen inches top to bottom on the sencillas, only about twelve inches on the Coronelas. While some earlier Spanish banderas had had the regimental name on them, the new models described in 1762 did not. The red silk cross was usually made of four distinct pieces being joined at the center of the flag. In most cases the entire flag was made the same way—four silk squares each with one section of the cross, sewn together such that the sections of cross met and joined at the center of the flag. The orientation of the short barbs on the cross does not seem to have been well regulated; usually they all point one direction as they would on two actual crossed tree trunks, but not uncommonly they point different directions on different portions of the flag.

While the Burgundy crosses vary from one to the next, the Royal coat of arms at the center of the Coronelas are remarkably regular in their presentation and manufacture from 1762 through the end of the Napoleonic period circa 1815. Some are a bit rounder than oval, but the colors used, the divisions of the

Corner of an original *sencilla*, or simple bandera, of Regimiento Aragón, showing the standardized golden-yellow frame of the coats of arms on most banderas, red and white cord and tassels, and red *corbata*, or bannerol. Detail from photo by Museo del Ejército, Toledo.

shield, the various charges in each division, are all virtually identical. The links of the collar of the Order of the Golden fleece are also very similar in design and shape, making allowance for the vagaries of hand-cutting and hand-sewing every bit of every flag. Each link has two cutouts, and these are filed with red, blue, copper-color, or no color at all, apparently at the whim of the maker. Only the flames between these links vary to any significant degree from one flag to the next. In general, they are portrayed as each flame having three sections of three tongues of fire, but this does not seem to be fixed, and how wavy, how serrated at their ends, how wide or narrow the flame spreads over the field of the flag, are all open to the taste or skill of the maker. The flames are either the same yellow as the links of the chain, or a light copper or salmon color, with a few outliers having flames of white or red. Non-standard banderas, privately purchased or presented to the regiment by well-wishers, more commonly had red flames, as did most of the Coronelas made after 1815.

The Royal Order of 1768 reduced the size of regimental banderas from nearly eight by eight feet to a much more manageable size of about fifty-six to fifty-seven inches per side, a size that could be easily approximated by either two twenty-eight-inch widths or three eighteen-and-a-half-inch widths, these being the two more-or-less standardized widths of silk used throughout Europe. In most Spanish references it is not clear what standard of measurement was being used; French measures were much in favor for military uses, but Spanish measurements were also employed, and French and Spanish inches (of course) were different. Nevertheless, based on standard silks readily available, the flags would come out fairly regular in size. Coronelas of the period appear to be mostly made of three equal panels of silk about eighteen to nineteen inches wide, usually joined vertically, while the sencillas were generally made of four pieces approximately twenty-eight by twenty-eight modern inches each, as described above. Banderas from this period measured by the Museo del Ejército in Toledo are all very close to these standard dimensions.

Banderas were nominally square, though a few Coronelas were slightly longer than wide, with a burlap-lined white silk pole sleeve added at the leading edge. A sizable minority of surviving Coronelas– approximately one-third—were attached to their poles sideways, such that the top of the crown was toward the pole, rather than "up." This made little difference on the sencillas, since the orientation of the barbed cross was not very standard. Rather than rows of nails like other continental armies, a silk ribbon at the top of the sleeve secured the flag to the staff.

Banderas were made of a single thickness of silk taffeta, pieced together, the cross and other designs appliquéd to the obverse and the silk cut away and all edges rolled under and sewn down on the reverse so that the appliquéd color showed through. The entire design, including all details of the coats of arms, were reversed on the back of the flag. All the elements of the complex designs of the royal coat of arms and the Collar of the Golden Fleece on the Coronela, as well as the secondary regimental badges or coats of arms on both Coronela and sencillas, were outlined with black cord stitched to both sides of the flag. (This is why the Spanish flags in this book appear almost like line drawings done in pen and ink with the colors filled in between the lines.) Other colors of the same heavy cord were sometimes used to delineate details, such as red and gray for folds on the white flags of the corner devices, or white or yellow to highlight an inset silk lion. Details too small for appliqué were embroidered. The red crosses on the sencillas were not outlined. Cord and tassels were usually red and white, bottle-shaped with an almost spherical body, and hung about one third the width of the flag. The poles were approximately eight to eight feet six inches including a small inverted-heart-shaped spear and a fire-gilt brass or iron butt ferrule. They were wrapped with red, green, or blue velvet ribbon that spiraled down from the lower edge of the flag to the metal butt ferrule, the joints covered and nailed down through a gold or silver braid. The Royal Order specified a red bannerol (*corbata*). This was a simple silk scarf, without a bow or fringe, attached just below the spear, and held in place by the cord and tassels. During the war in America, there were usually two bannerols—one red to denote Spain, and one white to signify the alliance with France.

A Note on Colors

As with other silk flags of the period, the Spanish banderas were a somewhat creamy or off-white, not a snow white or typing-paper white. Silk can only be bleached so much before it loses its strength. White silk typically yellows fairly quickly as well, so even if individual banderas were made of silks bleached more white than usual, they would soon acquire a light cream color in the field—though always clearly identifiable as white, especially as they have the intense red crosses on the sencillas, and all other colors outlined in black.

The other colors used in the banderas were generally clear primary colors taken from heraldry, though the blues usually tended to a light, medium, or sky blue, rather than an intense primary blue. Many coats of arms used gold and silver for their various parts, but it was understood that in textiles, white would be used for silver, and yellow would signify gold. The yellows could vary considerably in hue and intensity. Spanish banderas tended to use a very light yellow—on many original flags the yellow is so light as to be barely distinguishable from the aged white silk of the field. Some yellows had a decidedly gold or sometimes copper cast to them, but this was from the dyes used—they were not made with metallic threads.

A very unusual feature in the coloring of Spanish banderas is the use of a very light copper or salmon color to represent the flames between the links of the collar of the Order of the Golden Fleece on many of the Coronelas. In an actual metal collar, these flames were often enameled or jewel-studded in bright red, but prior to 1794 there are no known Coronelas of the standard pattern of flags pieced together from silks of different colors that have red flames. Most have either yellow of the same yellow silks used for the crowns, corner devices, and links of the collar, or a light copper color of the same value or intensity as the yellows. (A few simply have the flames outlined in black with the interior being the white silk of the field.) Copper is neither a metal or a color identified in standard heraldic traditions, nor can these copper-colored flames be just very faded red, as the red silks on the same flags are always uniformly discolored or faded, and there is no reason to think that the flame pieces would have been made of a very fade-prone red silk different from the other reds. This dichotomy in the two similar but different colors does not seem to change over time; there are roughly equal numbers using either gold or copper throughout the period. A count of thirty-five extant Coronelas of standard manufacture and pattern held in Spain and France, dating from about 1762 to 1815, yields eleven with flames the same yellow-gold silk as the crowns and links, sixteen with the flames of this unusual light copper or salmon color, six that appear to have no color in the flames (same white as the silk field), and two with red flames (both post-1794, well after the period covered by this study). A smaller number from the same period survive as only one or two of different non-standard designs, some all embroidered, some locally made approximations of the standard government pattern. As so few originals carried in North America have survived, the banderas here illustrated are all assumed to be of the standard Royal pattern, using copper, yellow, or white flames more or less in proportion to how often those are found in originals, and varying the colors within the links of the collars interchangeably, except on those banderas for which there is good reason to believe one particular combination is more likely than another. These exceptions, or any other deviations from the norm for which there is physical or documentary evidence, are described in the individual entries.

A Note on Sources

There are few primary published or manuscript sources for Spanish military banderas of the period including the American War of Independence comparable to the lists, tables, compilations, and publications for French drapeaux or German Fahnen. Like British sources, however, there are relevant Royal Orders, and random contemporary drawings and archival documents describing individual banderas. There are also a very large number of original banderas held by the Museo del Ejército in Toledo, and a smaller number in the Musée de l'Armée in France. While most of these date from the Napoleonic period rather than 1779–1783 and have regimental arms of myriad regiments besides those involved in the American War, they all display a remarkable degree of uniformity and product control, and apart from the corner devices are indistinguishable from those few that survive from the earlier period. Clearly they were manufactured under strict supervision, and probably using the same templates, materials, and in many cases the same artisans for the entire period. Most of the information used in the reconstructions here presented come from detailed information and very excellent photographs of the originals provided by Luis Sorando Muzás, the resident vexillological advisor at the Museo del Ejército.

Descriptions of the Banderas

The following entries are focused primarily on the banderas carried by the individual Spanish units in North America. Details on the history or lineage of a regiment and the battles it participated in are included only insofar as it is relevant to the banderas or tend to clarify why one source or conclusion was found preferable to another. The list of regiments is from the Museo del Ejército in Toledo, the average strengths are taken from various sources and records published in the books cited in the bibliography.

Regimiento Aragón

Regimiento Aragón was part of the garrison of New Orleans for some time after the transfer of Louisiana from France to Spain at the end of the Seven Years' War, then was transferred back to Spain where it participated in operations against Algiers in 1775. In 1780 the regiment arrived back in America from Spain as a full regiment of approximately 725 officers and men in two battalions. They would have been accompanied by four banderas—the Coronela and one sencilla in the first battalion, two sencillas in the second.

Coronela, Regimiento Aragón.

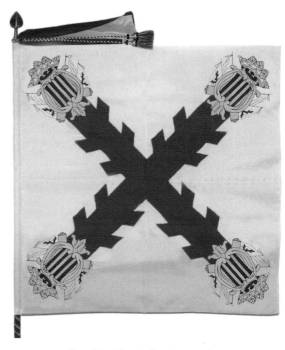

Sencilla, Regimiento Aragón.

The regimental strength at Pensacola, however, is listed as 278, suggesting that only a single battalion participated in the siege. Presumably this battalion carried its two banderas, although which battalion and which banderas are not known. The regimental badge or coat of arms on all four banderas was the ancient arms of Aragon: four red bars on a gold field, represented in textiles by yellow.

SPANISH BANDERAS BY REGIMENT

Regimiento del Rey (King's Regiment)

The Regimiento del Rey, the King's Regiment, arrived in Cuba in 1780. The regiment fielded about four hundred men at Pensacola, so probably represented the entire regiment organized as two smallish battalions, one carrying the Coronela and one sencilla, the second with two sencillas. The coats of arms in the four corners of all the banderas were the arms of Castile: golden (yellow) castle, on a red field. It is not known whether the castle on the banderas was appliquéd in silk or embroidered—later banderas with the same arms of Castile show examples of both methods. An existing bandera of Regimiento del Rey dated to 1811 shows the flames between the links in the collar of the Order of the Golden Fleece to be a muted copper or salmon color, the openings in each of the links filled with the same, so that is how it is portrayed here. Although the regiment had been complimented by the king with the sobriquet "Immemorial" early in the century, that designation was not officially used in the regimental title until well after the war in America.

Coronela, Regimiento del Rey (King's Regiment).

Sencilla, Regimiento del Rey (King's Regiment).

Dragones de América

Only a single squadron, fewer than one hundred men, of the Dragones de América (Dragoons of America) was with Gálvez's army in North America. One of the regiment's guidons, dated to 1754, has survived and is currently in the Museo del Ejército in Toledo. The somewhat convoluted history of the regiment is reflected in the guidon. Originally raised as Royal Irish Dragoons, the regiment entered Spanish service in 1703. In 1718 it was officially denominated in the Spanish service as "Dragones de Edimburgo" (Edinburgh Dragoons). It was still generally referred to as "Dragones Irlandeses" (Irish Dragoons), however, and when it received new guidons in 1754, they featured the Irish harp at their center. In 1761 the regiment was sent to Cuba, where it was disestablished in 1763. The new regiment established in its place, the Regimiento de Dragones de América, was awarded the old unit's guidons, which they continued to use until at least 1805.

The 1754 guidon as used during the period of the war in America is made of two layers of figured silk damask, deep crimson on both sides, and fringed with red and silver on all sides including the pole edge. There is a pole sleeve of the same crimson damask sewn outside the fringe, so that on this part of the guidon the fringe shows only on one side. Like guidons of other continental dragoons, the design on the flag is perpendicular to the pole. When the lance is carried pointing straight ahead, or "at the charge," the designs appear right side up; with the lance point high in the air, the design on the guidon appears sideways. The designs are heavily embroidered in silver and gold. One side shows an Irish harp on a green ground, surmounted by a Spanish crown and supported by two yellow-gold dragons. These are surrounded by military panoplies of flags, arms, drums, and bugles, all in metallic gold and silver, plus the motto of the British monarch, *HONI SOIT QUI MAL Y PENSE*, and two cyphers so complex that historians have been

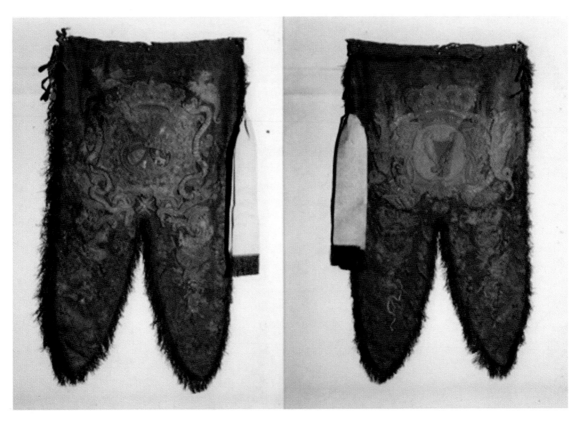

Guidon, Dragones de América, obverse, photo Museo del Ejército, Toledo.

Guidon, Dragones de América, reverse, photo Museo del Ejército, Toledo.

unable to identify exactly who they represented. The opposite side displays the coat of arms of Fernando VI, also crowned and surrounded by military motifs, with two golden dragons in the corners nearest the pole, and the regimental title of *REGIMIENTO DE DRAGONES IRLANDESES DEL REY* (Regiment of Irish Dragoons of the King) on a long scroll. The flag had both white and red bannerols—the white with gold bullion fringe at its ends.

The original cord and tassels have been lost.

While the known history of this guidon clearly places it with the regiment in Cuba, it is not certain whether it accompanied the squadron assigned to Gálvez or was present in the campaigns in North America.

Regimiento España (Regiment Spain)

Regimiento España had served in Cuba during the Seven Years' War, where one battalion had been captured at Havana. The regiment was reorganized in Spain and returned to Cuba in 1776. The first battalion, presumably with the Coronela and one sencilla, served in Louisiana in 1777, before the official declaration of war between Spain and Great Britain, and in 1780 the second battalion, probably with its two sencillas, participated in the capture of Mobile. A composite detachment of approximately 480 men of both battalions served with Gálvez in America and took part in the capture of Pensacola. Too large to be fielded as a single battalion, this unit was probably organized as two battalions and carried all four banderas.

The arms of the regiment in the four corners of each of the regimental banderas were a shield of sky blue, two globes at the center representing the two hemispheres, with a small Spanish crown in the blue sky above and an island upon a darker sea with waves below, between two white columns (the Pillars of Hercules), each crowned, a scroll partially wrapped on each column, with the motto *PLUS / ULTRA*. A surviving coat of arms of the regiment, completely detached from its original bandera, is mostly done in the appliqué and outline method, with only the smallest details in embroidery.

Coronela, Regimiento España (Spain Regiment).

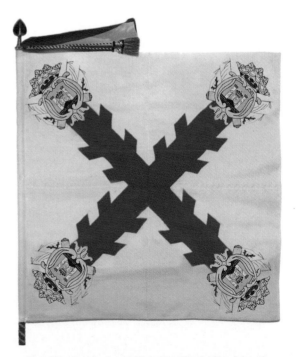

Sencilla, Regimiento España (Spain Regiment).

Regimiento Fijo de la Habana (Fixed Regiment of Havana)

Regimiento Fijo de la Habana was originally created in 1710 in Havana, Cuba, as a standing regiment of infantry under the same regulations and Royal ordinances as the Spanish regiments in Europe. In 1769 one battalion was transferred to New Orleans. The New Orleans battalion fought in the Mississippi campaigns in 1779. In 1780 one battalion of 244 men served at Pensacola. As this unit was recorded as having accompanied Gálvez from Cuba, it was probably not the same battalion as had been headquartered at New Orleans.

In 1753 the single-battalion Regimiento Fijo de la Habana had become a full regiment, thus would have carried four banderas, the Coronela and one sencilla in the first battalion, and two sencillas in the second. Presumably banderas of the new pattern were received sometime after their introduction in 1762. As a regular regiment, these were probably manufactured in Spain and would have varied from others of the same type only in the coats of arms in their corners. These consisted of a blue field with three towers and a key with Royal crown above and surrounded by the collar of the Order of the Golden Fleece rather than the usual gold frame. As with any coat of arms, there are many interpretations which would be completely correct based on the original word description. In this case, there is nothing in the original grant of arms to say whether the castles were gold or silver, and they have been portrayed both ways. The key, generally shown as gold, has been placed below the castles or among them, oriented up-and-down or side-to-side. The arrangement shown here is from an existing bandera circa 1836.

Coronela, Regimiento Fijo de la Habana
(Fixed Regiment of Havana).

Sencilla, Regimiento Fijo de la Habana
(Fixed Regiment of Havana).

Regimiento Fijo de Luisiana (Fixed Regiment of Louisiana)

The Regimiento Fijo de Luisiana was created in 1769 according to the same regulations and Royal ordinances as the Spanish regular units, to be permanently stationed in the colony of Louisiana, formerly French territory but ceded to Spain at the end of the Seven Years' War in 1763. During the period of the American War of Independence the regiment comprised two battalions, so would have had a Coronela and three sencillas. Its colonel before the war was Bernardo Gálvez, also the governor of Louisiana, who later became the overall commander of Spanish land forces when Spain entered the war as an ally of France in 1779. It is not clear what strength this regiment committed to Gálvez's campaigns from Louisiana to Florida, so it is not known how many banderas may have accompanied, or which ones.

The sencillas of the Louisiana regiment are well documented in two drawings made in 1786 for banderas of a third battalion raised in that year. As a regular regiment, all the regimental banderas would have been made in Spain and differed from others of the same pattern only in their corner coats of arms. One archival drawing shows the coat of arms of the province of Louisiana, the other shows a sencilla of the regiment, but there is no reason to believe that the regiment did not have its full complement of four flags in America, including a Coronela. The sencilla as portrayed in 1786 has all the barbs on the Burgundy cross pointing outward from the center, rather than all pointed in one direction as on two actual crossed tree trunks.

The regimental coat of arms on these flags is not confined by the usual frame with cannon and flags, rather it is displayed as a full coat of arms complete with central escutcheon, supporters, and crest—in this case the same Spanish coronet, or open-topped crown, common to other banderas. The central shield is an oval divided by a yellow band across its center. Above are the arms of Castile and Leon. Below is a reclining American Indian with a bow in his right hand, and a pitcher with water flowing from it, on his left. The supporters are two American Indians, each with a bow in his hand, a quiver of arrows, and a

Coronela, Regimiento Fijo de Luisiana (Fixed Regiment of Louisiana).

Sencilla, Regimiento Fijo de Luisiana (Fixed Regiment of Louisiana).

feather headdress. All three Indians are in natural colors, the rock on which the Indian on the shield sits is a neutral gray, the sky unaccountably grayish-orange, possibly the same copper-color used for the flames in the Order of the Golden Fleece on many Coronelas. As on other banderas with complex designs, the main sections of the corner coats of arms would have been made of the proper colors of silk outlined with black cable, with smaller details embroidered. On the sencillas is also the motto *HONOR / ET FIDELITAS*, embroidered in red above and below the cross of Burgundy. As the letters are embroidered directly onto the silk field, they read backward on the reverse of the flag. An interesting detail on the original drawing is the inclusion of a Spanish accent above the E in *FIDELITAS*, which would not occur in the original Latin spelling. Also in the original archival drawing, the cord and tassels are white, and the staff is wound in blue velvet, the color of the regiment's small cloths and uniform facings.

Regimiento Flandes

Regimiento Flandes is reported to have had 424 men present at Pensacola. This strength suggests it was organized as a full regiment with two battalions, with four banderas—the Coronela and one sencilla with the first battalion and two sencillas with the second. The regimental arms in the four corners of both banderas was a black lion rampant on a gold (yellow) ground.

Coronela, Regimiento Flandes.

Sencilla, Regimiento Flandes.

Regimiento Guadalajara

Regimiento Guadalajara served for some period in Louisiana after that territory passed from France to Spain at the end of the Seven Years' War. However, it was back in Spain by the time the new war was declared in 1779. The regiment then re-deployed to America and arrived in Havana in 1780. While its total strength is not known, it is recorded that a detachment of 328 men was sent to Gálvez's campaign against Pensacola. This unit was probably a single battalion of the regiment, or if a detachment of picked men or individually chosen companies, then probably organized as a battalion for tactical purposes, nonetheless. Two banderas no doubt accompanied, but whether they were the Coronela and one sencilla or simply two sencillas is not known. The arms of the regiment displayed in the four corners of each bandera were an armored knight on a white horse carrying a spear with red pennant, displayed on a starry blue sky. The number of stars does not seem to be determined and varies among the few existing originals, none of which date precisely to the period of the American war.

Coronela, Regimiento Guadalajara.

Sencilla, Regimiento Guadalajara.

Batallón de Morenos Libres de la Habana (Morenos Battalion of the Havana Militia)
Batallón de Pardos Libres de la Habana (Pardos Battalion of the Havana Militia)

Two battalions of Havana Militia are identified in different documents as having accompanied Gálvez in the siege of Pensacola: the Batallón de Morenos Libres de la Habana, and the Batallón de Pardos Libres de la Habana, traditionally translated as the Battalion of Free Mulattos of Havana, and the Battalion of Free Negros of Havana. It appears that some records consider these a single battalion—Haarmann gives their strengths at Pensacola as 135 and 139, respectively, while Quintero Saravia lists "The Battalion of Havana Free Blacks (Batallón de morenos libres de la habana)" at a strength of 262, roughly equaling the combined strength of the two battalions under their separate names.

According to the "Regulations for the Infantry and Cavalry Militias of the Island of Cuba, January 19, 1769," each of these battalions was to carry only two simple banderas, no Coronela. These harked back to earlier periods by having the names of the battalions marked on them, probably because these units did not have coats of arms. Unlike other Spanish banderas, each also had a motto. For the Morenos Battalion: "The two Flags of this Battalion will have the Cross of Burgundy; placed above it: Batallón de Morenos Libres de la Habana, and below: Vencer o Morir (Win or Die)." For the Pardos Battalion: "The two Flags of this Battalion will have only the cross of Burgundy (red), and above: Batallón de Pardos Libres de la Habana, and below: Siempre adelante es gloria (Always forward is glory)." It is likely that these militia banderas were locally manufactured rather than received from Spain. It is not known whether the lettering was in paint or embroidered. As military flags, they were almost certainly accompanied by cord and tassels, and after the declaration of war on Britain and alliance with France in 1779, they would have had both red bannerol for Spain and a white bannerol to represent France.

Bandera, Batallón de Morenos Libres de la Habana
(Morenos Battalion of the Havana Militia).

Bandera, Batallón de Pardos Libres de la Habana
(Pardos Battalion of the Havana Militia).

Regimiento Hibernia

Regimiento Hibernia was one of three Irish infantry regiments in Spanish service, the only one to serve with Gálvez in America. It is one of the few regiments for which an original bandera of the period still exists, a Coronela probably dating to 1790, but according to the vexillological advisor of the Museo del Ejército in Toledo where it is preserved, and based on the relatively high standard of quality control among all existing banderas from the period, there is little doubt that the flag immediately preceding it would have been virtually identical. As reproduced here, the original had yellow-gold flames between the yellow-gold links of the Collar, and blue in the cutouts in each link.

The regiment was organized in the towns of Corinena and Longares, in the province of Aragón in 1709 and received its official title of Hibernia in 1718. When banderas of the new pattern of 1762 were adopted, those of the Regimiento Hibernia were unusual in having two different coats of arms in the corners, rather than four coats of arms all the same. The two shields of yellow with red stripes represent the ancient kingdom of Aragón; the Irish connection is designated by the Irish harp on a blue ground. The harp is sometimes described as on a green ground, but in this case and in all known surviving banderas of the three regiments Irlanda, Ultonia, and Hibernia, the silks appear to have been originally blue, even if now faded or discolored to a more greenish hue. The only original staff of one of the Irish regiments in Spanish service, a sencilla of Regimiento Ultonia captured in 1809 and currently in France, is wrapped in crimson velvet.

Coronela, Regimiento Hibernia.

Sencilla, Regimiento Hibernia.

Regimiento Mallorca

Regimiento Mallorca is often overlooked on lists of Spanish regiments which served in North America. The regiment arrived in Havana in 1779, but sources focused principally on the Pensacola campaign mention Mallorca only as a small detachment that served with the naval or marine battalion there. This would suggest that no banderas of the regiment were present on the mainland. Quintero Saravia (see bibliography), however, cites Spanish sources for four companies of the first battalion plus two companies of grenadiers from Regimiento Mallorca with Gálvez in the Mississippi campaign. This would be basically the entire first battalion plus an additional company. Presumably this unit was organized as a battalion for tactical purposes, and since its basis was the first battalion of the regiment, it likely carried the regiment's Coronela and one sencilla. The arms of Mallorca in the four corners of both banderas were the red and yellow stripes of Aragon with a sky-blue diagonal bar from upper left to lower right across the whole shield. Whether sewn or embroidered, this would appear reversed on the opposite side of the flag.

Coronela, Regimiento Mallorca.

Sencilla, Regimiento Mallorca.

Regimiento Navarra

Regimiento Navarra arrived in Havana in 1778, before war between Spain and Britain was declared. It fought at Mobile in 1780. The regiment reported 672 officers and men at Pensacola in 1781. This suggests that it was present as a full regiment of two battalions, thus would have carried four banderas—the Coronela and one sencilla in the first battalion and two sencillas in the second. The arms displayed in the four corners of the regiment's banderas were the traditional arms of Navarre: on a red field, a chain of gold (yellow) links in the form of a square, with a green emerald at its center.

Coronella, Regimiento Navarra.

Sencilla, Regimiento Navarra.

Regimiento del Príncipe (Prince's Regiment)

Regimiento del Príncipe was transported from Spain to Cuba in 1779, and was listed as having 620 men available for campaigns on the North American mainland in January 1780. This was a full regiment, with four banderas, one Coronela and one sencilla in the first battalion, two sencillas in the second. Later records show only 257 men of the regiment at Pensacola, so apparently only one battalion was sent to Galvez's army. Whether this battalion would have carried the Coronela and a sencilla, or two sencillas, is not known.

Regimiento del Principe did not have the standard escudo frames in the corners of its banderas. Instead, each corner featured an elaborate cypher of RPE, for Regimiento Príncipe España, supported by gold lions, topped with full Spanish royal crown (not the slightly different crown indicating the heir apparent) including the globe at the top and arches with pearls, and surrounded by the collar of the Order of the Golden Fleece as well as the collar of the Order of Carlos III. A surviving example of this design, apparently dating to a bandera circa 1809, is embroidered onto a large silk cartouche or patch. One of these would then have been sewn into each corner of each bandera, showing an outline either of simple stitching around the entire design, or possibly a decorative border. However, no other known banderas of the 1762–1815 pattern show such a method of construction. Even corner badges with fairly complex designs have their details embroidered directly onto the field of the flag, not on a separate patch to be applied as a single element. The banderas shown here have the designs embroidered directly on the silk field.

Coronela, Regimiento del Príncipe (Prince's Regiment).

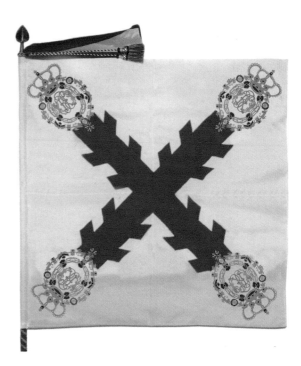

Sencilla, Regimiento del Príncipe (Prince's Regiment).

Regimiento Soria

Regimiento Soria had an average strength of approximately 600 in America, indicating that it was a full regiment of two complete battalions. At Pensacola the regiment fielded 495. It would have carried four banderas, the Coronela and one sencilla in the first battalion, and two sencillas in the second. The arms displayed in the four corners of all four banderas were a red field with a silver (white or gray embroidered) Spanish castle with three turrets, with a knight at its door, the castle encircled by a white oval border with the motto *SORIA PURA CAVEZA DE EXTREMADURA*. It is not clear whether at this time the knight was portrayed as mounted or on foot. By the time new banderas were issued circa 1833, the arms had assumed their modern form with a bust (head and shoulders) of the king at the top of the central turret on the castle, rather than a figure at the door.

Coronela, Regimiento Soria.

Sencilla, Regimiento Soria.

Segundo Batallón de Infantería Ligera Voluntarios de Cataluña

The exact identity and title of the Cataluña battalion in America is unclear, being denominated Segundo (Second) Catalonia Light Regiment in some documents, as Second Battalion of Catalonia in others, and simply as the Regimiento Ligeria (Light Regiment) Voluntarios of Catalonia in others. The unit is listed by the Museo del Ejército, Toledo, as 2º Batallón de Infantería Ligera Voluntarios de Cataluña, in English: Second Battalion Light Infantry Volunteers of Catalonia.

Quintero Saravia lists the regiment as having been formed as two battalions in 1762, with the first battalion of 228 men serving at Pensacola in 1781. It has been stated elsewhere that a light regiment had only a single battalion, and as it is generally agreed that only a single Catalonia battalion was committed to the Pensacola campaign, only two banderas would have accompanied. But as a regiment, albeit of only a single battalion, and despite its title, these were probably one Coronela and one sencilla. The regimental coat of arms displayed on the banderas was the same as that of Aragón, four red stripes on a yellow field.

Coronela, Segundo Batallón de Infantería Ligera Voluntarios de Cataluña.

Sencilla, Segundo Batallón de Infantería Ligera Voluntarios de Cataluña.

Notes

Introduction

1. William H. Prescott, *History of the Conquest of Peru* (1847), Preface.
2. Ibid.

British Regimental Colours in North America

1. Preston, *Braddock's Defeat*, (New York: 2015), 247, 270, 300, 404 *f.*71, 410 *f.*3, 416 *f.*85.
2. Ibid.
3. Milne, 92.
4. Lawson, Vol. 2, 172.
5. Lawson, 172.
6. *Extract of a Letter from General Montgomery, dated camp before St. John's, October 20, 1775*, Library of Congress, Continental Congress Broadside Collection.
7. Davis, 36.
8. Jackson to Morgan, Jan. 20, 1795. In James Graham, *Life of General Daniel Morgan, of the Virginia Line of the Army of the United States* (New York, 1856), 472.
9. Morgan to Greene, Jan. 19, 1781. Ibid, 310.
10. Greene to Morgan, Mar. 20, 1781. Ibid, 372.
11. Huntington to Morgan, Ibid, 320.
12. *Narrative of Col. Marinus Willett,* quoted in Henry Steele Commager, *The Spirit of Seventy-Six; The Story of the American Revolution as Told by Participants*, 565.
13. Journal of William Colbraith, quoted in Commager, 564.
14. British Colours at Saratoga, *Journal of the Society for Army Historical Research,* Vol. 45, No. 182 (SUMMER, 1967), 102–104.
15. Gates to Congress, December 3, 1777.
16. P. D. S. Palmer, *The Colours of the 17th or The Leicestershire Regiment of Foot* (1930), 13.
17. Ibid. See also, Edward Arthur Howard Webb, *A History of the Services of the 17th (the Leicestershire) Regiment: Containing an Account of the Formation of the Regiment in 1688, and of Its Subsequent Services, Revised and Continued to 1910* (1911). 256. The loss at Stony Point is also mentioned in Milne.
18. Lieutenant General J. P. Riley, "The Colours, Part 1: The Regular Battalions" in *Regimental Records of the Royal Welch Fusiliers*, 2015.
19. Thomas Carter, *Historical Record of the Twenty-Sixth, Or Cameronian Regiment* (London(?), 1867), 86–87.
20. Strachan, 218.

21. Ibid., 219.

22. Quoted in Hiller B. Zobel, *The Boston Massacre* (New York: 1970), 99.

23. Strachan, 219, 220.

24. Ibid., 232.

25. Lawson, Vol III, 119.

26. Ibid., Vol. II, Appendix, 98.

27. Strachan, 243.

28. Jackson to Morgan, Jan. 20, 1795. In James Graham, *Life of General Daniel Morgan, of the Virginia Line of the Army of the United States* (New York: Derby & Jackson, 1856), 472.

29. Matthew H. Spring, *With Zeal and with Bayonets Only*, 156, 319, footnote 108.

30. *Pennsylvania Journal* or *Weekly Advertiser*, February 14, 1781. For additional details and sources of original correspondence relating to these captures, see entry for Seventh Regiment.

31. Ross M. A. Wilson, "Notes on the Colours of the British Marine Corps During the 18th Century," *Military Collector and Historian*, Vol. 40 (Summer 1988), 59–61.

French Regimental Drapeaux in North America

1. *État général des troupes de France, sur pied en Mai 1748, Avec le traitement qui leur est fait tant en quartier d'hiver qu' en campagne, suivant les ordonnances du Roi. (General state of the troops of France, on foot in May, 1748, With the treatment given to them both in winter quarters and in the country-side, following the King's orders)* (Paris: 1748).

2. Wyczynski, Michel, "The Expedition of the Second Battalion of the Cambis Regiment to Louisbourg, 1758," *Nova Scotia Historical Review*, Vol. 10, No. 2, p. 94–110.

3. Alfred Marbot et Joseph Anne Dunoyer de Noirmont, *Costumes militaires français depuis l'organisation des premières troupes régulières en 1439 jusqu'en 1815* (Paris and London, 1830), Plate 918.

4. The shield and motto are from the arms of the family Biron. Lauzun was born Armand Louis de Gontaut, the son of the duc de Biron, but, of course, could not hold that title as long as his father was alive. The Lauzun title had been inherited by his grandmother when her uncle, the last of that name, had died. The title duc de Lauzun was then formally "restored" and bestowed on the young Armand Louis in 1766 by Louis XV, so most of his military career was under that name. Thus, the Legion's regimental etendard has the arms associated with the family Biron rather than Lauzun, which had technically died with its last male heir in 1723. Just to confuse things, however, Lauzun did become duc de Biron in 1788, and it is under this name that he was generally referred at the time of his execution during the French Revolution in 1793.

5. The arms of Hohenack and Ribeaupierre, known as Rappoltstein in German, also appear in the combined arms of the Waldeck Regiment raised as an auxiliary to the British. See Waldeck in German section.

German Regimental Fahnen in North America

1. Georg Ortenburg, *Braunschweigisches Militär* (Cremlingen, Germany: 1987).

2. Donald V. Holst and U. P. Böhm, "Hessische Fahnen im Gefecht von Trenton 1776," *Zeitschrift für Heereskunde* (Nov–Dec 1990), 141–51.

3. Quoted in Rodney Atwood, *The Hessians: Mercenaries from Hessen-Kassel in the American Revolution* (New York: 1980), 235.

4. Atwood, 235.

5. Donald V. Holst and U. P. Böhm, "Hessische Fahnen," 141–51.

6. *Die deutschen Hülfstruppen im nordamerikanischen Befreiungskriege* (Hannover: 1863), 121.

7. Holst, footnotes 24, 25.

8. Johannes Reuber, *Tagebuch des Grenadiers Johannes Reuber*, trans. Herbert H. Freund (Lancaster, PA: Lancaster History Library, n.d.).

9. Most of these plates can be found online on the site of the Bibliothèque Nationale Française. Some pages, or possibly a second volume under the same title, is not posted. A very comprehensive article titled "Dutch Colors and Standards, The War of Austrian Succession, Parts I and II" was published by Dan Schorr in the Winter 1993 and Summer 1994 issues of the wargaming magazine *The Courier*. The illustrations accompanying the article are very close copies of the original plates, but done only in black ink. The colors of all the component parts are described in the text.

10. The arms of Hohenack and Rappoltstein, known in French as Ribeaupierre, also appear on the arms of the drapeaux of the Royal Deux Ponts Regiment. See French section, American War of Independence.

Annotated Bibliography

The below listing includes many recent and popular books as well as manuscripts and other documents pertaining to the period covered and used in the preparation of this study. Some titles are duplicated because they are better or worse on specific nations. List does not include many individual titles that may contain one or more useful references to individual regiments or flags. Publication information for such sources is either in the text or in endnotes.

General Studies on Regimental Colors

Davis, Gherardi, *Regimental Colors in the War of the Revolution*, New York: privately printed, 1907, supplements 1910. Classic study and a standard reference. Davis corresponded with British and German archives and historians. Photographs of many originals. Some drawings of British colours based on Milne's out-of-proportions illustrations.

Davis, Gherardi, collected papers and manuscripts, held by New York Public Library. Original correspondence and many beautiful watercolors of British, French, and German flags.

Ketchum, Richard A., ed., *The American Heritage Book of the Revolution*, New York: American Heritage Publishing Co., 1958. Several beautiful watercolor paintings by Gherardi Davis of French, British, and other flags from the period.

Lossing, B. J., *Pictorial Field-Book of the Revolution*, 2 volumes, New York: Harper & Brothers, 1852. Includes some drawings and information on captured British and German flags, but the drawings are not especially accurate. Only listed because it is an early history, often cited, and reasonably well-known.

Richardson, Edward W., *Standards and Colors of the American Revolution*, Philadelphia: University of Pennsylvania Press, 1982. Very complete and well researched history and text. Covers American, British, French, and German colors. Illustrations leave much to be desired and further many misconceptions on actual appearance of original flags. Reconstructions of many flags look like the period in which book was published rather than eighteenth century. British King's Colours wrongly drawn to post-1881 patterns.

Wise, Terence, *Military Flags of the World, 1618–1900*, New York: Arco Publishing, 1978. Exactly what the title implies. The illustrations are diagrammatic rather than realistic and the information on individual flags or types of flags varies greatly. Some entries appear to be from first person research and/or inspection of existing flags. Overall, must be used with caution and info questioned or cross-referenced.

Sources on British Regimental Colours

Davis, Gherardi, *Regimental Colors in the War of the Revolution*, New York: privately published, 1907, supplements 1910. Only very brief text on British colours, the details of which Davis found "uninteresting." Davis corresponded with Milne (see below). Some Davis drawings influenced by Milne's out-of-proportion drawings.

Dawnay, Major Nicolas Payan, *The Standards, Guidons and Colours of the Household Division, 1660–1973*, London: Midas Books, 1975. Good background on British colours. Though it covers only colours and guidons of the Guards regiments, many of the photos and drawings show details of construction of flags and some accoutrements such as finials.

Dunbar, Francis J., and Harper, Joseph H., *Old Colours Never Die: A Record of Colours and Military Flags in Canada*, Toronto: F. J. Dunbar & Associates, 1992. Excellent source for colours of regiments associated with Canada. Includes photos of originals and some accurately made reproductions.

Lawson, Cecil C. P., *History of the Uniforms of the British Army*, 3 volumes, London: Kaye & Ward: 1940, 1941, 1960. Includes some information on colours, including firsthand sketches of originals no longer available to public inspection. Text of all warrants, letters, other documents relating to uniforms, the colors of uniform facings, and regimental colours.

Lemonofides, Dino, *British Infantry Colours*, Surrey, UK: Almark Publishing Co. Ltd., 1971. Nice small work with good guide to colors of uniform facings and changes between old regiments and new post-1881 titles. Most illustrations influenced by Milne's out-of-proportion drawings.

Lossing, B. J., *Pictorial Field-Book of the Revolution*, 2 volumes, New York: Harper & Brothers, 1852. Includes some drawings and information on captured British and German flags, but the drawings are not especially accurate. Only listed because it is an early history, and reasonably well-known.

Milne, Samuel Milne, *The Standards and Colours of the Army*, London: privately printed, 1893. Very complete study of British colours prior to the regimental amalgamations of 1881. Includes text of most of the warrants relating to colours from 1743, 1751, 1768. Milne drew the central designs of the colours far larger than they would appear in life to give greater care to the details. He explained this in the introduction. Unfortunately, later scholars have looked only at the illustrations and redrawn British colours in very incorrect proportions.

Richardson, Edward W., *Standards and Colors of the American Revolution*, Philadelphia: University of Pennsylvania Press, 1982. A standard reference in many ways, good historical information, but the drawings leave much to be desired. On British King's Colours, Richardson is simply wrong.

Ross, Andrew, *Old Scottish Regimental Colours*, Edinburgh and London: William Blackwood & Sons, 1885. Excellent color plates made from photographs of originals.

Strachan, Hew, *British Military Uniforms 1768–96*, London: Purnell Book Services, 1975. Includes excerpts from regimental inspection returns, many of which include dated comments on colours. This has proved invaluable in discovering which pattern colours many individual units would have carried, based on when they were issued.

Sumner, Ian, *British Colours & Standards, 1747–1881*, 2 volumes (Vol 1, Infantry; Vol 2, Cavalry), Oxford, UK: Osprey Publishing, 2001. Good overall view of period addressed but takes illustrations from many different sources and many show the out-of-proportion characteristics of Milne's drawings.

Sources on French Drapeaux

Chaligny, *Tableau Militaire des Drapeaux, Étendards et Guidons des Troupes au Service de la France*, Paris: unknown publisher, 1771.

Charrié, Pierre, *Drapeaux et Etandards du Roi*, Paris: Le Léopard d'Or, 1989. Best overall work on French military drapeaux, though to be so inclusive, most regimental drapeaux are described only in text, not with illustrations. A few of these descriptions have questionable information, uncredited, at odds with all earlier sources. Charrié's alphabetical listing of all named regiments makes it possible to untangle the various changes and re-use of many of the regimental titles.

Chartrand, René, *The French Soldier in Colonial America*, Bloomfield, Ontario: Museum Restoration Service, 1984. Flag illustrations based primarily on the manuscript plates of *Drapeaux des regiments francais et d'autres troupes 1745–1776*, which Chartrand characterizes as "Official pattern book."

Chartrand, René, *Canadian Military Heritage, Volume I & II,* Montreal: Art Global, 1993.

Chartrand, René, "Les drapeaux militaires en Nouvelle-France," *Material Culture Review/Revue de la culture materielle*, Vol 42, Fall/Automne, 1995. Illustrations based primarily on the manuscript plates of *Drapeaux des regiments francais et d'autres troupes 1745–1776*.

Chartrand, René, and Eugéne Leliépvre, *Louis XV's Army (2) French Infantry,* Oxford: Osprey, 1996. General introduction to French forces of the period. Drapeaux not specifically addressed.

Chartrand, René, *Quebec, 1759*, Oxford: Osprey, 1999.

Chartrand, René, *Ticonderoga, 1758*, Oxford: Osprey, 2000. Includes color illustrations of three of the four known circa 1762 watercolors belonging to Parks Canada of regiments that took part in the French and Indian War.

Davis, Gherardi, *Regimental Colors in the War of the Revolution*, New York: privately published, 1907, supplements 1910. Pioneering work on colors carried by all combatants of the war. Includes water-colors of French drapeaux, but probably incorrect on their sizes.

De Bouillé, Louis, *Les drapeaux francais*, Paris: Librairie Militaire de J. Dumaine, 1875. A general history of French military flags. Few illustrations. Word descriptions of regimental drapeaux of eighteenth century taken primarily from Chaligny's Tableau of 1771 and Montigny's plates of 1772.

De Roquebrune, Robert La Roque, "Uniformes et drapeaux des egiments au Canada sous Louis XIV et Louis XV," *Revue de l'Université d'Ottawa 1950*, Ottawa:1950. De Roquebrune gives a different list of regiments than those usually cited and appears in some cases to describe drapeaux of earlier or later regiments of the same names. Can be unclear on period colors, describing isabelle as brown (*brunes*), and feuille morte as isabelle, thus using the three names more or less interchangeably.

Delaistre Jacques-Antoine, *Ancien habillement de l'infanterie*, Paris:1721.

Delaistre Jacques-Antoine, *Drapeaux de l'Infanterie tant Françoise qu'Etrangère au service de la France. En l'année 1721*, Paris: 1721. This work is sometimes attributed to M. d'Hermand, but the individual plates appear to have been executed by the artist/engraver Delaistre.

Desjardins, Gustave, *Recherches sur les Drapeaux francais*, Paris: 1874. Good general information on French drapeaux. Illustrations are re-drawn from Chaligny's Tableau of 1771.

Diderot, Denis, et al, *Encyclopédie, ou dictionnaire raisonné des sciences*, Supplement 1785.

Döhla, Johann Conrad, *Tagebuch eines Bayreuther Soldaten des Johann Conrad Döhla aus dem Nordamerikanischen Freiheitskrieg von 1777 bis 1783,* Bayreuth:1913. Translated and published by Bruce E. Burgoyne, as *A Hessian Diary of the American Revolution*, Norman, OK: University of Oklahoma Press: 1993. Often cited for Döhla's eye-witness account of French drapeaux at Yorktown.

Drapeaux des regiments francais et d'autres troupes 1745–1776, collection of plates/prints originally held by Minister of War, Paris, now in Musée de l'Armée, Archives Raoul et Jean Brunon, Chateau de l'Emperi, Salon-de-Provence, France.

Elliot, Rita F., and Elliot, Daniel T., "Savannah Under Fire, 1779: Expanding the Boundaries," in *Archaeology Coastal Heritage Society*, Savannah, GA, 2011. A short summary from a study done under auspices of National Park Service. Includes a very complete list of French troops involved.

État général des troupes de France, sur pied en Mai 1748. Avec le traitement qui leur est fait tant en quartier d'hiver qu'en campagne, suivant les ordonnances du Roi. Paris: 1748. Text only.

Ketchum, Richard A., ed., *The American Heritage Book of the Revolution*, New York: American Heritage Publishing Co., 1958. Several beautiful watercolor paintings of French and other flags from the period.

Letrun, Ludovic, trans. Alan McKay, *French Infantry Flags from 1786 to the End of the First Empire*, Paris: Histoire and Collections, 2009. Beautiful illustrations. Covers the period directly after the wars in North America, but includes many of the drapeaux that would have been carried there.

Littret de Montigny, Claude-Antoine: *Uniformes militaires, où se trouvent gravés en taille-douce les uniformes de la Maison militaire du Roi*, Paris: Chez l'auteur, 1772. Very stylized renderings of uniforms and drapeaux. Littret de Montigny did many of the engravings for Diderot's *Encyclopédie*.

Manuscript, *Les Triomphes de Louis Quinze, Roy de France & de Navarre*, Paris: n.p., c.1748, Bibliothèque Nationale Française.

Manuscript, *Troupes du Roi, Infanterie française et* étrangère, *année 1757*, 2 vols., Musée de l'Armée, Paris: c.1765–1770.

Maury, Arthur, *Le Coq Gaulois: les Emblèms et les Drapeaux de la France*, France: n.p., 1904.

Mouillard, Lucien, *Armée Française, Les Régiments sous Louis XV, Constitution de tous les corps de troups, à la solde de France pendant les guerres de succession* à *l'empire et de sept ans*, Paris: L. Baudoin &

Cie, 1882.; Trans. G. F. Nafziger, *The French Army of Louis XV, In the War of the Austrian Succession and the Seven Years War*, translated text, facsimiles of original plates, pub. West Chester, OH: Nafziger Collection, 2004. For some unknown reason, the infantry drapeaux are portrayed with the staff to the right, meaning that the view is of the reverse of the flag, thus the colors are reversed from other illustrations of the same flags. Swallow-tailed cavalry flags are portrayed with the poles to the left, as one would expect.

Rey, M., *Histoire du Drapeau, des Couleurs et des Insignes de la Monarchie Francaise*, Paris: Chez Techener, 1837.

Richardson, Edward W., *Standards and Colors of the American Revolution*, Philadelphia: University of Pennsylvania Press, 1982. Generally good info on French drapeaux, including color plates.

Schermerhorn, Frank E., *American and French Flags of the Revolution*, Philadelphia: Pennsylvania Society of Sons of the Revolution, 1948. Generally follows Desjardins, but some unique and questionable interpretations. The crosses on the drapeaux are drawn far too narrow, and the author inexplicably claims the drapeaux had gold fringe on three sides.

Susane, Louis, *Histoire de l'anciénne Infanterie française*, Paris: J. Corréard, 1856. Many plates from this book are available online, some with the details of uniforms and flags painted in different colors one from the next.

Tableau des trophees conquis par les Hollandais de Anna Beck 1713, pub in Charrié, p. 81.

Tableau Militaire, de tous les Drapeaux, Étendards, et Guidons des Troupes . . . 1773, pub in Charrie, p. 82; formerly available online, website no longer available.

Van Blarenberghe, Louis-Nicolas, *The Capture of Yorktown*, Château de Versailles, 1785.

Wyczynski, Michel, "The Expedition of the Second Battalion of the Cambis Regiment to Louisbourg, 1758," *Nova Scotia Historical Review*, Vol. 10, No. 2, p. 94–110.

On the Web

Chartrand, René, "Les drapeaux militaires en Nouvelle-France," *Material Culture Review/Revue de la culture materielle*, Vol 42, Fall/Automne, 1995: https://journals.lib.unb.ca/index.php/MCR/article/view/17656/22306.

Nec Pluribus Impar: *A Web Magazine About the History, Wars and Armies of the Seventeenth and Eighteenth Centuries*, http://vial.jean.free.fr/new_npi/index.htm. A great site in French, some pages in English as well, covering primarily European militaria, uniforms, equipment, and colors, by war, nationality, and regiment.

Sources on German Fahnen

Davis, Gherardi, *Regimental Colors in the War of the Revolution*, NY: privately published, 1907, supplements 1910. Classic study and a standard reference. Davis corresponded with British and German archives and historians. Photographs of original Hessian and Ansbach-Bayreuth Fahnen.

Davis, Gherardi, Collected papers and manuscripts, held by New York Public Library. Complete original correspondence (in German) from archives in Hesse and Braunschweig. Many beautiful watercolors of British, French, and German flags.

Hill, Steven W., "Hessian Flags in the American War for Independence, 1776–1783," *Military Collector and Historian, the Journal of the Company of Military Historians*, Vol. 55, No. 4, Winter 2003–2004. A point-by-point description of the process of reconstructing the Hessian Fahnen as depicted in this book. Some conclusions on which flags belonged to which regiments have been updated since article was written twenty years ago. Includes documentation from German archives of many specific points on equipping of Hessian regiments, and photos of original Fahnen and fragments in Philadelphia. Available online as pdf.

Korn, Hans-Enno, *Fahnen und Uniformen der Landgräflich Hessen-Kassel'schen Truppen im Amerikanischen Unabhängigkeitskrieg 1776–1783 (Flags and Uniforms of the Landgraf Hesse-Cassel Troops in the American War of Independence, 1776–1783)*, Kassel: Verein für Hessische Geschichte und Landeskunde, 1977. Selected plates from the Thalmann manuscript listed below. Korn suggested that the brightly colored flags depicted in the manuscript were the Leibfahnen of the named regiments. Text in German.

Londahl-Smidt, Donald M., *German Troops in the American Revolution, (1) Hessen-Cassel*, Oxford: Osprey, 2021. Very thorough short study of all Hessian regiments and secondary units. Lists regimental Fahnen for each regiment, but only illustration of a specific Fahne is incorrect in shape and details. It obscures or omits the distinctive undulating corner blazes, making the flag look more like a contemporary Prussian flag. The color *pfirsichblüt* is translated as purple, which would give a very false impression to most British or American readers.

Lowry, James W., *A Yorktown Surrender Flag—Symbolic Object*, Harpers Ferry: National Park Service, 1989. Very complete survey of the four Ansbach-Bayreuth Fahnen belonging to the federal government.

Manuscript, *Les Triomphes de Louis XV, Roy de France et de Navarre*, in the collections of the Bibliothèque Nationale Française. Includes plates of Waldeck Fahnen captured 1746–47.

Ortenburg, Georg, *Das Militär der Landgrafschaft Hessen-Kassel zwischen 1783 und 1789 (The Military of the Landgraviate Hessen-Kassel between 1783 and 1789)*. Potsdam: n.p., 1999. Reprint of *Abbildüng derer Uniformen von dem Hochfürstl: Hess: Casselischen (Illustrations of the Uniforms of the High-princely Hesse-Cassel Military)*, manuscript plates originally created circa 1785. Very useful source (text in German) with reservations. See text in section on Hesse-Cassel and Hesse-Hanau.

Ortenburg, Georg, *Braunschweigisches Militär*, Germany: Cremlingen, 1987. Comprehensive study (in German) of Braunschweig uniforms, organizations, flags. Includes photos of some original archival documents.

Thalman, G. F., *Abbildung und Beschreibung des Fürstlich Hessen-Casselischen Militair-Staates unter der Regierung Landgraf Friedrich des zweiten, bis zum Jahre 1786, gezeichnet von G. F. Thalmann. (Illustration and Description of the Princely Hesse-Cassel Military State under the Reign of Landgrave Friedrich II up to 1786, drawn by G. F. Thalmann)*, Cassel: 1786. Manuscript in several folios at Hessischen Staatsarchivs Marburg, Germany. Many of the individual plates can be found online but must be used with caution. See text.

Sources on Spanish Banderas

Calleja Leal, Guillermo, and Calleja Leal, Gregorio, *Gálvez and Spain in the American Revolution*, trans. Donald Snowden, Valencia, Spain: Albatros Ediciones, 2016. A very thorough history; includes information on individual units, unit strengths, and casualties. Occasional mentions of Spanish banderas and mentions of captured British and Waldeck colors.

Haarmann, Albert W. "The Spanish Conquest of British West Florida, 1779–1781," *Florida Historical Quarterly*, Vol. 39, No. 2, Article 2 (1960), pp. 107–134. Good brief summary of the Spanish campaign to Pensacola. Basic background, no unit-specific information.

Haarmann, Albert W. "The Siege of Pensacola: An Order of Battle," *Florida Historical Quarterly*: Vol. 44: No. 3, Article 6. (1965). Concise history of the siege; includes list of Spanish units present. Slightly different figures for Spanish unit strengths than later publications.

Quintero Saravia, Gonzalo M., *Bernardo de Gálvez, Spanish Hero of the American Revolution*, Chapel Hill, NC: University of North Carolina Press, 2018. Another very thorough history, based on Spanish original sources, detailed down to individual units, unit strengths, and casualties. Thumbnail histories of each Spanish regiment are included in the notes. Includes contemporary illustrations of battalion color (sencilla) and coat of arms of Regimiento Fijo de Luisiana (Fixed Regiment of Louisiana), photo of British flag taken at Pensacola, mentions of capture of British and Waldeck colors.

Réunion des Musées Nationaux, website, https://www.photo.rmn.fr/CS.aspx?VP3=SearchResult&VBID =2CMFCIXID2XCSX&SMLS=1&RW=1920&RH=929. Grand Palais photo agency, a public institution under the authority of the French Ministry of Culture, officially responsible for photo collections of France's national museums. The link may not go directly to search results, but will allow a search in English or French, for captured Spanish flags (or several other nations).

Sorando Muzás, Luis, pamphlet, *Banderas y Trofeos en las Campañas de los Gálvez (1779–1783)*, illus. Francisco Vela (Museo del Ejército, Toledo, Spain).

Sorando Muzás, Luis, *Catálogo: Banderas, Estandartes y Trofeos del Museo del Ejército, 1700–1843*, Zaragoza: Museo del Ejército, 2012. Comprehensive museum catalog, complete with color photographs, of every bandera held by the Museo del Ejército.